Frontiers

Frontiers

Histories of Civil Society and Nature

Michael R. Redclift

The MIT Press
Cambridge, Massachusetts
London, England

MIT Press books may be purchased at special quantity discounts for business or sales promotional use. For information, please email special_sales@mitpress. mit.edu or write to Special Sales Department, The MIT Press, 55 Hayward Street, Cambridge, MA 02142.

This book was set in Sabon by SNP Best-set Typesetter Ltd., Hong Kong and was printed and bound in the United States of America. Printed on Recycled Paper.

Library of Congress Cataloging-in-Publication Data

Redclift, M. R.
Frontiers : histories of civil society and nature / Michael R. Redclift.
   p. cm.
Includes bibliographical references and index.
ISBN-13: 978-0-262-18254-6 (alk. paper) — 978-0-262-68160-5 (pbk. : alk. paper)
ISBN-10: 0-262-18254-8 (alk. paper) — 0-262-68160-9 (pbk. : alk. paper)
1. Environmental management. 2. Civil society. I. Title.

GE300.R43   2006
304.2–dc22

2006042035

10 9 8 7 6 5 4 3 2 1

Contents

Preface

This book was prompted by a growing unease with the discussion of nature and society in academic discourse. It was written in an attempt to set the discourse on a different path. My unease can be boiled down to three distinguishable problems, which the book seeks to address. These are the continuing deficit in historically grounded, but comparative, discussion of the links between the environment and society; the problem in establishing how physical space is culturally assimilated; and the need to question the one-sided discussion of the environment as a socially constructed object. All three of these concerns led me to the theme of frontiers.

First, in my view, the discussion of anthropogenic environmental change has become divorced from the civil society transformations with which it is always associated. The environment, like gender, is increasingly treated as a kind of intellectual ghetto, only loosely connected with the momentum of social change. Often the connections between the environment and social structure, when they are made, suffer from solipsism and, in their specificity, they fail to illuminate wider processes. Alternatively, the discussion of nature and culture is sometimes pursued in an abstract theoretical fashion, which ignores historical and political realities if they temper the conclusions of academic discourse. This book seeks to address the common ground in the histories of civil societies and nature.

Second, the discussion of space and place, in contrast, has been one of the most promising areas of geographical thought in recent years, and has attracted many who are not geographers to think seriously about the links between spatial and social relationships. This has shown itself in recent work on globalization, for example, and writing on networks and flows. The question of physical space and its cultural assimilation under capitalism has benefited particularly from critiques of Henri Lefebvre, whose work is discussed in chapter 2. This promising discussion can be employed to good effect in analyzing the discourses surrounding "frontier," as myth, analytical framework, and material reality.

The frontier encapsulates this concern with the intellectual potential of rethinking space and place. The originator of the Turner thesis in North America, the historian Frederick Jackson Turner, wrote of the prevailing disorder on the "primary" frontiers that interfaced with wilderness areas where civil societies had still not been properly established. My aim in this book is to suggest that the social noncompliance that Turner identified with these primary frontiers is not a stage in a sequential, civilizing process but a symptom of deep-seated social conflict. In the last two chapters I discuss the other side of the frontier, evidenced in the Mayan rebellion of the Caste War, as well as the attempts to resist the further development of tourism in the Yucatán peninsula today. It is often asserted today that some peoples' versions of history are ignored or erased in favor of more dominant narratives. I argue that unless we see the frontier as essentially two-sided, we relegate minority histories to oblivion.

Third, the literature on nature and social construction has given considerable attention to the way in which we construct our view of nature, but much less attention to the way in which nature influences and transforms us. This book is an invitation to view human societies and their environments as part of a wider process of dialectical change. From this perspective the material forces that are galvanized under late capitalism, especially by migrant populations, have the capacity to influence both ecological and cultural changes. Envisioning nature as an object of conquest or material exploitation has, in turn, created antithetical concerns, among them the belief in nature conservation and environmental sustainability. This book suggests ways in which spatial structures, and a sense of place, are increasingly subordinated to new forms of cultural hegemony. The frontier is both a boundary *and* a device for social exclusion, a zone of transition *and* a new cultural imaginary. As argued in chapter

2, we might think of the frontier more in terms of process than form, within a critical realist frame of reference.

What drew me to consider these frontiers over others? The obvious answer is personal experience. In all but one of the cases I discuss much of the material rests on contemporary, or near-contemporary fieldwork: the Spanish Pyrenees in the late 1960s, coastal Ecuador in the mid-1970s, and Mexico primarily during the last decade. The exception is British Canada in the midnineteenth century, which I have accessed primarily through the original archive papers of Francis Codd, a young English doctor who arrived in Canada in 1847, and the accumulated writing about this period and its migrant populations.

While conducting field research, I was aware that frontier was a term being employed to describe the very experiences that I came to see as very disparate. This proved to be part of the intellectual challenge that prompted me to write this book. Each of the cases I describe raises issues about the effects of migration on boundaries and space, and the use that is made of natural resources. They also flagged up the continuing significance of cultural and geographical place to those whose livelihood depended more or less directly on the natural resources that surrounded them. I was also aware in each case of rival imaginaries: local Aranes/immigrant, British and Irish immigrants/native populations, coastal sharecropper/landlord, *chiclero/chicle* contractor, Maya/tourist. At the same time these binary distinctions did little to capture the complexity and reflexivity of social relations in each of these places, nor their populations' links with nature.

I came to see these frontier histories as contested zones, where rival versions of civil society (or its denial) vied with each other, and where it was often their definition and management of nature that was most at odds. These frontier histories demonstrated a process of renegotiation between the increasing penetrative power of the market and the establishment, or defense, of cultural identity. The battlefield was usually the land base (including the forests). Later in the book I consider how far global responsibilities might affect these negotiated responses, as transnational institutions increasingly wrest control of the environment from local people, in the name of all of us. This, however, is one of many important concerns that lie at the margin of this particular endeavor.

This preface was written in a small town called Jimena de la Frontera in southern Spain. It is one of several towns and villages in the area, all bearing the name *frontera*, that describe the territories held by Christian and Muslim populations in the thirteenth and fourteenth centuries when Spain's "reconquest" of its own territory from Islam was the precursor of its conquest and possession of the New World. As this book is poised between the Old World and the New, this seems an appropriate point to begin. It also serves to remind us that the divisions between Christianity and Islam represent perhaps the biggest challenge even today for those who choose to take frontiers seriously.

Michael Redclift
Jimena de la Frontera
Spain

Acknowledgments

Among those who have contributed most to this book I must mention Oscar Forero (chapter 6) and the Economic and Social Research Council/ Arts and Humanities Research Council in the United Kingdom (chapters 6 and 7) for supporting the research undertaken in Quintana Roo under the Cultures of Consumption Programme between 2003 and 2005. The Department of Geography at King's College, London, is one of the most conducive environments for critical research, and also deserves my thanks. Nanneke Redclift has, as always, been a constant source of inspiration and intelligent criticism throughout the five or so years during which the book was written. I dedicate it to her.

Frontiers

1

Nature and Civilization

This book begins with three very different accounts of the frontier, and human engagement with nature, within the space of a few months in 1847. These accounts are separated by geography, and each elicits distinctive concerns, but their comparison can help us to clarify the issues that stand at the heart of this book. As we will see in the next chapter (chapter 2), much of the discussion of the environment and the development of civil societies has been disjointed and unconnected. However, the suggestion that they bear a dialectical relationship to each other, and might illuminate each other's development, deserves serious attention. The essentially diachronic relationships between nature and civil society are the core material for this book, and constitute its theoretical object. These questions raise conceptual and methodological issues, as well as matters of historical substance and interpretation.

In this chapter, however, the point of departure is different. The following cases provide a reference point that is distinctive, in that they record synchronic events—the unraveling of a relationship between nature and civil societies at a single point in time. These accounts thus enable us to develop a perspective on "frontiers" that is both more conceptual and more speculative. The subject matter is not so much the growth of institutions, and forms of organization for managing nature, as the cultural exchanges that take place when individuals locate themselves within nature. Later in the book it is argued that these spatial re-locations, and the constructions of "place" with which they are associated, can help us bridge the gap between versions of space in material terms, and those which prioritize the human subject and consciousness.

1847: Walden, New England

Henry Thoreau was twenty-seven when he went to live in the wood cabin by Walden Pond in New England. The following three years or so were spent building the cabin, learning new rural crafts, observing and writing about nature. By 1847, as John Updike writes, in a new commentary on *Walden*, "he emerged from his cabin as essentially the Thoreau known to literary history" (Updike 2004, xi).

Thoreau's example, and the power of his prose, have influenced successive generations in the United States and beyond, as much for his practical example as for his literary sensibility, or his importance in the canon of great American writers. He had many advantages on his side: the son of a well-to-do pencil manufacturer, and a Harvard graduate, Thoreau was hardly one of the world's dispossessed. He came by the cabin rent-free, since it was located on land owned by his mentor, Ralph Waldo Emerson, and he had no dependents to support. In many respects Thoreau's vision of simplicity and minimalism was one he could afford to choose for himself.

The vision remains, however, one of the most compelling available to people, especially young people, in a world increasingly ordered by corporate finance and extravagant consumer preferences. Thoreau was one of a number of writers in the midnineteenth century for whom the natural world was not just a source of artistic inspiration but a spiritual and moral force. Although Thoreau enjoyed some dealings with local society, the time spent in his cabin, in surveying the pond, and in learning necessary skills for survival was essentially a voyage of individual fulfillment. As Updike rightly argues, Thoreau's *Walden* is one of the great works of American individualism, as well as a testament to a heightened environmental consciousness that has developed in the intervening century and a half.

Thoreau expresses his philosophy, and his intentions, very clearly in an early section of *Walden*:

For many years I was self-appointed inspector of snow storms, and did my duty faithfully; surveyor, if not of highways, then of forest paths and all across-lot routes, keeping them open, and ravines bridged and passable at all seasons, where the public heel had testified to their utility. . . .

(Later) finding that my fellow-citizens were not likely to offer me any room in the court house, or any curacy or living anywhere else, but I must shift for myself, I turned my face more exclusively than ever to the woods, where I was better known. . . . My purpose in going to Walden Pond was not to live cheaply nor to live dearly there, but to transact some private business with the fewest obstacles. . . . (Thoreau 2004, 21)

What follows is an account of what one does *not* need to survive comfortably in close communion with nature.

First, Thoreau considers clothing—"no man ever stood the lower in my esteem for having a patch in his clothes"—and concludes—"a man who has at length found something to do will not need a new suit to do it in" (Thoreau 2004, 22–23). Next, he looks at shelter, which he admits is "now a necessary of life, though there are instances of men having done without it for long periods in colder countries than this." He notes that Adam and Eve "wore the bower before any other clothes." If housing is what we need then human ingenuity can provide from nature: "a comfortable house for a rude and hardy race, that lived mostly out of doors, was once made almost entirely of such materials as Nature furnished ready to their hands" (Thoreau 2004, 29). The avoidable reality of much of "modern" (midnineteenth century) life was that people were forced to spend half their lives paying for their dwellings. The link between what labor and nature afforded, and how we might live securely, demanded major shifts in the economy, that would lead to greater personal independence, fewer debts, and more "socially useful labor time" (to coin a marxist phrase). We were prisoners of our societies if we failed to live frugally; conversely, frugality was a means to liberation.

For Thoreau the core of the problem does not lie at the door of the house; it lies with those who inhabit it: "while civilization has been improving our houses, it has not improved the men who are to inhabit them" (Thoreau 2004, 34). Most men hardly consider what a house really represents; as a consequence they "are needlessly poor all their lives because they think that they must have such a one as their neighbors have." Some men even require furniture, although he "would rather sit in the open air, for no dust gathers on the grass, unless where man has broken ground" (Thoreau 2004, 36). In fact he does acquire furniture, of course, but exclaims, "Thank God, I can sit and I can stand without the aid of a furniture warehouse."

It is these thoughts on "economy" that underpin the rest of Thoreau's account, the meticulous observation of nature, the passing of the seasons, and the delight in new skills learned. Thoreau gives expression to questions that resonate today, and do so through a process of cultural transmission—his admiration for nature is matched by his own resourcefulness and pride in what he can do. These values have passed into the cultural cortex of societies founded upon a frontier myth and celebrated for generations by the descendents of immigrants. Although he is not oblivious of the local society that he has entered, the enduring power of Thoreau's vision lies somewhere else—in the realization that landscape is the product of human ingenuity as well as so-called wild, uncivilized nature.

Much of the impulse behind environmentalism today can be attributed to this vision, and to its re-awakening in every new generation. Thoreau's pond was not a geographical frontier, and it lay close to a very settled, well-established human population. But it constituted a frontier of the mind, a metaphor for the human condition in its most elemental form, which continues to resonate today. Henry Thoreau completed two years in the woods and finally left Walden on September 6, 1847.

1847: Pembroke, Ontario

Eight days later, on September 14, 1847, a young English doctor, Francis Codd, wrote to his parents from Pembroke, the most westerly part of populated English-speaking Canada at the time (Redclift 2000). While Thoreau was addressing the benefits of freeing oneself from the chattels of civilization, and living comfortably within modest means, Francis Codd was experiencing the North American frontier in a very different way. He was twenty-four years of age, almost the same age as Thoreau and, like many middle-class immigrants to Upper Canada in the 1840s and 1850s, very ambivalent about the absence of civilization in their countries of adoption. These seemed to be characterized by violence, irreligion, and anarchy, as well as sublime natural beauty:

[September 14, 1847] As to coming home again I am determined to do so if I can, although I am sure it is not my wisest course. . . . If I come home this fall I shall not wish to stop longer than next March. If I could get all my bills in, the matter would be plain enough, but that I have no hopes of. . . . Two men fought with their jack knives at the mouth of the Petawawa a week ago and one was killed on the spot, the other was taken prisoner at Portage du Fort and is now in jail at Perth, he is said to have killed two men before in the same manner. . . . Last Tuesday I attended the funeral of a patient on the Allumette Island, the corpse had to be taken six miles down the lake on a canoe. The man was buried on a hill about 200 feet over the lake, a most beautiful spot with a splendid view from it, but it was the corner of a wheat field and there was no clergyman. . . . Last week I went up to Fort William in my boat and came back the same day, the channel is full of rocks and the weather was very stormy, moreover the Indians stole my grog and my bread got wet, so I had quite enough of it before I got home and swore I would never go again, but I think I shall. The wild fruit is still not finished. I have been out twice and gathered two pailsful [sic] of gooseberries, and the blackberries also are numerous, and grapes, and wild plums. . . .

This brief extract conveys something of Codd's emotions and thoughts. Law and order has scarcely been established, since the more civilized parts of Canada still lie to the south and east. His patients are unwilling or unable to pay their debts, and there is a marked lack of sophistication and "civilization" among most of the company that he joined. On the other hand, the social values of frontier life, elevated to a myth in much of the discourse initiated by Frederick Jackson Turner, and discussed in chapter 2, are rooted in the belief in independence and self-reliance as quintessentially American values. Such virtues are never very far from the surface in Francis Codd's letters, and resonate with the views expressed by Thoreau.

These first impressions are combined with enthusiasm for what Codd sees as the exuberance of nature. Some of the most vivid references to the physical beauty of the Canadian forests are contained in the earliest surviving letters. On February 12, 1847, on his journey to Pembroke, Francis comments on the beauty of the Upper Allumette Lake. Soon he is involved in trading fish and venison with the Indians and, by August of the same year, enjoying the fruits of nature as we have seen, picking raspberries, blueberries, wild plums, grapes, and gooseberries. By the fourteenth of September 1847 he is referring to islands within the river system of the Ottawa River, "weighed down with wild fruit." He writes as if he has stumbled upon the Garden of Eden, rather than someone who has forsaken "civilization".

Nature's bounty, however, has another, harsher, face to it. While celebrating the harvest of wild fruit he bemoans the isolation of his adopted country—"I am tired of this wild, uncivilized place . . ." he complains, and wishes that he lived somewhere that was ". . . more in the world." On a hunting trip in August 1847, when he gets lost, he is awaken by what he believes to be a bear, and makes a hasty retreat. He clearly enjoys the fact that this account will terrify his parents sitting in front of the log fire in Letheringsett, in Norfolk, England.

In later letters, when he can hunt and shoot better, and has built himself a canoe, he displays a more confident and resourceful approach to what was previously threatening about the wilderness. From Renfrew in December 1849, he describes his love of shooting and fishing "to hunt deer successfully requires great knowledge of their habits and of the country and Indian patience and perseverance." A year later, on December 2, 1850, he records that he has killed a deer and is now the envy of the "other sporting white men" in the village. "Don't laugh!" he tells his parents, reflecting on his hard-won skills, and the improvement in his status.

Together with his growing engagement with nature, there is a growing sense of responsibility for the rule of law. He begins, on June 19, 1847, declaiming against the absence of law and order: "(there is) no law or civil power within 100 miles of here," he writes. In the same letter he mentions the ugly brawls between raftsmen, in which he as the local doctor inevitably becomes involved. The people cannot be trusted "for the most part they are a most infernal set of rogues . . . and there is no court of law nearer than Perth." By September 1849 he is complaining that the raftsmen threatened to avenge him for one of their number that died in his care: "I find my revolver a very agreeable and necessary companion."

However, in the same letter he mentions that a Division Court has been established at Renfrew for small debts and, in the next letter, that it is held several times a year. Two years later, in 1852, he is much more optimistic, and very much involved in the establishment of civil institutions. He writes, on January 14:

[A] magistrate in this country is . . . a very different animal from the same in England—he need not spend a dollar a year the more for being a magistrate— many of our magistrates are plain farmers who can read and write decently, but their authority seems to be just as much respected as in England.

Within the compass of five years, between 1847 and 1852, the frontier that showed little evidence of civilization, has given way to a sense of a civilizing mission. He had written "many of *our* magistrates," with an almost proprietary tone, in defense of their legitimacy for the local community. Later he reports that he has been a witness in a murder trial held in Perth and, in an undated letter, he records how squatters on Allumette Island had threatened to shoot someone who had thought of buying the island from a land speculator. Francis Codd implies that such squatters, however violent their response, are not to be condemned for defending what is theirs by rights, if not in the eye of the law. Clearly, law and order arrives through legitimate claims but the rights of possession are real, and should be respected. Occupying land and clearing forests are the legitimate activities of settlers, and they bestow responsibilities of ownership on those who settle. It is not lightly that he mentions to his brother Henry, on October 16, 1850, that "surveying is as good as any profession, and must continue so while there is any wild land to be settled, that is for hundreds of years to come." It is clear that in Francis Codd's view the frontier, and its settlement, implies a new set of rights and obligations corresponding to natural justice rather than the letter of the law.

Unlike Thoreau, Francis is faced by a paradox: as a recent migrant his ability to appreciate "wildness" is intimately linked to the "civilized" qualities he feels he lacks in his new environment. He has not come to Canada to avoid civilization but to help "civilize" his country of adoption. In the next few years he takes increasing pleasure in the wild nature that surrounds him in the Ottawa Valley, but his letters constantly return to other aspects of frontier settlement. Above all, land settlement is seen as a necessary, civilizing process, and such pioneering sentiments were very different from those of the society that he had left behind in midnineteenth-century Norfolk.

From the beginning Francis enjoins his father to sell up his "livings" (parish) in Letheringsett in Norfolk and to join him in Canada. More than two years later, in December 1850, he writes that he is "anxious to hear how you decide about emigration but (I) do not wish to bias you." Should his father decide to emigrate, he says [in March 1851], "It is far worse to be in debt in England than live modestly without debt in Canada." And he goes on to cite himself as an example of this axiom: "Do you think if I had been in the same situation in England I should have met with as much help in the shape of credit as I have had in Canada," he insists. The "wild" and "uncivilized" society of the frontier is also one that asks few questions about peoples' past, values them for what they do, and rewards hard labor. "It takes a man several years to open his eyes to what may be done with a little capital in Canada," he writes in 1852.

There is nonetheless a sharper point to his observations about civilization, that goes far beyond good manners and social breeding. The Ottawa Valley was the scene of deep-seated cultural conflicts, based largely on religion or ethnic membership. Notably absent, however, is any serious attempt to engage with the condition of the Indians, those native Canadians whose land the settlers have effectively confiscated. Unlike Thoreau, who recommends Indian knowledge and ways (and who adamantly opposes slavery), Francis Codd is racially blind in many of his comments. In January 1848 he records a great ball being held in Pembroke at which an Indian the worse for alcohol, interrupts the Highland Reels "with a war dance of his own" and is forcibly ejected from the company. At no point in his letters does Francis consider the humiliations that might lie behind such behavior, or the abuse and degradation to which the Native American population were routinely subjected.

The British government had never accepted the sovereignty of Indian lands in the eighteenth century, but it had promised, by the Proclamation of 1763, to accept aboriginal title and to consider the interests of the native population before settlement was allowed. Essentially this was a device to reduce conflict on the borders with what became the United States. The British government's only motive in appearing to help native Canadians was to have allies in its disputes with the Thirteen Colonies to the south. By 1814 Britain had rescinded on its undertaking to the indigenous people of Canada, and extinguished Indian titles in preparation for further British settlement (Buckner 1993).

It is clear, then, that what Francis means by a "civilized country" has little to do with the treatment of native Canadians, or relations between Catholics and Protestants, and still less with the political interests in the United States to the south. His sense of a civilized universe is one that is permanently settled, and in which civil institutions are established. This society stood in clear contrast to the wilderness that in Francis's day had still not been properly surveyed. Indeed, he is talking about "civilization" in both environmental and social terms. Civilization concerns navigable rivers and cleared forests, as well as the civil institutions that settlement gave rise to. However, it excludes the rights of other peoples, particularly of the indigenous groups that were gradually being annihilated at the time.

Beinart and Coates (1995) have written about the "vagaries of ecological interactions," as part of the process through which civil society was created, but what ensued in Upper Canada cannot easily be attributed to a desire for sustainable settler communities. Most settlers in Upper Canada in this period had no wish, and little opportunity, to be self-sufficient. Their farming practices were driven by the market, and whatever they did in the Old World, they never sought to be self-sufficient farmers in the New.

Today the area from which Francis Codd wrote (the Algonquins Regional Park) is largely a protected area, a nature reserve protected from the full development of the market, in which amenity, nature conservation, and recreational tourism coexist in a managed way. In the midnineteenth century it was merely a staging post in the advance of white settlement, northward and westward. The frontier spirit was one of inexorable expansion and mastery over nature.

As we will see in chapter 4, what is interesting about the frontier settlement is not so much the democratic opening that it represented, *pace* Frederick Jackson Turner, as the social closure that it avoided. Coming from societies that were resource scarce, settlers like Francis Codd viewed nature's plenty as an opportunity for short-term gain. Their vision of a just society, in Wynne's (1999) phrase, was a departure from midnineteenth century Britain, itself on the threshold of social reform but a far cry from sustainable production in this or any era. However, land settlement and title were important building blocks in the communities that flourished in this period, and which Francis Codd describes. They provided the key to a more inclusive sense of citizenship (although one that excluded women and the indigenous peoples). A serious and sustained effort followed, to reproduce recognizably civilized values and institutions within a situation that had been transformed, and in which modes of behavior, discipline, and social control were very different from those of the societies from which the immigrants had come. This was also a frontier of the mind, as Thoreau's had been, but it spoke less to individual self-sufficiency than to the virtues of human settlement, good governance, order and civic responsibilities.

1847: Yucatán, Mexico

Just as Francis Codd was establishing himself in Upper Canada, other events were unfolding several thousand miles to the south. On the Yucatán peninsula of Mexico a struggle emerged between the indigenous Mayan people and their white, Mexican masters, which established quite different boundaries between civil societies and their management of nature. The frontier geography of the Yucatán was eloquent testimony to the ability of the conquerors to racialize and legitimate their conquests, of both people and territory. The frontier in this case was erected between the autarchic Maya that sought to separate itself from white society, and the group that oppressed them. The separatist Maya were to survive for more than half a century, and even the Mexican Revolution (1910) failed to redraw the lines of conflict and social exclusion. They were the followers of the Talking Cross (*Cruzob*), a millenarian cult that inspired the rebel Maya to continue their struggle for liberation from the whites, and whose descendents maintain their loyalty to the Cross in isolated parts of Quintana Roo today.

The origins of this separatist rebellion illustrate the conflict of interest behind the frontier that was erected between them. In July 1847 the Mexican authorities shot one of the leaders of the Mayan people, Manuel Antonio Ay. This took place in the city of Valladolid, a citadel of white supremacy surrounded by Mayan villages and the focus of repression against the indigenous population. In his possession they had found a letter giving information about a Mayan uprising that was being planned by Ay and fellow conspirators, Jacinto Pat and Cecilio Chi.

The assassination of Ay was a miscalculation of historic proportions, and set in motion a series of events that constituted arguably the last great indigenous rebellion in the Americas, the Caste War of Yucatán (Reed 2001). In the course of this conflict the Mayan people sought a future free from white domination, and a life according to the precepts of their own (highly syncretic) religious beliefs. Ultimately they were unsuccessful in these aims, but their struggle continues to this day. The civil and religious authority to which they were subjected had failed to deliver the promise of Mexican Independence twenty years earlier. Since the Conquest the whites had alienated most of the land that the Maya had occupied for centuries. For the Maya in Yucatán in their conflict with the whites what was at stake was nothing less than their own conception of the links between nature and a social and the religious order that respected its primacy.

When Mexico became independent, the principal beneficiaries were the white Creole elite. The Spanish governor of Yucatán resigned without a fight, and the peninsular joined the Mexican Union. However, not surprisingly, the majority of the indigenous population also entertained hopes of a much better future. Fewer than 300,000 Mayas had survived the brutality of the Spanish Conquest, but in the succeeding three centuries their numbers had gradually begun to climb once more. The total population of the Yucatán peninsula, which was at its lowest in 1700 at about 130,000, had risen to over half a million by 1845, two years before the outbreak of the Caste War.

The Yucatán had always retained a degree of independence from the rest of Mexico, partly because of its geographical position, a peninsular jutting into the Caribbean. Indeed, until independence in 1821 Spain had administered it separately from the rest of Mexico. After independence the historical trajectory of the peninsular departed ever more radically from that of the Mexican Republic. In 1839 Santiago Imam launched a revolt that formally separated Yucatán from the rest of Mexico, but this brief flirtation with independence did not succeed for more than a few months. He promised the abolition of taxes on the Maya, and the expectation of these reforms, some of which were incorporated into the 1841 Constitution, ignited high expectations among the Mayan peasantry. They can be seen, with hindsight, as having prompted millenarian convictions, which were channeled in the direction of Mayan independence and cultural autarky during the subsequent century.

Most of the indigenous Mayan farmers were dependent on corn as their food staple, and their cornfields (the *milpa*) were the center of their ceremonial life. After 1825 this subsistence economy was increasingly placed in jeopardy by the expansion of a new cash crop, sugar cane, which was being grown on large estates. Sugar cane required high-quality land, but the financial returns on investment were extremely profitable, and large landlords began to employ increasing numbers of dispossessed and marginal *campesinos*. Many of the Mayan peasants, already subjected to onerous taxes and labor obligations by the whites (*dzul*), fled into the jungle to the east of the peninsula, today's province of Quintana Roo. In the forests of the east and south, Mayan resentment at the trick played on them by the dominant white population nurtured and grew. To most of the peasant farmers the fact of independence from Spain had opened possibilities of easing their subjugation, and earning them rights as free and equal citizens. Their unease grew into unrest and eventually in 1847 they rebelled in Tepich, a small town to the south of Valladolid.

The white authorities were alerted to an impending rebellion by the movement of population within the territory between Valladolid, the center of white supremacy, and Tepich and Tihosuco, to the south. The Indians were anticipating conflict by leaving the colonial towns where they were subjects, and occupying the dense forests where they could disappear from view. A movement of organized resistance was born.

The frontier that had been drawn by the Caste War existed for both sides in this conflict, the rebel Maya and the whites. For the whites the rebel Maya came to occupy the "other" side of this line. The land controlled by the followers of the Talking Cross was effectively outside the Mexican national patrimony and this constituted a threat to the white *mestizo* majority. Not only was the forest hostile to the whites, impenetrable and dangerous, it came to be ruled by Mayan leaders who cultivated economic relations with timber entrepreneurs and chewing gum intermediaries, including the Wrigley's company. The boundaries between the separatist Maya and the Mexican state were clearly drawn. However, the commercial possibilities of the forest opened up quite different trajectories that served to break down frontiers, rather than erect them. As we will see in chapter 7, the Maya discovered the commercial potential of chewing gum, just as the American manufacturers were developing an important new consumer product. As a consequence the frontier created by conflict was dissolved by the penetration of global capital. At the same time the institutions that the Maya had used to defend themselves, and their way of life, were fatally undermined.

Nature and Civil Society

Although they share the same historical timeline, the events discussed above describe very different social conjunctures, and widely disparate relationships between society and nature.

Thoreau was retreating temporarily from the demands and constraints of society, into a world where labor was born of necessity and necessarily unpaid. His example of survival skills and wonderment in the beauty of nature inspired successive generations, and even contributed to an ideology of frontier independence and individualism, though the location of Walden was far from any recognizable geographical frontier.

Francis Codd's arrival in Canada West had been precipitated by events over which he felt he had little control, and he found himself in a geographical space that was fast becoming civilized, very much to his benefit. He and his neighbors were building a civil society out of the process of physical expansion, and the gradual divorce from British institutions and practices. Nature for him, although an object of admiration, was not part of his philosophical vision, as it was for the author of *Walden*. However, the transformation of the forests by immigrant settlers played an important part in the way he came to view his adopted society, It demonstrated, above all, the human mastery of nature.

Finally, the Mayan rebellion of 1847, the Caste War, called for an alternative to the society based on racial divisions that had been the prize of the whites on independence. Their rebellion was an autarchy founded on different principles from those of the whites. In Mayan cosmology humans were an integral part of nature, and their mission was to acknowledge natural forces and work with them, rather than to subordinate nature to human ends in the Judeo-Christian tradition. To the rebel Mayan the frontier was only welcome as a zone of refuge. The frontier with white Yucatan marked a boundary of civil and religious oppression from which they had to retreat. To both parties in the conflict, civilization was manifest only on their side of this frontier, which was represented by religious observance, respect for family and kin and for civil and religious institutions.

Table 1.1 brings together these distinctions and sets out the structure of the ethnographic and historical material discussed in this book. The horizontal axis describes the four main processes that determine the development of the frontier: migration and settlement, the management of resources, the development of civil institutions and the effects of globalization. The vertical axis refers to each of the specific cases discussed in successive chapters: the Spanish Pyrenees (chapter 3), midnineteenth century Canada (chapter 4), coastal Ecuador (chapter 5), and the Yucatán peninsula (chapters 6 and 7). In each case it is suggested that migration and land settlement were prompted by ideologies of nature, which reflect the social and ethnic characteristics of the settlers as well as the environmental characteristics of the area. Civil institutions developed out of a dialectical process with nature, through which its transformation helped to shape the civil society that came into being. There was no simple process of environmental causation or determinism but rather a reflexive process from which human agents constructed both a society and their means of imagining it. The frontier thus became a canvas on which both nature and civil institutions developed, and co-evolved (Norgaard 1984). In the Conclusion these ideologies of nature are re-examined, in the light of this broader canvas.

It is not my intention to pass lightly over the implications of these very different kinds of data, and the reflections to which they give rise to some extent mirror the evidence base. It is also important to set out

Table 1.1
Nature and civil society: Historical transitions

	Migration/settlement pattern	Resource use/management	Civil institutions/social capital	Globalization
Spanish Pyrenees, 1700–2000 (*chapter 3*)	Transhumance (sheep) traditionally; post-1940, migration from Catalonia, Andalucia, Galicia, etc. (construction, power, tourism)	Management of community owned forests and high grasslands; land sales for tourist development after 1968	Traditionally the *corvee* (communally managed); after 1960s increasing control of central government; today Catalan control and institutions	Tourism, especially ski resorts
Upper Canada, 1845–52 (*chapter 4*)	Land settlement: migrants from Britain and Ireland	Timber industry, forest clearance, small family farms	Land settlers seek political representation in Canada	Tourism to Algonquin Regional Park
Guayas basin, Ecuador, 1970–80 (*chapter 5*)	Migration from Ecuadorian sierra to coast; migration to Guayaquil	Internal frontiers of export crop production (cocoa, bananas) and rice for domestic market	Squatter land invasions lead to cooperatives and selective state control of rice production	Global agricultural markets
Yucatán, Mexico, 1700–2000 (*chapters 6, 7*)	Migration of rebel Maya from white control (Cruzob); migration from other Mexican tropics for chicle in forests; migration for land clearance (ejidos) after 1940	Forest products, particularly chewing gum (chicle) until 1950s; then large-scale land settlement under state aegis (ejidos)	Mayan civil institutions through separation; local institutions increasing subject to Mexican state	Global extractive markets (chicle); mass and niche tourism; global conservation of biosphere reserves

the rather bold methodological assumptions that underlie the analysis of such large categories as civil society and nature, and the considerable time span covered in this book. It will be clear to the reader that the evidence base varies markedly between chapters. The chapters on the Spanish Pyrenees, coastal Ecuador, and the Yucatán peninsula Mexico (chapters 3, 5, 6, and 7) all draw on field research that I have undertaken at different times: the late 1960s (Pyrenees), 1975 (Ecuador), and the period since 1995 (Yucatán). In these chapters the historical context plays a large part in the narrative, and history is largely treated as a narrative account. The voice adopted by the writer is that of a social scientist, informed by contemporary and archival material but resting heavily on field accounts and evidence. Occasionally it is made clear that different histories are at work, and the narrative format is inadequate.

It will become evident that these observations do not apply to the chapter on Canada in the midnineteenth century. The evidence here was gathered from collections of letters and contemporary chronicles, and it covers a much narrower period of time, as befits primary records and archives of this type. There is particularly heavy reliance on the accumulated letters of Francis Codd, extracts of which have already been published elsewhere. The voice in this chapter, while not that of the settlers themselves, is not far removed, and it certainly serves to silence that of other participants in the frontier drama, notably native Americans.

To some extent similar observations could be made about chapter 6, on *chicle* production in Mexico, since the state archival sources in Chetumal, as well as other historical material, play a considerable part in the recreation of the period, and the lives of the *chicleros*. This research, which was funded by the Economic and Social Research Council and Arts and Humanities Research Council of the United Kingdom, also draws on oral history, the testimony of ordinary people in the zone most of whom had never been interviewed before. Without seeking to take the part of the Mayan people, the account has sought to question the integrity and value of the Mayan brand name, which itself usurps a people's history.

There are clear advantages and disadvantages in using such a wealth of different material, both primary and secondary, from different historical periods and across cultures. The histories referred to in the sub-title of this book are not simply chronologies or narratives; they are highly selective episodes in the main, which it is hoped throw light on wider issues of interpretation. It is clear that other kinds of selection might yield very different results, and the analogies drawn throughout the book would not work. Another, and perhaps more serious charge, is that the way the book is written serves to disguise the raw data, since many of the accounts already embody a position on events and processes, that of other authors, contemporary chroniclers, or protagonists.

To these charges I would respond in the following way. The primary purpose of this book is to look beneath events, and peoples' accounts of them, and to place these accounts within a relatively unfamiliar context—that of the formation of different kinds of civil societies, in conjunction with "natures" constructed to a large extent by human hands. Indeed, each of these histories is discussed very explicitly in terms of the dominant theoretical project that prompted this book: the rela-tionship between material changes in the natural environment and the way we construct this world sociologically. It is not a book that sets out to present representative, or even historically adequate, accounts of places and societies. Rather, it sets out to demonstrate that the value of a social constructivist position on the environment is enhanced if it is located within a critical realist agenda. It is to this end that the dialectic is introduced, and reconsidered, as a means of illuminating sometimes unpredictable social changes.

In the following chapter (chapter 2) this theme, the relationship between the development and maintenance of frontiers and that of civil society, is investigated conceptually and theoretically. It takes us into areas that are not usually associated with the historical debates sur-rounding Turner and the so-called Turner thesis. Two theoretical issues are given particular attention. First, the way in which ideas surrounding private property, derived from the work of Hobbes and Locke, were used to justify the geographical expansion of empires onto land already occupied by other, indigenous cultures. From this perspective the devel-opment of civil societies is clearly dependent on the evolution of private property and the growth of individualism, two of the defining aspects of modernity.

Second, drawing on the work of the French marxist philosopher, Henri Lefebvre, attention is given to the way in which space is seen as a social construction as well as a material reality, which carries cultural and political significance. It is argued that frontiers can be seen as both material realities and as social constructions, whose ideological utility often develops slowly, without clear lines of demarcation. Frontiers are important as myth and as metaphor, as well as in their material transformation. The argument of this book is that we need to re-examine conventional categories, and begin to view frontiers as a metaphor for wider interactions or hybridizations between nature and society.

Chapter 3 examines the origins of common-pool resource management in the Pyrenees, and the difficult balance between delicate ecological systems and the pressure of growing human populations. It also discusses what happens when market forces and the controlling power of the Spanish state undermine these civil institutions. Chapter 4 follows a new spatial dimension of a frontier society: its expansionary role in the New World. It is concerned with the forest frontier in English-speaking Canada in the midnineteenth century and the inexorable process of settlement, which brought social conflicts but also a desire to establish social order in an apparently disordered world. The geographical contour lines are redrawn in midnineteenth-century Canada in ways that demonstrate the civilizing potential of the frontier, for better and for worse.

Chapters 5 and 6 consider another range of frontier situations created by the expansion of the global market economy. In these cases the impetus for frontier expansion is not the expulsion of population from the Old World, nor the European settlement of the New, but the expansion of market forces in the New World. Coastal Ecuador has witnessed political conflicts, over land and water resources, which reflect the demand for products such as bananas, cocoa, and rice. In these circumstances the political forces released by these conflicts have threatened the stability of already highly divisive civil societies. In the example that is discussed in detail, rice sharecroppers pursued their own interests in land to the point of invasions, as well as pressures to change the law itself. In coastal Ecuador, like the Yucatán peninsula described in chapters 6 and 7, the weakening of local control over the environment, and stronger links with international consumer markets, have led to civil unrest as an oppositional force. In the Yucatán the Mayan population resisted the control exercised by powerful landholding classes. The frontier in both cases became a historical battleground between classes and races that enabled the conflicting parties to each provide an account of events that legitimized their own claims. It provided them with myths about space and territory that they handed on to successive generations.

Finally, in chapter 7, I turn to the present, to examine a frontier that is being settled today by tourists and entrepreneurs on the Mexican Caribbean coast. The chapter argues that the process of tourist discovery needs to be set against the context of other, earlier frontiers, specifically that of *chicle*, and compares the way in which nature is valued under very different regimes. In looking at the Mexican Caribbean today it becomes evident that spatial and cultural relationships, between nature and civil societies, are increasingly linked to consumer markets, lifestyles, and tastes. It is the reflexive consumer, advertising copywriter, and global tourist who invented the Mayan Riviera, and with it a conception of frontier that assimilates the past. The evolving tourist frontiers of the Mexican Caribbean use images of bounteous nature that often obscure the flows of resources from periphery to center that have defined the region for centuries.

In this poststructuralist reading of environmental change, spatial relations and natural resources are the product of new, often compressed conceptions of time and space within a framework of economic and cultural globalization. The frontiers at issue are consequently as much the products of peoples' imaginations, as of geography and space. In a sense such hybridized cultural phenomena are consumed like other tropical products. One of the questions to be discussed in later chapters is to what extent these newly delineated frontiers represent the past, and its geography, and in doing so blur the line between what is natural and what is not.

2

Civil Society and Nature: Materiality or Cultural Construction?

In this chapter the relationship between nature and the development of civil society is examined from an historical and analytical perspective, drawing on a number of diverse literatures in the social sciences. It begins by examining the tradition of thinking about frontiers within the context of North American historiography, the so-called Turner thesis attributed to Frederick Jackson Turner, in the late nineteenth and early twentieth centuries. It is suggested that distinctions can be made between this avowedly modernist position and others that place emphasis on the frontier as an ambivalent area of economic exploitation and that make use of a broader historical and geographical canvas. Beginning with the experience of settled populations and longstanding forms of resource use, such as those found in much of mountain Europe, we can conceptualize some frontiers in terms of their institutional governance: in which communities utilize collective forms of livelihood, such as livestock transhumance, to demarcate their zones of responsibility and to manage their fragile ecosystems. As we will see in the case of the Spanish Pyrenees in chapter 3, this includes the management of forests and grasslands under forms of collective or cooperative management.

At another geographical scale, however, international frontiers exhibit greater ambivalence, social and political conflict is endemic, and the management of natural resources is more contested. We can then employ the concept of frontiers to demarcate spatial relationships in a different way, by exploring the successive waves through which the global economy impacts on the global periphery, where extractive forms of production source new patterns of consumption in the developed, increasingly consumer-driven economies. These geographical frontiers on the peripheries of empires and zones of colonial exploitation have brought commodities like coffee, bananas, and chewing gum to the table of the urban populations of Europe and North America. Transnational frontiers link consumption with production activities and may, as in the cases examined later in the book, served to transform forest economies in Latin America.

Finally, this chapter also sets out its analytical tools, by shifting the discussion away from discrete historical experiences and toward more theoretical models of the frontier. It explores the way in which the concept of frontier also taps into the imaginary, providing images and associations that take us beyond a set of economic and physical processes into new forms of cultural construction. This concern with identifying cultural processes across societies is not a purely discursive activity, devoid of real political consequences, but an invitation to view human societies and their environments as part of a wider dialectical process. As we will see, the discussion necessarily acquires greater theoretical complexity once we begin to explore the links between space and the way it is constructed socially.

The social construction of the frontier, through language and imagery, is now a powerful element in the development of tourism globally, and the legitimizing of international conservation policies and practices. This leads us to consider several analytical questions about the way space is conceptualized, as part of the process of understanding the frontier both as a locus of exchange between nature and culture, and a means to the creation of new cultural and consumer practices. The chapter ends by considering to what extent a dialectical approach to the frontier leaves us with a choice between a materialist and a social constructivist approach.

The Geography of Frontiers and the Turner Thesis

Much of the literature on frontiers, especially in geography, has distinguished between definitions of what a frontier constitutes, as a form of boundary or a zone of transition, and the social and cultural characteristics of the frontier. The discussion of frontier has sometimes sought to demystify the supposedly *natural* quality of frontiers as lines of demarcation. Broek, an early theorist, writes in *Frontiers of the Future* (1941) about what he terms "physiographic frontiers," which he describes as geographical frontiers without the so-called mystery attached to natural frontiers. He goes on to observe that "The word 'natural' (has) served as a double-barreled gun—scientific and emotional—to win land and to influence people" (Broek 1941, 11). As we will see, this is a recurring theme of much of the frontier literature, and of relevance to much of the discussion below.

If a frontier is conceptualized as "a boundary marked by nature . . ." (Broek 1941, 12), then the frontier itself is often thought of as imbued with "natural" qualities, the physical geography of the place takes on wider, essentially cultural, meanings. This process through which *other* aspects of frontier life are said to assume the qualities of nature is perhaps the first defining characteristic of frontiers.

Another dimension of frontiers that has attracted considerable interest is their place as zones of transition. Commenting on work by an earlier scholar (Fawcett) written at the very end of the nineteenth century, one leading writer on frontiers states that they are "distinct regions of transition; while it is admitted that all regions are transitional, it is only when transitional features are the dominant characteristic that the region is a true frontier" (Prescott 1965, 15). This emphasis on transition suggests that *process*, rather than form, needs to be considered as a defining characteristic: frontiers are about geographical zones that are changing their identity.

The idea of transition places frontiers not merely on the geographical margin but in a state of becoming something else. This transitional quality in turn reflects important shifts in the juridical and legal status of the frontier, as it passes from being a new territory to an established part of the political map. The frontier, then, tends to reflect ambiguity toward the authority of the state, a view expressed by Prescott in the following way:

[S]ettlement frontiers can exist only where *de jure* boundaries have been established to define the state area. The frontier then marks the limit to which the state's authority has extended in occupying its legally defined territory . . . primary settlement frontiers are historical features . . . the primary settlement frontier marked *de facto* limits of the state's political authority . . . primary frontiers were also characterized by rudimentary civil institutions, an absence of law and a presence of rebellion (Prescott 1965, 34–36).

In this view the social conditions, which are encountered on the frontier, are themselves the product of political ambivalence: the state exists but almost in vestigial form. At the same time, while the institutions of civil society are not fully developed, the frontier provides opportunities for dissent, and social conflicts. What Prescott terms the "primary settlement frontier" is really a zone of noncompliance, where individuals and families have sought to establish their own rules, within the wider, but tenuous protection of the state.

The idea of normative, and juridical boundaries, then parallels that of political frontiers and separate jurisdictions. In the view of some authors the *primary* frontier needs to be distinguished from other, later frontiers. In the case of the primary frontier the range of activities is essentially linked to subsistence in that the natural environment is the primary means of livelihood—whether through hunting, farming or mining, for example. According to Prescott, "the range of potential economic activities in a primary frontier is generally greater than in . . . secondary frontiers" and include fur trapping, timber felling, semisubsistence cultivation, grazing, mining, manufacturing, and service industries (Prescott 1965, 35). The term "primary frontier" also refers to rudimentary commercial networks and transportation links, seen as a primary stage in occupation. The use of the term subsistence is also important, since most farmers on the North American frontier were engaged in constant relations with the market—they were not self-provisioning peasants in the European nineteenth-century mold.

Turner's contribution to the debate about the American frontier was important in a number of ways, which have subsequently attracted considerable criticism (Taylor 1972). First, Turner argued that in the advance of the frontier one could observe what he called "the meeting point between savagery and civilization . . . the outer edge of the wave" (Turner 1920, 3). This contact between civilization and savagery involved a struggle, to establish human dominance. "[I]n short, at the frontier the environment is at first too strong for man . . . little by little he transforms the wilderness, but the outcome is not the old Europe . . ." (Turner 1920, 3–4).

From this initial conflict Turner goes on to argue that the struggle for dominance results in the development of American values. The passages in which he refers to this process are interesting:

The peculiarity of American institutions is the fact that they have been compelled to adapt themselves to the changes of an expanding people . . . to the changes involved in crossing a continent, in winning a wilderness. . . . American social development has been continually beginning over again on the frontier. . . . [T]he most significant thing about the American frontier is that it lies at the hither edge of free land. . . . [I]n the settlement of America we have to observe how European life entered the continent, and how America modified and developed that life and reacted on Europe. . . . [T]he frontier is the line of most effective Americanisation. . . . Little by little he transforms the wilderness, but the outcome is not the old Europe. . . . [H]ere is a new product that is American . . . the advance of the frontier has meant a steady movement away from the influence of Europe, a steady growth of independence on American lines (Turner 1920, 3–4).

This passage provides the core of Turner's argument, and the case for which he has been criticized. In his view the nature of frontier settlement—the existence of so-called free land and the need to transform and tame nature—has helped to forge American culture and institutions. As he puts it in a later passage "[at the frontier] the complex European life [is] sharply precipitated by the wilderness into the simplicity of primitive conditions" (Turner 1920, 9).

The primitivism does not persist, of course. In time it gives rise to new frontiers—after the pioneer comes the next group of emigrants, who purchase land, who add field systems, who build better roads, and build bridges over streams. Turner was well aware, indeed it is central to his thesis, that there are sequential frontiers: the trader's frontier, the rancher's frontier, the miner's frontier, the farmer's frontier, and so on. Each of these frontiers, however, has imbued something from what came before, and each is testimony to the ability of American society to make, and re-make, itself.

The third element in Turner's argument—after the taming of wilderness, and the forcible establishment of civil society, imparting distinctively American institutions—is that this process breeds *individualism*, the backbone of democracy. The individuals who pit their wits against nature are able to exercise a degree of independence from outside control, something that was unknown in Europe:

[T]he most important effect of the frontier has been in the promotion of democracy here and in Europe . . . the frontier is productive of individualism . . . complex society is precipitated by the wilderness into a kind of primitive organization based on the family. The tendency is anti-social. It produces antipathy to control, and particularly to any direct control . . . steadily the frontier of settlement advances and carries with it individualism, democracy and nationalism. . . . (Turner 1920, 35)

As we will see later, several of the points that Turner made in relation to the role of the frontier in the United States resonate too in the Canada of the 1840s and 1850s. In particular, the challenge represented by an apparently limitless natural environment was certainly one that played a large part in helping shape early Canadian institutions. The conflict between what Turner calls civilization and the savagery of the wilderness were themes of settlers and visitors to Upper Canada in the mid-nineteenth century.

At the same time we must ask ourselves how much of Turner's thesis is rhetorical, and has served to reinforce, rather than question, underlying assumptions about North American history. We can perhaps discern strong and weak variants of the Turner thesis. The strong version sees the frontier as giving rise to democratic political forms, that are uniquely American. Subsequent writers have pointed to other settler societies in the Americas and elsewhere, in parts of Africa and the Antipodes, all of which retain some of the features described by Turner, and many of which claim to be equally democratic. Clearly, the way in which the United States can lay claim to democracy involves a series of important variables that the Turner thesis ignores, notably the integration of millions of European immigrants into the American cities of the late nineteenth and early twentieth centuries. One can also criticize the Turner view of democracy from another perspective, as a narrow and privileged one that is essentially ethnocentric.

Critics of the Tuner thesis have engaged in a number of debates with what became one of the orthodoxies of American scholarship before the Great Depression. They suggest that Turner chose to ignore more longstanding traditions—particularly religious and political traditions—that came from Europe, and also helped to shape American democracy (Taylor 1972). One distinguished American historian, Louis Hacker, has argued that the West furnished the means for the United States to sell food competitively on the world market (and undermining European agriculture in the process), which in turn enabled the United States to borrow capital for its own industrialization. The history of the United States, claimed Turner's critics, has less to do with the supposed virtues of frontier individualism and more to do with the advance of corporate power, and American capitalism.

More detailed historiography has also suggested that the idea of sequential frontiers is sometimes confusing, since many of the stages referred to by Turner existed at one and the same time in the American West. This is an observation supported, to some extent, by the evidence from Francis Codd's account of Upper Canada, in chapter 4. Of course, there are real dangers in stretching the American case to cover British North America—where the idea of what Turner termed a "composite nationality" (i.e., American) was absent. In particular, the element in the Turner thesis that deserves more attention is that which was almost passed over without comment earlier this century, when it became dominant. This is the only half conceived connection between the way civil institutions and society develop, and the way that nature is transformed.[1] This is the part of the argument to which we return, and at more length, later in this book. As we will see, the more we examine what frontiers have come to mean, the less satisfactory is this rather limited, utilitarian view.[2] This chapter examines three alternative models for conceptualizing the frontier, each of which has application to distinct historical and geographical circumstances: frontiers as boundaries, as areas of human settlement and commodity production, and as cultural imaginaries. Before examining these models in more detail, however, we need to consider the role of land and property, core institutions in the development of frontiers and civil societies.

Land, Property, and Civil Society

Today we associate land with property, but the links between them bear witness to a considerable evolution over time. Modern views of landholding depart radically from those of ancient and pre-modern societies. There is archaeological evidence of links between property regimes and land, in the land registers from the ancient Egyptian, Chinese, and

Babylonian civilizations, as early as 2200 BC. Such evidence does little to illuminate the intrinsic characteristics of property, however, since the relationship between human populations and resources has varied widely. In some cases the property regime involved people working on the land, for example, in the first Roman codifications and in medieval societies where human labor constituted part of the property held. In other cases social groups or individuals were the objects of property in a particular place or, more commonly, property regimes were expressed through myths and ritual observances, which were not codified in law (Neale 1998; Duchrow and Hinkelammert 2004).

The idea that property can be closely associated with land is hardly a novelty. Land forms the basis of social reproduction, it provides the livelihood basis for most people, especially in pre-industrial societies, and it carries importance for their identity, whether in symbolic or naturalistic form. As societies evolve, so do property regimes, and their growing complexity helps create subjects and agencies for dealing with rights and obligations to land.

Thinking about the link between land and property also evolved together with examples of practices, providing a complex set of alternative philosophical and legal positions. In Western thought it is possible to trace human reflections on property back to the early works of Plato (in his *Republic*) and to Aristotle (in his *Etica nicomaquea*). Similarly in the writings of early Christian theologians, such as Augustine and Thomas Aquinas, it is possible to find references to the distinction between collective and individual property. For all these authors the problem of property and land ownership was indissolubly linked to that of the ethics and morality of human behavior and societies (MacPherson 1978). Much of this early thinking, however, was primarily concerned not with property relations as we might see them today, as institutions for managing economic resources and competing claims from individual groups of people, but with the political legitimacy of property.

The European Renaissance marked a series of major social changes that had great bearing on property relations. The advent of modernity in the fifteenth century brought the consolidation of centralized power by monarchies, and their territorial ambitions. With the expansion of mercantilist capitalism the boundaries of political influence shifted outward and, underpinned by the Protestant reform movement, so too did the process of individualization. It has been argued that these twin processes of territorial expansion and the individualization of the subject constitute the two principal elements in modernity (MacPherson 1978). The development of new structures of power was connected with the transformation of social structures, in terms of social classes, the consolidation and expansion of markets, and new relationships between centers and peripheries, towns and rural areas.

The development of modernity implied increasing control over the land by centralized states, usually employing military means. These states established and enforced property regimes, which often challenged and transformed traditional rights to resources, and helped secure a new relationship between central governments and civil societies. This was particularly evident in the support given by the newly emerging financial bourgeoisie to the monarchy, and the successful subordination of social classes whose own control over the land loosened that of the central monarchical state.

Spread over several centuries, the major shifts in law and politics, were also reflected in thinking about the role of the individual in society. In northwest Europe, and later in North America, industrialization and rapid urbanization brought immense social upheaval and new largely secular discourses. In the late nineteenth century these culminated in the development of classical political economy and, later, other social sciences, distinguished from the natural sciences by their often explicit political concerns. As the new secular discourses replaced the old religious understandings, so the justification for the old order was more difficult to maintain. The relative demise of religion, as the basis of all authority, led thinkers from Adam Smith onward to assume that the economy was part of the natural order, and its rules, universally true.

The social revolutions of the eighteenth and nineteenth centuries in Europe had already assisted in the diffusion of ideas associated with the social contract theorists of the seventeenth century, notably Thomas Hobbes (*Leviathan*, 1651) and John Locke (*Essay on Civil Government*, 1689). These volumes established the basic ideological elements on which the later political economists were able to construct their rationale of society (MacPherson 1962, 1978). For Hobbes, property was a natural right of the individual, and society existed to help secure it in a context of scarce resources and human conflict. In his view, this natural right was a reflection of the naturally possessive instinct of the human individual, and the individual's control over his labor power. Later Locke developed Hobbes's approach and added a new critical aspect: the right to property had no natural limits. Durchov and Hinkelamert (2004) have observed that the short period that separates Hobbes and Locke was marked by the beginning of English colonization of the Americas. The exploration of North America by the English settlers, appeared to reveal a land frontier that was endless, making Hobbes's argument about property rights under scarce resources appear redundant. In addition Locke's argument seemed to justify the occupation of land held by indigenous people, since they appeared not to exert any property rights to their land, at least in the way suggested necessary by natural philosophy.

The coincidence of the discovery of a new continent, the rise of overseas economic markets, and the justification of private property in the writings of Hobbes and Locke helped the development of an idea that was relatively new: that only individual or private property was natural. As a natural phenomenon individual property lay outside history, and it possessed the common and universal quality that societies sought to protect in the form of a social contract. Within this highly individualistic frame of reference attempts at the social control of private property were backward, and hindered prosperity, they ceased to be natural. The only real check on the rights of private property lay with the individual's intrinsic genius and industry; his ability to produce and acquire. This was later incorporated within political economy, as the liberal economists of the nineteenth century argued that possessive individualism was a positive force that helped support markets through rational choice. Smith was acquainted with the work of Hobbes and Locke and, although he rejected the social contract theory, he defended the view that civil society was a spontaneous order based on the individual's acceptance of authority (Malloy 1995). Smith added to this the belief in the individual as a rational calculator by focusing on utility as a concept, something that contributed later to the full development of a liberal theory of property.

In this book the term civil society is accorded importance not as a narrowly defined concept but as an element in a wider set of relationships through which property rights have been exerted over nature. The constraints of limited natural resource endowments thus inhibit economic development in some societies while opening up apparently limitless resources that offer the promise of prosperity in other societies. The dialectical process, between nature and society, provides a momentum for the development of both civil institutions and the forcible transformation of nature. As we will see, each frontier discussed exhibits degrees of social conflict. In some cases, these conflicts are between competing definitions of property and civil society, held by different ethnic and religious groups; in others, they are struggles within the logic of modernity itself, between social classes with distinct economic interests, notably in their control and management of land.

Boundaries: Communal Resources and Governance

As noted above, one of the first ways in which the term frontier is employed is in the sense of boundaries. Frontiers have often been envisaged as lines of demarcation, as boundaries that separate different civil and political institutions. A closer look at these frontier/boundaries also suggests something else, that they are often zones of extensive interaction, rather than of settlement, transitional zones where the exercise of governance and the powers of civil authorities are closely guarded and geographically delimited. The Pyrenees, in the case discussed below, has been such a frontier for millennia, partly offering a natural boundary between territories but also providing examples of resource management (of forests, sheep, and high pastures) that served to define the authority of local governance. These were frontiers in which communal civic institutions evolved together with forms of environmental management designed to be sustainable, in the light of the resource systems' considerable ecological fragility. A discussion of the frontier benefits here from the acknowledgment that civil societies have grown up alongside specific systems of environmental management, and have co-evolved with these ecological systems (Norgaard). Governance, which includes the rights of individual community members, is almost indistinguishable from the routine management of the natural resource base.

The emphasis on the legitimacy of governance at the local level, as a means of managing nature, has been discussed in the literature on social capital. It is useful to clarify these arguments because most of the historical cases with which this book is concerned suggest elements of this discussion—in particular, the extent to which societies need to act collectively to ensure sustainable environmental management, and the part played by social conflict in the integrity and legitimacy of civil societies. In much of this discussion civil society is equated with social capital.

It was within the corridors of the World Bank that the term came into general usage. Following on Robert Putnam's study of Italian regional politics and development (1993) the World Bank adopted the concept of social capital as a way of explaining the need for strong horizontal ties between social actors, if development gains were to be made. The concept then assumed importance for a variety of reasons, some of them internal to the Bank: it provided a parallel to that of the environmental economists (natural capital) and held the promise of deliverable, measurable indicators, like those being developed by the Bank for human populations at the time (Dasgupta and Serageldin 2000; Serageldin and Steer 1994). The World Bank saw social capital as a measurable good, rather than a way of exploring social process, while at the same time it enabled a link to be made between participation in development, and development theory (Bebbington 2004). Social capital risked being all things to all people as a result.

One response to this emasculation of politics under the aegis of neoliberal economic orthodoxies was that the idea of social capital appears to have been radicalized in some quarters, drawing on the more structuralist analyses of development and underdevelopment that characterized the 1970s and early 1980s. As Bebbington notes, "the concept of social capital necessarily implies a recognition that all forms of economic, political and social action are embedded in deeper institutional and social structures" (Bebbington 2004, 41). This position, with which most critics of social capital concur, locates the concept within given historical situations: "social relations and their patterning cannot be looked at independently of location, history and political economy"

(Bebbington 2002, 802). Subsequently the debate surrounding social capital has emphasized aspects of this historicity, including the need to acknowledge the importance of power relations, class, ethnicity and gender (Harriss 2002; Fine 2001). In his earlier synthetic account Woolcock (1998) had emphasized the way in which the concept of social capital served to bridge disciplines and facilitate discussion from different intellectual positions, much as sustainable development had done a decade earlier. These critics of social capital (like those of sustainable development) often insist that whatever its deficiencies, the concept still has utility, provided that its use is not confined to policy thinking within the World Bank (Fox 1996; Fine 1999; Smith and Kulynych 2002).

As I have suggested, the critics of social capital cited above have argued effectively for a concept that is more rigorous and culturally refined than many of its original architects might want. My purpose is to demonstrate in the cases that follow, that civil societies have grown up in which the management of natural resources is intimately linked with wider histories of class conflict and market relations. Whether it is possible to engineer cooperation among international institutions, such as the World Bank, and local communities, in a way that strengthens their social capital remains unclear.

Settlement and Commodity Frontiers: Spaces of Unintended Consequence

In other circumstances the idea of boundary gives way to a much more expansionary concept in which the natural environment is plundered or transformed to meet human purposes, but often at a considerable geographical distance. The histories of empire have been precisely histories of such ecological expansion, often giving rise to exchanges of genetic materials, as well as products, to a different form of dialectic.

However, it is important to distinguish between settlement frontiers. One variety, in which European colonists played the major part, saw migrant populations occupying land with the intention of establishing permanent settlement and new social institutions. In Upper Canada, under the force of British and Irish immigration, the native population offered little resistance to white rule and never represented a serious threat to the hegemony of white settlers. To some extent, however, the destruction of the forest and the population of theoretically empty lands brought consequences for the new civil society that came into being in Canada. The settler population invented what David Nye has called a "second creation" story about itself—although one that was markedly different in certain respects from that of the United States—and placed emphasis on lines of continuity with the British Empire until well into the second half of the twentieth century (Nye 2003). In the process they often created what David Nye (2003) calls "foundation narratives," which brought them into conflict with indigenous groups and values ("counter narratives" in Nye's term). This is seen most vividly in the case of the United States, but also in Canada, Australia, and Afrikaans-speaking South Africa.

However, it is clear that to develop a more robust, conceptually rewarding notion of frontiers, we need to move beyond the historical and geographical context provided by Turner. Another variety of settlement of new lands that is discussed more fully in chapters 5 and 6 is that of global commodity frontiers. These are conceived as locations in which ecological transformations take place as a consequence of purposeful human action, but whose consequences are rarely anticipated. In the cases that follow much of the settlement undertaken by migrant populations in Latin America was on land that was looked upon as empty, implying not simply that it was devoid of human population but rather of civilized humans, since indigenous people were largely invisible to colonialism. The settlers who occupied the internal frontiers of much of Latin America usually did so for short-term profit, through the extraction of rent (on both servile labor and on land) or in the search for precious materials and commodities. In Marxist language this process refers to "primitive accumulation."

Coastal Ecuador was a very different case from that of British Canada, since much of the migrant population was itself partly indigenous. Land was not settled in favor of whites from Europe, but of elite groups that had lived in the country for generations, and fought their way to power on the back of global commodities: cocoa, bananas, and rice. Their authority lay in their control of a labor force largely made up of people of mixed race, and their attention to the environmental consequences of their plantation activities was minimal. The process, which explains their economic hegemony and rationale, was the extraction of rent, on both labor and land. For much of tropical Latin America, unlike the so-called settler societies established by populations of British and Irish descent, the land frontier was essentially a means of extracting value from primary commodities, but at several removes. The city continued to dominate the interior in Latin America, providing a vivid cultural contrast between civilization and wilderness that continues to resonate today. Today, too, many more such settlers in the interior are poor, and politically subordinated people.

Indeed, the exploitation of the tropics under North American tutelage was a distinctive experience, very removed from that of European colonialism. Richard Tucker (2000) charts this history with great conviction. In his book, *Insatiable Appetite: The United States and the Ecological Degradation of the Tropical World* (2000), Tucker begins by asking himself how and why American history came to be so inseparably linked to global ecological destruction. Not until the very end of the nineteenth century, after the military victory over Spain, did the United States "open the door to the creation of an American empire in Latin America and the islands of the Pacific" (Tucker 2000, 2).

Tucker draws a useful parallel between the newly established American "empire" and that of the European states. He notes that for well over half the period during which European influences dominated the world economy (from Europe's discovery of America in the late fifteenth century to the end of the nineteenth century) "North America was itself a frontier for the extraction of resources by European powers" (Tucker 2000, 3). The United States and Canada had experienced empire first hand, at the receiving end of ecological transformations largely initiated by the British.[3] The resource frontier shifted, however, in the 1890s, as the United States grew as an economic power and raised its own domestic consumers, and their consuming appetites.

One interesting example is that of the banana. Until the mid-nineteenth century fresh fruit and vegetables were always eaten during the harvest season. However, by the 1890s, and the expansion of steamship and railroad networks, tropical products had arrived at the

American table, bringing much needed vitamins and enriching the diet. As Virginia Scott Jenkins writes: "The idea of pricing bananas low enough so that everyone could buy them and still make a profit for the producing company preceded Henry Ford's Model T" (Jenkins 2000, 56). The success of bananas in the American diet, like that of chewing gum described in chapter 6, is largely attributable to advertising and mass communications. Americans, and later Europeans, did not acquire a taste for eating bananas from Africans or Central Americans. These tastes suggest the beginnings of a consumer society in which products were designed for a consumer with insufficient time and a modest, but steadily increasing, disposable income.

Apologists for consumer society today, however, continue to berate the "unproductive" labor of less "civilized" peoples, and to compare it unfavorably with the gains from mass consumption:

Americans exchange work for goods on much better terms (than Papuans). They grow 48 times as many sweet potatoes per workday as Papuans. They catch 118 times as much fish as Papuans and 144 times as much as Australia's aborigines. Such considerable differences reflect the gap between primitive economies and more complex capitalist ones. (Lebergott 1993, 64–65)

Interestingly Lebergott does not attempt to quantify how much more damage to the environment is done by American consumers, or the extent of their ecological footprint.

From the late nineteenth century Americans took the baton from Europeans in the exploitation of the tropics. Their control of the seas in the Western Hemisphere, and the growing appetites of their consumers, ensured that their entrepreneurs were able to fill their pockets, and their households furnish and stock their houses and yards. What Tucker calls the "hungry giant" extended its reach, by using the capital generated in the American heartland to penetrate the environments of the Caribbean and Latin America. This process of commercial expansion was made easier by the territorial expansions, largely at the cost of independent Mexico, in 1848 and 1853.[4] In the second half of the nineteenth century the United States stood head and shoulders above any other power in the Western Hemisphere, and by the beginning of the twentieth century was exercising its muscles in the growing global economy.

Unlike Great Britain and other European powers the United States did not seek direct political control on the imperial model. It sought instead to dominate commerce and to exploit the resource frontiers of the Americas without subjecting their populations to American social institutions. It did so by filling the power vacuum that Spain, in particular, had left in its wake. The remaining vestiges of European empire were easily outmaneuvered: "Even where European colonies remained— Spanish Cuba, the Dutch East Indies, and British Malaya—the power of Yankee capital was gradually established" (Tucker 2000, 4). Now it was Americans, rather than the Europeans, who were zealously civilizing the tropics, just as they were civilizing their own native populations, almost to the point of extinction.

North American economic hegemony had other effects, which have remained and generated important consequences today. The new sciences of agronomy, pasture, and livestock management and forestry were given a critical boost by public funding and private patronage in the United States. They helped take the surveyor into new lands, and onto new frontiers. Francis Codd, whose personal narrative was discussed in the previous chapter, had instructed his brother in England to train as a surveyor so that he could come to Canada and survey what was seen as a limitless territory, and one that was barely mapped in the 1850s. But mapping, of course, was not an altogether innocent activity. With the mapping of the frontier came the management of its resources and the extension of political authority to newly settled areas, a model that was later extended to tropical lands overseas.

Tucker also makes another comment on this expansionary process that has relevance for this discussion. He suggests that the process of commercial expansion into the tropics had secondary ripple effects, which "are virtually impossible to measure with any precision, since the boundaries of systemic change are partly a matter of definition" (Tucker 2000, 5). The tropical frontier carried implications for the domestic parts of the system, introducing changes in the economy and society of the United States, just as colonialism left its impact on the colonial powers of Western Europe.

One author who has sought to develop a model that incorporates the tropical, extractive frontier and the metropolitan economies of North

America and Europe is Stephen Bunker. In *Underdeveloping the Amazon: Extraction, Unequal Exchange, and the Failure of the Modern State* (1985) Bunker argues that most marxist analysis, with its emphasis on the labor theory of value, ignores the real contribution of natural resources and ecological systems to economic development. This contribution is conceptualized in the idea of energy flows, and he argues that the continued maintenance of industrial modes of production is at the cost of primary resource systems, such as those of the Amazon:

Uneven development between regions and the capacity of one region to subordinate another reflect not only the unequal exchange of labor values but also the very different of energy flow-through in social organization and infrastructure. (Bunker 1985, 245)

The argument that frontiers extend in ways that are not confined to geography is a central tenet of this book, but the use of energy flows, while innovative, raises some awkward questions. Among the most important of these is the vexed question of whether thinking in terms of flows enlarges discussion through the use of an appropriate metaphor, or (as Bunker seems to suggest) offers a genuinely synthetic approach that integrates questions of power and social structure with those of materiality (Buttel, Mol, and Spaargaren 2006).

New spatial relationships helped to facilitate changes not only in the natural environment but also in the engine of economic growth itself. To fully appreciate this process, we need to look beyond the tropics to the consumer markets of the developed world, where temperate agricultural products played a central role in the popular diet. The temperate frontier had dramatic effects, in North America and Europe, that matched those of the tropical frontiers developed primarily around resource extraction. To fully understand this process, we need to return to the centrality of consumption.

During the second half of the nineteenth century the labor force grew rapidly in the industrial economies, first of Great Britain, but later in continental Europe and the United States. The distinctive features of consumption under these regimes were cheap staple foodstuffs, particularly grains. In the development of capital they constituted an important element in labor costs and, indeed, in the reproduction costs of labor as

Sidney Mintz pointed out in his study of the supply and demand for sugar, *Sweetness and Power* (Mintz 1986). Much of the reproductive costs continued to be borne by small scale, usually domestic, activities, but the fully fledged wage labor economy developed features that were to eclipse the simple production of commodities, a process initiated much earlier in the history of industrialization (Goodman and Redclift 1991; Aglietta 1979).

In the period before the First World War, industrial capitalism consolidated its expansion in overseas markets on the global periphery. Merchant capitalists extended the frontiers of agricultural production in the temperate grain-producing areas of the New World, utilizing the technological advances of the second half of the century: the railroad, telegraph and steamship. This led to a spatial restructuring of the global economy, not only to deliver tropical products to the homes of new classes of consumers but also to ensure their staple diet. The gradual formation of a world grain market after 1850 was made possible by territorial and productive expansion, in the North American prairies, and later in Australia, New Zealand, and the River Plate countries. This ensured cheap supplies of staple foodstuffs for the expanding urban labor forces of both Europe and North America.

The consequences of these changes for European agricultural producers were not foreseen. By the mid-1870s world grain prices had collapsed, undermining large-scale capitalist agriculture in Britain, which had followed a policy of free trade since the repeal of the Corn Laws, and leading eventually to the encouragement of working tenant farmers, commented on by Marx in the third volume of *Capital*. Family labor forms of production came to dominate agriculture, even in those parts of the temperate world that had never experienced a peasantry. These producers achieved a growth in world output of grains, and extended the margin of cultivation to incorporate new land. This extensive frontier was made possible by reserves of potentially productive land for cereals in temperate latitudes, and by the exploitation of family labor, much of it made up of European settlers, or first generation Americans. The frontier referred to by Frederick Jackson Turner may, or may not, have helped generate democratic ideals, but it certainly facilitated the expansion of internal markets for wage-goods in the United States and its emergence as the foremost capitalist power.

The development of a new "more complex international division of labor after 1850" meant that local harvest crises had a diminishing impact on economic activity, besides dispelling the specter of famine and food riots that had haunted the European ruling classes in the "hungry" 1840s (Goodman and Redclift 1991, 95). With simultaneous access to geographically separate zones of production, in different latitudes and continents, industrial capital was freed from the seasonality of individual national agricultures, facilitating a continuous production of staple foods, analogous to that of industry. For the first time overproduction of grains assumed structural proportions as new agricultural frontiers were incorporated into the world market. In the United States alone the extension of cropland trebled between 1840 and 1888 (Hobsbawm 1979). At the same time overproduction reduced food prices for the masses and, in most industrialized countries, improved working-class standards of living in the period just before the First World War. Eventually food, like other commodities, was to be subjected to fordist principles, and popular diet to large-scale market extension (Friedmann and McMichael 1989).

This process of territorial expansion, and the concomitant improvement in popular diet, provides a definition of frontiers that departs from some of the more narrowly conceived versions that we have inherited in the literature. But the engine of economic growth that led to the extensive frontier did not stop with the grain-elevator companies and commodity exchanges. Increasingly the production of key wage-goods was transformed by new technologies, first mechanical, then chemical, and finally increasingly biological. Beginning in the United States and Great Britain, public funding played a critical role not only in the growth of domestic agriculture, but its export overseas, where the development of the applied agricultural sciences and technology was linked, during the Green Revolution years of the 1970s, with increasing irrigation and market inducements such as the provision of agricultural credit. Now it was the export of the model, rather than the product, that was driving the process of global market integration, and claiming new frontiers.

Frontiers and the Imaginary: Cultural Conceptions of Place and Space

The third sense of frontier is primarily about the effect of the interaction between human-made and wild nature on the cultural imaginary, the way that societies see themselves and others. Frontiers in this sense are metaphors for wider interactions or hybridizations between nature and society. They refer to an imaginary conception of place and its uses, and the way in which the creation of landscape reflects both the material circumstances of societies and their social constructions. In chapter 8 this conceptualization is developed in the context of global tourism and conservation in the Mexican Caribbean. These processes are not simply subject to sequential changes but also appear in other frontier situations today, such as that of the Spanish Pyrenees, discussed in chapter 3.

In exploring the relationship between physical space and its cultural assimilation, we owe a particular debt to the French philosopher and political activist, Henri Lefebvre. It is Lefebvre more than any other thinker, who has sought to explain the importance of space, as a dynamic force, and a universal factor in the development of modernity, and its discontents. His writing informs our understanding in a number of interrelated ways that can be usefully distinguished from each other but require careful analysis of their contribution to the wider discussion.

Consciousness and the Visual Plane

The first analytical issue is that of space. Lefebvre's work took the visual plane and gave it an emphasis previously denied it. Space was approached in terms of what lay beneath the surface of appearances, using the metaphor of the visual image present by art. Drawing on his interest in art history, and his own engagement in the early surrealist movement in the 1920s, Lefebvre notes that during this period "space opened up to perception, to conceptualization, just as it did to practical action," and the artist increasingly considered not only objects *in space* but also the concept of space itself (Lefebvre 1991, 205). This new consciousness was developed through re-imagining the canvas, by manipulating the planes through which space was viewed, and reconstituting the depth of space unavailable on a flat canvas. It enabled the viewer to discount the façade, the privileged aspect of a work of art, which lays it open to view, and to determine its multiple planes. This understanding of what we see—and may be denied—is particularly useful in interpreting the frontier, since it enables us to appreciate several perspectives at one and the same time. It argues for considering space as both multidimensional and constructed by the viewer. Space may involve representational understandings, such as perspective provides in Renaissance art, that are linked to societies' evolutions. As we have seen the commodity frontiers provide evidence to our eyes but also require an understanding of what we see, *Verstehen* to use Weberian terminology, that has as much to do with the viewer as the object viewed.

Social Space and Social Practices

The second contribution that Lefebvre makes to our understanding of space and the frontier is his insistence that we cannot observe spatial relations that are not also social relations. We produce space just as we produce nature in the development of economic relations. Lefebvre introduces the idea of global space, as "a void waiting to be filled, a medium waiting to be colonized" (p. 205). In his view this sense of space represented a challenge for capitalism, and capitalism eventually filled it with the desiderata of late modernity, commercial imagery, brands and logos. The void that he refers to is occupied with images that we construct, or are constructed for us, to encourage the growth of commodities and a commodity culture. Space in this sense is not the passive location that serves as the site for social activity; in the form of social space it is the means by which the economic and political system establishes hegemony and gains legitimacy.

In effect, Lefebvre is arguing that space is part of the process through which societies transform nature. This implies contradictions that capitalism cannot easily solve, since social space is a unitary concept embodying the *physical, the mental, and the social* (p. 11). Space, in other words, is seen as a way of drawing together different facets of both the physical and the cultural. The idea of physical qualities to space is not difficult to grasp—it is the everyday construction that we understand. However, Lefebvre is also writing about concepts of space that exist within our heads, and are part of mental processes. What he terms the "space of social practice" is occupied by sensory phenomena "including products of the imagination, such as projects and projections, symbols and utopias" (p. 12). On this reading space is a highly complex concept that embodies cultural as well as physical properties, and cannot be understood unless these properties are interrelated. In addition, because the construction of space is an active, transitive process, involving cultural meanings as well as territorial dimensions, it is best seen as a process linked to the development of societies. He comments that the redrawing of space in visual terms, and the construction of social space "gave rise to a very specific dialectic" (Lefebvre 1991, 125).

Interpreting Space: The Dialectical Character of Social Space

Finally, Lefebvre takes this dynamic process through which space is socially constructed, and suggests that we consider the way in which space is read or decoded. Lefebvre comments that "already produced space" is capable of being decoded in a variety of ways depending on the subjects, or members of a particular society, for whom their space has particular significance, and who use language, both formally and as semiotics, to communicate its value. He sees the dialectical character of codes as "part of a practical relationship, as part of an interaction between 'subjects' and their space and surroundings" (Lefebvre 1991, 18). The idea presented is an intellectual challenge rather than an axiom, and it leads us to ask whether we ever fully understand the social practices inherent to spaces and the languages that are used to describe them.

The central idea in Lefebvre's thinking is that space appears to have taken on a reality of its own within capitalist society where it is regularly divested of its social nature. For him as a marxist this is unacceptable, and, indeed, a mystification, since this is only *appearance*, and fails to capture the social forces that actually produce space. It suffers from the illusion of transparency, which places the design of space in the foreground, and serves to hide the shadows behind the light, representing space as an innocent domain. Hence ideas like those of discovery and settlement can be reinterpreted, from this perspective, as ways of concealing as much as they reveal.

Another implication of this illusion of transparency has clear implications for thinking about sustainability and the conservation of nature.

Lefebvre argues that although nature is disappearing, its symbolic weight persists and takes on meanings that obscure what is happening through its destruction. He suggests that we are obsessed by nature (which he compares with childhood) because we can only appreciate it through the cultural filter of memory:

Everybody wants to protect and save nature; nobody wants to stand in the way of an attempt to retrieve its authenticity. Yet at the same time everything conspires to harm it. The fact is that natural space will soon be lost to view. Anyone so inclined may look over their shoulder and see it sinking below the horizon behind us. (Lefebvre 1991, 30–31)

This approach opens up a number of important insights for the discussion of the frontier. The dialectical character of social space enables us to reclaim it from its supposed innocence and to subject it to human purposes and understanding once more. Myths of nature surround us, but these myths serve to hide social and political realities, as well as to illuminate them. By mythologizing meaning, they render nature less accessible to rational thought. At the moment the concern for nature conservation suggests that nature is not seen solely in instrumental terms. In Lefebvre's view it is a "negative utopia," the raw materials from which social systems fashion their productive resources and their particular spaces.

If we begin by acknowledging that space is a social product that comes into being by engaging both the human imagination and human physical processes, as Lefebvre suggests, then whatever we might conceive imaginatively about nature prior to human intervention cannot be detached from human purposes. This approach suggests a Promethean transformative role for humans in relation to nature, as depicted by Marx himself, but critically it departs from classical marxism in identifying distinct dialectical forces in human societies, that reject the way nature is itself being destroyed. Consciousness of the destructive consequences of globalization and the commoditization of space is evident in several of the chapters below, and returned to at different stages in this book.

At this point Lefebvre puts forward a way of distinguishing within this process, between the realities of social space and the powerful imagery with which it is viewed. There are three categories to be employed. First, what he terms *spatial practice* refers to the processes of production and reproduction within a society that ensure its continuity and a degree of cohesion. These practices ensure that the individual absorbs society's relationship to space. Second, there are the *representations of space* that link the relations of production in a society to its knowledge and the language (codes), with which a society explains itself. This is the space of scientists and engineers, of architects, planners, and academics, who use their own professional linguistic codes to communicate the codes of practice. Third, there are what Lefebvre terms *representational spaces*, and these spaces embody complex symbolism and constitute the space of most inhabitants. It is the routine lived space that most people are conscious of occupying. It utilizes and overlays physical space, "making symbolic use of its objects" (Lefebvre 1991, 39). At the same time it is this representational space that is socially and politically contested, that is subjected to the power of the human imagination and the will to establish lived alternatives.

The Dialectic: Materialities and Social Constructions

It has been suggested that a more conceptual approach to space requires further consideration of the dialectic, as the process through which social and material changes can best be understood. This in turn requires some historical explanation. The principal strength of the dialectic, as a process of reasoning, is that it enables one to grasp two opposed propositions as simultaneously valid. In Plato's dialogues, Socrates argued by means of cross-examination, seeking to reveal the inherent contradictions in the other person's position. The method was taken up by Hegel and was influential during much of the nineteenth century in European thought (Berthold-Bond 1993). For Hegel, the entire span of Western history was one enormous dialectical process, charting a difficult path toward rational institutions and citizenship from origins in confusion and self-alienation. This progressive movement demonstrated the primacy of ideas, of the principles that were coming into being during the nineteenth century: it was idealist and teleological.

Engels, in his essay on Feuerbach claimed that he and Marx had "turned the dialectic off its head . . . and placed it upon its feet again" (Engels's *Essay on Feuerbach*). They had transformed the dialectic from a way of understanding thought to a law of motion of the material world. As Kautsky (1927) showed, Engels regarded movement and development not as reciprocal effects of two factors, the individual and the environment, on one another but rather at the initiative of the individual who alone produces the antithesis to his thesis. If Hegel's mistake was to place the mind upon a historical pedestal, that of Marx and Engels was to see human action alone as constituting history. Not able to fully anticipate the difficulties that science was to pose for the environment, still less the environmental crisis, Marx and Engels were unable to fully acknowledge the part played by nature in determining human life chances, partly as a *consequence of* human interference (Redclift 1983). At the end of the nineteenth century air and water pollution were realities, as they had been for centuries, but they did not threaten human progress and even survival in the way similar processes do today—global warming, the ozone hole, bio-engineering, and the threat of species extinction.

But, if Marx and Engels can be criticized for not anticipating the extent to which changes in the material world can also make history, they cannot be criticized for being overly dependent on a social constructivist perspective. As Dickens (1997) has shown, Marx's picture of the relationship between nature and human exploitation continually reminds us that environmental analysis should not be limited to social construction in its strongest variants. In Marxist terms all knowledge is necessarily socially constructed, but his realist approach insisted that knowledge is not *only* socially constructed. Indeed, "there are powers and tendencies in the human and natural worlds which exist over and above social constructions. Chemical formulae, or the laws of thermodynamics and Darwin's evolutionary biology, are not *only* socially constructed" (Dickens 1997, 188). A Marxist version of the role played by humans in making history would not reduce scientific claims to the particular claims of interest groups, as some social constructivists claim (Hannigan 1995). Paradoxically unease with extreme constructivism has prompted recent attempts to acknowledge the unitary science that Marx had advocated (Bhaskar 1989; Collier 1994; Sayer 1992). This entails giving recognition to the causal mechanisms in the natural world, in the physical and biological, as well as the social, fields. Recent work on actor-network theory and environmental flows is a case in point (Latour 1987; Law 1992; Buttel and Mol 2006).

In this book the dialectical method is used within a realist ontology that recognizes that although we construct the environment socially, it is also brought into being as the result of a combination of forces, not all of them human-induced or intentional. Indeed, one of the themes to emerge in several of the chapters of this book is that many of the consequences of the interplay of nature and civil society have been unintended. Following Lefebvre, nature is considered as social space, in the sense that nature often embodies human purposes. At the same time civil society is infused with nature. The civil institutions that managed the land and the forests in the Spanish Pyrenees grew and evolved from the practices of successive generations of peasant farmers and shepherds. Land settlement in the Canadian Algonquins produced civil institutions out of the conversion of the forests to settlements. At the same time the process led to a mythology about the Canadian frontier that is difficult to separate from the historical process. Development of the frontier left representational spaces that are important in the region today.

We might then ponder the value of approaches to the frontier that pose social construction and materialism/realism as alternative heuristic devices. As we will see, the narratives contained in subsequent chapters often invoke dualisms in their conceptualization of civil society and nature, such as *frontier/civilization, community/markets, commodity/ conservation, and conservation/tourism*. However, in employing a dialectical approach to the analysis of civil societies and nature, we are operating on several planes simultaneously. We hope therefore to avoid the awkward dualisms with which the discussion of the environment and society is often plagued. Our objective is to examine not only the history through which the frontier has been colonized and settled, but also the way in which this history has been imagined, committed to memory, or written about. It is also to look behind the veil of appearances, as Lefebvre advocates, discovering the territory of the mind.

3

Common Property and Civil Society in the Spanish Pyrenees

This chapter examines the relationship between the organization of communities and the management of the environment in the geographical and historical context of the Spanish Pyrenees. In the previous chapter a distinction was made between geographical boundaries, between boundary regions and other types of frontier. It was suggested that boundary regions were often zones of extensive interaction, or transitional zones where the powers of civil authorities and the exercise of local governance is closely guarded and defended. In these areas communal civic institutions often evolved together with precise mechanisms of environmental management. In the case of the Pyrenees a natural frontier was the shifting canvas for pastoralists and the management of community-owned forests. The experiences of communities in the Pyrenees suggest elements in the wider picture that should not be lost, especially since, as we will see in the next chapter, European experiences were exported through migration to the North American continent.

In mountain Europe the delimitation of political frontiers in the nineteenth century was a relatively recent phenomenon that built upon existing local boundaries and jurisdictions. In the local societies of the Pyrenees in the seventeenth century, civil rights and obligations clearly pre-dated national sovereignty and national identity, although they became assimilated later in the latter part of the twentieth century. These local societies revolved around the management of common property. This chapter argues that to understand the role of civil society and the constructions placed on nature in mountain Europe, we need to examine the delicate ecological balance that enabled mountain communities to survive, even when placed under considerable internal and

Figure 3.1
Viella, Val d'Aran, 1967

external pressure. The emergence of civil institutions and ecological practices in managing forests and high grasslands was a key element in reducing both social and environmental vulnerability.

Frontiers and Boundaries

On a map the boundary between France and Spain clearly suggests a physical object, the Pyrenees, as a natural line of demarcation between the two countries.[1] The political boundary also suggests a frontier—a defensive position from which two states viewed each other, and "stood face to" an enemy, the original meaning of the word frontier, according to French historians (Sahlins 1989). However, as Peter Sahlins explains, the concepts of boundaries and frontiers were not regarded as similar, still less interchangeable, until sometime in the late sixteenth century. The Treaty of the Pyrenees, signed in 1659 named the Pyrenees Mountains as the official division between France and Spain, but when tasked with a clear line of division by the Treaty, the commissioners who were appointed fell back on more ambiguous concepts of jurisdiction. In his eloquent book Sahlins discusses one such case, that of the Cerdanya, in the eastern Pyrenees (Sahlins 1989).

The Cerdanya region includes parts of both Spain (Catalonia) and France today, and shares a common language and a common culture. The focus of this chapter is another Pyrenean region, not far to the west, and still technically within Catalonia, the Val d'Aran. In the seventeenth and eighteenth centuries, when many of the stone Aranes houses, which still stand today, were being built, most issues of jurisdiction had little to do with boundaries between nation states. In the *Libro del concordat*, a book highly prized by some of the village authorities in the valley to this day, and written in Catalan and Latin in the mideighteenth century, the boundaries referred to are between *comarcas*, or communities and their lands. The rights to which members of the communities were entitled were rights to pasture, to shares in the abundant forests, and to the related civil duties and responsibilities. To be a citizen in the Pyrenees in the eighteenth century usually meant to hold rights as a local resident (*vecino*) and, as we will see, to a share of natural resources and the way in which they were exploited. The institutions of civil society were embedded in the everyday practices of what we would term resource management today.

By the 1940s the isolation of the Val d'Aran in the winter had been ended when a road tunnel was constructed to the south, under some of the most formidable mountains in the Pyrenean chain, and giving access to the valley throughout the year. The workers who built this tunnel, and who worked in the hydroelectricity-generating plants that followed, came from other areas of Spain, particularly Andalucia and Galicia. It was not until the 1960s that the valley became Spanish in the wider cultural sense, and even this process was partially reversed in succeeding decades with the resurgence of Catalan nationalism. Street names that had traditionally been given in the local *patois*, a Gascon dialect, used Castilian Spanish in the 1960s and at the very end of the twentieth century used Catalan, the language of the wider region, but never the mother tongue of the native population.

The point that Sahlins is making in the Introduction to his book is that there was no simple evolution in the Cerdanya, from a frontier zone to a linear boundary, between 1659 and 1868, the period that he is considering. Zones imply distinct jurisdictions imposed by states for their own convenience, while boundaries suggest lines of demarcation between states. Before the French Revolution gave the impetus to consider national sovereignty as a paramount ambition, and for other European peoples the fruit of nationalist struggles, in the nineteenth century, boundaries and frontiers were held to be distinct. In the case of the Pyrenees, "in 1659 it was a boundary defined by the jurisdictional limits of specific villages. Much would happen before it became a delimited boundary defining national territorial sovereignty" (Sahlins 1989, 2).

Common Property and Civil Authority

The institutional complex that governed the use of natural resources, and the rights of citizens in the Pyrenees, is usually referred to as the *corvee*. There is a rich ethnographic history of the *corvee* that spans a variety of European states and includes several mountain regions (Berthoud 1972; Burns 1963; Cole and Wolf 1974; Weinberg 1975). One of the principal features of the societies being described is their heavy reliance on land that is held in common, particularly pastures and forests. The *corvee* was a system that drew on the labor and resources of individual households, enabling them to undertake the pasturage of animals on the high lands above the forest line, to share in the timber from the forests, and to pool their resources to hire necessary specialists, such as shepherds. It was houses, rather than families or individuals, that were the key element in the collective, since houses owned the private land and undertook ritual positions within the community. It has been pointed out in the literature on common property resources that there is no requirement for an individual to exercise the rights to manage public goods; rather this right is vested in an entity that is frequently a public body (Bromley and Cernea 1989; Bromley et al. 1992). Similarly a public body can claim to represent the general population—it makes representational claims (McKean 2000). Thus "common property is not access to all but access limited to a specific group of users who hold their rights in common" (McKean 2000, 30). In some Pyrenean settlements even today, like those of Anso and Hecho in Aragon, *vecinos* organize much of the village's activities collectively—from the *crèche* for children to the dairy cooperative and timber yard. In most cases today these communal-level institutions are more or less vestigial, but they were once paramount in maintaining delicate ecological balance. The Val d'Aran, discussed below, provides one example of how common property resources were managed historically, and the circumstances under which this management broke down or became obsolete.

Common-pool resources can only be managed effectively if a number of conditions apply. Often it is difficult to define the stocks and flows of these resources with precision accordingly; custom plays a large part in day-to-day management (Dolsak and Ostrum 2003). If social relations are based on mutual trust, itself usually the product of long-term acquaintance, then procedures are much more likely to be understood fully and accepted. This is particularly the case where common management, although beneficial for users, implies an externality for non-users. In the case of the Val d'Aran, for example, it was decided that *vecinos* should not keep goats because they were a threat to young saplings. Most community members were able to comply with this rule, which was accepted, and goats were no longer kept within the valley. However, restaurant owners and others complained that it made it difficult to offer their customers *cabrito* (kid goat), a delicacy in Spain.

The Aranes and Catalan languages spoken in the Val d'Aran, and discussed in the next section, provide evidence of the centrality of the vocabulary of common-pool resources; expressions exist for a variety of customary practices based on reciprocity, sharing livestock, sharing harvests, and managing the forests. This corresponds with the first common feature of such systems—that if one person harvests or deposits in a resource, this must not detract from the ability of others to use it. Without these understandings common-pool resources would be subject to overuse, degradation, or even complete destruction (Dolsak and Ostrum 2003).

The second characteristic is one with which contemporary environmental policy makers are very familiar: that of so-called free riders, individuals who benefit from a rule without contributing to the costs of provision. To avoid the problem of free riders, the management of common property resources usually require mechanisms to exclude potential beneficiaries who do not agree to operate by the rules. In the case of the natural resources of a Pyrenean valley, it is much easier to exclude free riders than in other contemporary situations—such as agreements to reduce levels of carbon emission into the atmosphere. On the whole, the more "uniform, simple and small-scale the resource is, the easier it is to design institutions governing it and to prevent its overuse and deterioration" (Dolsak and Ostrum 2003, 11).

Finally, common-pool resource management is most likely to be used where the shared resource is not seriously under threat, and its conservation is demonstrably of interest to all. If the threats to the resource base are negligible, there is no incentive to introduce common management; where it is excessive, then common management is unlikely to work. In addition, in the case of the Pyrenees, most users of common property had only limited social contact with other groups, who unlike them were not peasant farmers or pastoralists. The problem faced for the management of most common property resources today, especially for governments, is that very few users are socially circumscribed in their behavior, and most have equally strong social ties to groups unconnected to the resource. The importance of common property in the evolution of the frontier in mountain Europe is illustrated by the case of the Val d'Aran.

Boundaries and Frontiers—The Val d'Aran

The Val d'Aran forms the northwest edge of the province of Lerida, which together with the provinces of Gerona, Barcelona, and Valencia makes up Catalonia, today part of Spain. To the north and west lie the French departments of Ariege and Haute Garonne, and to the west and south the Spanish province of Huesca, a part of the region of Aragon. The valley's topography is, however, very different from both the neighboring French and Spanish valleys: it is higher and more mountainous than those of France, and wetter and greener than those of Spain. Arriving in the Val d'Aran from the dry south is like entering a different, hidden world: it is mistier, more enclosed, and less Mediterranean than the valleys that surround it on the Spanish side.[2]

The built environment of the valley is also unlike that of its neighbors. The houses are made of stone and the roofs of gray slate—the appearance is that of a winter landscape, where populations need protection from the cold of winter rather than the heat of summer. Many of the houses date from the seventeenth and eighteenth centuries, when the villages composing the valley built secure foundations, not only for a social order but also a material order. The thick stone walls and carved wooden balconies seem to suggest confidence and stability, as well as a degree of similarity—what distinguishes these houses from each other is not their style but their scale. Those that belonged to the local community leaders, the Justices of the Peace or Mayors, have more elaborate balconies and are somewhat bigger. However, their stone barns and courtyards all display the characteristics of an agricultural system that used different land resources throughout the year, developing and maintaining a delicate ecological balance between nature and human populations. Today many of these barns and courtyards have been converted into second homes for the vacation population of skiers and walkers, and the land within the villages has been used for the construction of holiday chalets and restaurants.

The valley is unlike other Pyrenean valleys in that it runs roughly from east to west, rather than north to south, for it is formed from the overlap of the two main Pyrenean ranges that enclose the valley of the river Garona, better known as the river Garonne, which ultimately flows into the Atlantic at Bordeaux. It is only sixty kilometers long, with a total area of about 470 square kilometers, and is surrounded by more than a hundred mountain peaks over two thousand meters high. To the east is an area of great lakes that now form a part of the national park of Aigues Tortes, and increasingly popular not only with mountaineers but campers, ramblers, and nature enthusiasts. Cultivated pastures and fields (*campos* and *prados*) dominate the view from the valley floor, reaching a height of about 950 meters. Above them are forests of pine and beech, and above the forest zone, at a height of over 2,400 meters, are the high natural pastures. Traditionally these high pastures, which are covered in snow for much of the year, were important grazing grounds for sheep and goats from other areas, the system known as transhumance, which underpinned the livelihoods and the income of the village communities in the valley.

In political terms the valley lies within Spain, but morphologically speaking it is on the French side of the Pyrenees. Of the natural passes from the valley to France few are clear of snow until the summer months, and only the Pont de Rey, at 528 meters, is low enough to remain open for most of the year. Thus in the past the Val d'Aran was physically isolated from Spain for much of the year, and as influenced by France as by Spain. Although the governance of the valley was contested for centuries, it acquired a form of autonomy of its own and remained largely untouched by the kings of Aragon and France alike (Campistol 1951). This relative autonomy was more pronounced than most Alpine and Pyrenean valleys, but by no means unique (Cole and Wolf 1974).

The valley's ambivalent geographical position as a frontier zone led its inhabitants to prize their liberties and independence over everything else. Many of the poems written in the Aranes dialect (properly speaking a variety of Gascon) record the struggles for liberty and strike a martial tone:

E despus de't cumbat tusten canterem
era Victoria, pro james plura
se cauque cop duspus de et plurerem
sigue ta's enemica ana enterra . . .
[And after every battle we always sang our victory / we never cried because of defeat. / The only time we ever cried was when we were burying our enemies.]

For most of the Middle Ages the valley was under the political rule of the kings of Aragon and later the kings of Castille. However, in ecclesiastical terms it lay within the jurisdiction of the Bishopric of St. Bertrand de Comminges, and a religious official from France was posted to the valley. Most significantly perhaps, it never came under seigniorial control, or owed prestations to a feudal lord, although taxes were paid to the king.

Although the valley was semi-autonomous in many respects, it was never agriculturally self-sufficient and . relied on exchanges with neighboring areas. Wheat, in particular, had to be imported, in exchange for livestock, from areas as far north as Toulouse (Foster 1960). There is thus little evidence of long-term stability, of an ecological system whose fine adaptation had resolved any imbalances with human population. In practice, the Val d'Aran, like most Pyrenean valleys, experienced periods of imbalance, when demographic pressures undermined the sustainability of its agricultural systems and natural resources were stretched. Nevertheless, the broad characteristics of the circum-Alpine region, described in two early papers by Burns (1961, 1963), were clearly in place by the seventeenth century: mixed agropastoral systems, with periodic transhumance of animals, the fragmentation of holdings to ensure equity in resource provision, and primogeniture as the pervasive system of inheritance. Communities were tightly organized around complementary land uses; agriculture followed seasonal patterns and was linked closely to communally owned and managed resources, particularly the forests and the high grasslands.

Transhumance in the Pyrenees: Managing Resources at the Margin

The economy of the Val d'Aran revolved around livestock until the advent of tourism in the 1960s, and the systems of livestock management were closely tied to the natural resources managed by each village. According to Campistol (1951), there was a rise in population during the fourteenth century, and this served to underline the need for nonlocal resources that could supplement the delicate ecological balance of each *comarca* (the land under the control of one or several villages). Cattle and mules were bred in the valley for sale outside, but by far the most important way of supplementing the communities' income was the institution of transhumance, under which flocks of sheep and goats from outside were given rights to pasture the high grazing land during the summer months.[3]

In point of fact these patterns of transhumance represented one of the key points of contact between the mountain Europe represented by the Pyrenees and the Mediterranean belt to the south. Most of the flocks that entered the valley under transhumance came from Aragon in the west, and they were often large, as many as four thousand sheep were

involved in some cases. Their origins in Spain date from the period of
the Visigoths in the sixth and seventh centuries. Among the most important of the contracts governing transhumance in Spain was the Royal
Mesta, the *Honrado Consejo de la Mesta*, which was signed in 1273,
and sought to guarantee the growth of the Spanish wool industry under
Ferdinand and Isabella.

The control of rights to pasture was often retained by collections of
villages, or leagues, rather than individual communities. Pastoralism,
and specifically transhumance, can thus be seen as a bulwark against
seigniorial control, providing a much greater degree of independence for
frontier communities. The climatic and ecological fragility of mountain
communities created the need to organize and control access to common
lands, and the consequent development of a strong corporate tradition
on the part of communities, guaranteed their independence. Nevertheless, there are dangers in being too environmentally deterministic, since
many of the areas of Spain that practiced transhumance were highly

Figure 3.2
Sheep grazing, Spanish Pyrenees, 2003

inegalitarian, and most of the population subject to the control of feudal lords. Although the ecology of the valley was one factor in explaining political relations there were others of equal importance. The geographical isolation, patterns of conquest, role of the church in landholding and relatively low levels of production, all made the political control of mountain frontier regions unattractive to powerful landlords. At the same time the livelihoods of most people depended critically on how the balances between population and natural resources were maintained. Key elements in this balance were provided by pastoralism, and especially transhumance.

Pastoralism and Transhumance

To appreciate the role of shepherds in communal resource management in the Pyrenees, it is necessary to outline the recent background to pastoralism. Shepherding is a good example of a resource system that was sustainable before this concept was widely used or understood. Pastoralism in northern Spain predates settled agriculture, and represented a subtle, but fragile, adaptation to the exigencies of climate and terrain. (Gomez Ibanez 1975). The drovers' routes were the first paths to cross the region. The key ingredients of pastoralism are easily explained. Mountain communities entered into mutual exchanges with lowland livestock producers to provide rights to pasture at different periods of the year. When the grasslands were inadequate for the lowland stock in summer, the animals were transported to the mountains where pasture was rented from local communities (*comarca*).

In the valley of Salazar and Roncal (west of Anso) Pyrenean communities traditionally pastured their animals in Bardenas Reales, and wintered them in Lower Aragon or the plains of Lerida. In the valley of Roncesvalles (north of Pamplona) the sheep spent the winter months over the French border. From Anso, in Upper Aragon, the flocks were transported to the province of Teruel, and to Lerida. From other Aragonese valleys they went to Somontanos in Huesca (now an important wine-producing region) and even as far as Zaragoza and Lerida. The livestock from the valley of Bohi traveled further south, to Huesca and the banks of river Ebro. These patterns were duplicated throughout the

Spanish Pyrenees, and their documentation enables us to identify key regions where transhumance was practiced, and research will be undertaken (Valleys of Ancho and Hecho, the valley of Bohi, among them).

The herdsmen from the lowlands exchanged pasture, comarca for comarca, with those of the mountains—literally changing places with them, for periods of the year. This led to very close cultural and political links between communities often hundreds of kilometers apart. In the case of shepherds from Upper Aragon, the Ribagorza and the Val d'Aran, the flocks traveled over one hundred kilometers into Andorra during the summer months. According to Blanchard (quoted by Violant I Simona 1949) in the 1890s there were in excess of 1,300,000 sheep involved in transhumance throughout the mountain regions of Spain. Some of these flocks were placed in the care of hired shepherds, while their owners transported others. Ten or more shepherds managed the largest groups. In the spring the flocks returned to the mountains, augmented by the lambs, which had been born over the winter.

The system under which shepherds with large flocks rented pasture from a comarca, was called *parrades*, or *comana*. As the transhumance progressed, two representatives from each village acted as guides. Members of communities through which they passed were allowed to purchase the animals' manure, and to obtain milk from the flocks. The host communities provided security for the livestock, and arranged the shepherds' keep. There was a hierarchy among the shepherds, with young journeymen shepherds (*rabada*, *regatxo*, or *maynatse* in the Ribagorza, Bohi, and Aran, respectively) learning their skills from the head shepherd, or *mayoral*.

One of the pioneers of English folksong and dance, Violet Alford, described the central role of shepherds and shepherding in Pyrenean culture in the 1930s. It was clear that at the time the organization of pastoralism, and the role of shepherds, constituted the linchpin of rural social structure:

In Upper Aragon each valley has its *fueros*, is in fact a small republic. . . . Flocks are communal and their care is communal work. Down on the wind-swept uplands. Immense flocks of tiny sheep spread about the tumbled plains, draw meager nourishment from gray-green lavender and rosemary. In the mountains the flocks are scarcely visible, on high pasture in the day, shut into the folds at night. . . . Later (in, the dance) the Pastorada (shepherds dance) begins, . . . On this day the leading shepherd (Mayoral) is king, and judge of the village, may say what he likes, and nobody takes it amiss. . . . The leader naturally takes his title from the main interest of the village. "The sheep are the people" (it is said), and the communal affairs of both are in the hands of social-religious brotherhoods. . . . These hard-headed shepherd brethren organize patronage, sales of beasts and wood, aid the sick, oversee funerals and funeral feasts, and meet to do their business in the church porch. (Alford 1937, 203 and 209–10)

In the 1930s Pyrenean shepherding was still experiencing its Golden Age. Transhumance was an activity that underlined the shepherds' role in the maintenance of agro-ecological zones, and the entire rural economy of the Pyrenees.[4]

By the 1940s large-scale transhumance was no longer the principal form of shepherding in the Pyrenees, and villages concentrated on a more limited form of pasturing, utilizing their own communities' boundaries (*terminos*). Even when many of the sheep left the mountain communities for lowland terrain, some (as many as a third) remained behind in the village. In some areas, including Upper Aragon, shepherds remained with their flocks in the mountains during the winter, returning to the stables when the weather was severe. In the Ribagorza and Sort (in Catalonia) sheep were usually left outside, even in severe weather. In the Val d'Aran large-scale transhumance was never practiced, and the sheep were kept inside the stables throughout winter, from November to April, where they were fed on the dry meadow grass. The importance of the practice to the valley lay in the income it guaranteed from other areas less well endowed with summer grazing.

During the summer the communal flocks, from several neighboring villages, were grazed on the high grassland above the tree line (about 6,500 feet altitude) where one shepherd, paid by the villages, tended them. Most of the communities practiced this form of more limited transhumance during the early twentieth century, and it was not until the 1940s that transhumance in the Val d'Aran came to an end. By this time the communities of the valley were being transformed by another process, which left an indelible mark on them and which ultimately served to break down much of the collective organization that had grown up since the Middle Ages. This was the beginning of mass immigration to the valley.

Migration and the Village Community

It has been suggested that to understand the role of transhumance in the Spanish Pyrenees one needs to consider the resource management strategies made necessary by the ecology of the zone, which enabled shortfalls in the natural resources of village communities to be made up for by income from sharing grazing rights. The second major element in the equation also represented a supplement to the income derived from peasant agriculture—this was the use of migration from the valley as a source of remittances for the household (Redclift 1971, 1973).

Seasonal and permanent movements of population from the Spanish Pyrenees were well established before the eighteenth century, and frequently occurred at times of scarcity, when population pressure forced villagers to migrate. There were two principal types of permanent migration. First, since inheritance was normally impartible, with only one child inheriting, the surviving children who did not inherit a house and land often found it necessary to migrate when family income was under pressure. Second, among the better-off families it was the practice for younger sons to move into careers, particularly medicine and law, which required training outside the valley.

Both types of migration often led to permanent relocation, and provided a magnet for young people who remained in the mountains. Those who lived in the pueblos at higher altitude migrated more frequently, and usually had less reason to return, since the land they worked was of poorer quality. There was, in effect, a process of territorial differentiation, which served to weed out the more vulnerable population of communities closer to the tree line.

Migration was also seasonal in nature, and closely related to the agricultural calendar. Migrants usually left after the festival of All Saints Day on October 31, and returned home for the busy period of harvesting in June or July, when the demand for labor was at a premium. The most frequent pattern was for the men and boys to leave, while the women remained at home to look after the farm. During the winter snow lay on the ground from November until April, and the agricultural work was very light, enabling holdings to be managed by a single women in many instances. During some historical periods, such as after the

First World War, the shortage of agricultural labor was particularly acute in France, and much of the deficit in southern France was made up of migrants from the Pyrenees and similar regions.

Seasonal migration from the Pyrenees was looked upon as part of the normal round of agricultural life, rather than as an emergency strategy. Income from migrants was used to augment the basic family subsistence, rather than to accumulate capital for investment, and such entrepreneurship as existed was only loosely connected to patterns of migration. People remembered migrating as a strategy designed to keep the community together, rather than disperse it, and the great majority of migrants did not consider moving away permanently from the valley. When they worked in France, it was usually as wage-laborers, a position considered less prestigious than that of an independent peasant farmer. Unlike many migrants in Europe, migrants from the Val d'Aran gained neither in status nor in skills from the experience. Migration had little effect on the distribution of land, or the differentials between households. It was essentially a stop gap, designed to secure the fortunes of households whose livelihoods depended on the resources that surrounded them: meadows for winter feeding of livestock, forests for wood, and high pasture for summer grazing and transhumance.

Communal Resources: Pastures and Forests

The distinctive ecological zones that made up valleys like the Val d'Aran, each played a part in the household economy, enabling families to utilize different resources at different times of the year. The lowland areas were divided into land set aside for cereal cultivation, mainly wheat (*campos*), and the land used as meadows, and harvested twice a year in June and September. Only the best land was suitable for the second (September) harvest, and the *prados* was not of sufficiently good quality was used for autumn grazing. The hay from the prados was stored during the winter in haylofts above the stables, where the livestock was quartered during the winter.

Individual families owned the campos and prados, but the high pastures were communally owned by the *municipios* (local villages) and each *vecino* (community member, literally "neighbor") had the right to graze their animals on the high pastures. Since most families with live-stock had limited access to the summer grazing on the valley bottom, the high pastures represented a considerable resource for the average farming household. Unlike the pattern in the Alpine *Almwirtschaft* however, the individual family did not manage their own flocks on the high pastures; they grazed together with those of other *vecinos*, under the direction of a hired shepherd.

Between April and July each year the flock was taken a short distance up the mountain, and returned again to the village in the evening. Between July and October, however, the animals remained permanently on the high grazing, in the care of a hired shepherd, at a distance of several hours walk from the village. This left the farming population free to concentrate on the harvest and, during the 1960s and 1970s, to concentrate on the burgeoning dairy economy that was the principal source of earned income.

Between the lowland meadows and the high pasture was the forest belt. Ninety percent of the forests were made up of fir trees (*abeto*, or *abeis pectinata*), but the forests also contained beech trees on the lower slopes and pine on the south-facing areas. The sale of these woods had been an appreciable asset to the villages; in the 1950s, when wood prices were high, they had been a considerable resource for each community.

Until the Spanish Civil War (1936–39) the woods were regarded as the property of every *vecino*, and people exercised this right on a regular basis—cutting firewood, but also trunks for making into furniture, and repairing their houses. The wealth of a community was judged not so much by the fortunes of its inhabitants as by the size and quality of its forests. By 1939, however, the closing of international frontiers and the cessation of external trade prevented the importation of wood. The resulting increase in demand for wood within Spain prompted the indus-trialization of the industry until in 1959 wood was again imported.

The effect of modernization on communal access to the community-owned forests was marked, and control passed from the villages to the *Distrito Forestal*, the provincial Forestry Commission. Michael Kenny (1966), in his discussion of "pine luck" in Castile, where the forests were also corporatively owned, emphasized that although material stakes in the forests were important, their value also has to be linked to their part in the social structure of village communities. Kenny argues that the forests evoke identity with place, which he regarded as a key feature of Castilian village communities. Even for emigrants returned to the village, when the allocation of lots was decided, it was a ritual that expressed their links to other families. However, in the Val d'Aran the extensive forests had, by the late 1960s, ceased to be of much importance for most people. The road access to the forests was poor, there was no legitimate right for individuals to cut wood, and few private entrepreneurs willing to do so. Communal rights were not exercised through the active participation of villagers. Rather, they were exercised by a village council (*Ayuntamiento*) that acted on behalf of the community and used what revenues it gained for public works. For different reasons both the communal pastures and forests remained frozen assets, no longer effectively under the control of local people.

As long as communal resources were used on a daily basis, as essential ingredients of household management, then rights were respected and obligations were acknowledged. However, the history of both grazing land and forests suggest that once economic interdependence has ceased to be important, households were slow to recognize the value of collective resources. Their energies and attention were largely taken up with work in the cash economy—selling milk to the dairy cooperative and, increasingly from the 1960s onward, benefiting from the tourist industry. Collective resources were a source of dispute between individual families and their local leaders, and the agencies of the state, such as the Forestry Commission. The value of locally managed public goods, such as forests or grazing land, was rarely recognized by the national state or its dependencies, partly no doubt because of ideological objections to the idea of locally managed common-pool goods (McKean 2000). As discussed in chapter 5, however, state intervention can also often be seen as a necessary way of exercising economic control over a vital or strategic resource, as it was on the Ecuadorian coast.

Transformations Post–Spanish Civil War

A number of factors have served to transform the environments in which Pyrenean farmers and shepherds lived and worked earlier in the twentieth century. In 1960 over 40 percent of the Spanish labor force worked in agriculture, and by 1995 less than 10 percent did so. The rural exodus was particularly marked in regions of smallholdings (*mini-fundia*) like the Pyrenees, where small farmers had too little capital and too little land to make a livelihood. Their sons and daughters left for the cities, and returned to their homes for summer vacations (Redclift 1973; Hermans 1981). In many parts of the Pyrenees it had already proved difficult for inheriting males to find marriage partners, and many farming families had no children to inherit. These processes were discussed at length in a series of publications during the 1970s (M. Redclift 1971, 1973; N. Redclift 1978; Greenwood 1976). Moreover during the 1960s and 1970s, under Franco, the industrial economy began to grow, a process that has continued impressively for the last twenty-five years.

The effects of these enormous social and economic changes are clearly visible in Pyrenean village communities today. In 1994 tourism represented over 10 percent of Spanish gross domestic product, higher than in any other industrialized country (Barke, Towner, and Newton 1996). The conversion of houses and barns to second-home ownership, or for summer vacations, was particularly marked in the Spanish Pyrenees (Roige, Estrada, and Beltran 1997). Ski installations were built during the 1960s and 1970s, and today they are among the best in Europe— leading in turn to hotel developments, chalets, and other recreational activities. The search for more up-scale tourism, in Spain, has precipitated new forms of tourist, often linked to the growing regional and national consciousness, developed especially in Catalonia and the Basque Country (Wallman 1977; Barcena 2000). There is even the promotion of more sustainable forms of tourism ("eco-tourism") in some parts of the region where old walled towns (like Jaca and Pamplona) in the foothills of the Pyrenees attract visitors interested in traditional aspects of regional cultures, particularly cuisine, costume, and vernacular architecture (Ehrentraut 1996).

Within the National Parks (the first of which dates back to 1918, but most of which have been established in the last thirty years) there is increasing interest in observing wildlife and botanical species, and in establishing the ground rules for future coexistence between tourism and nature conservation. Each National Park has a strategic plan, for zoning activities, but these activities serve to attract more visitors. Outside the boundaries of the parks, designated "protected areas" are subject to the same pressures as elsewhere. In 1971 ICONA was created (National Institute for the Conservation of Nature) with responsibility for areas, including parts of the Pyrenees, but with few practical powers. The organization became dedicated, instead, to fighting forest fires, and issuing shooting and angling permits.

A Ministry of the Environment was not established in Spain until 1993, taking its lead from some of the autonomous governments. This was particularly the case in Catalonia and the Basque Country where environmental issues were beginning to be given more attention. On the whole, however, environmental protection and management is in its infancy in most parts of Spain. However, in the Pyrenees interest in regional customs is increasingly popular and linked to both regional pride and a burgeoning sustainable tourism industry. Many of the components of mountain existence—architecture, food, and an appreciation of nature—are assuming a heritage quality, similar to that which they enjoy in other European countries, including Britain (Roig, Estrada, and Beltran 1997; Ilberry and Kneafsey 1998; Ekman 1999; Gray 2000).[5]

In Spain today a Supra-regional Transhumance project has been developed in the Rioja region under the auspices of the European Union. It includes "an invitation to tourists to go in search of the transhumance heritage adventure." In San Ramon de Cameros a twelfth-century wool-spinning workshop has been restored and ancient shepherd paths have been marked out for ramblers. The European Union's project partners "intend to develop a European cultural itinerary based on pastoral farming" and to find partners in other European Union countries (European Union Regional Policy, March 2000).

Sustainable Livelihoods and Environmental Knowledge

It was noted above that although ecological sustainability was, with hindsight, a feature of Pyrenean pastoralism, this was not fully acknowledged until the late twentieth century. There is now a considerable literature on sustainability, with an emphasis on rural economies and environments (Redclift 1987; Redclift and Sage 1994; Redclift 1996; Redclift 2000). There is also a burgeoning literature concerned with local environmental knowledge (Ellen, Parkes, and Bicker 1997; Ellen 2000). Other research has distinguished between the costs and benefits of both expert and local knowledge, and different environmental rationalities (Leff 2000; Ellen 2000).

It has become clear that in examining rural *livelihoods*, a distinction must be made between practices that support *environmental sustainability* and those that enhance the social resilience of households, without necessarily carrying ecological benefits. Shepherding in the Pyrenees was traditionally an activity that served to integrate both of these dimensions—the shepherd's work was intimately related to most facets of the agricultural calendar, and sustainable resource uses. The pastoral economy rested on a division of land uses, between the summer meadows (used to feed livestock in winter) and the upland pastures. As we have seen the shepherd's role also carried cultural and political significance—in establishing *termino* boundaries, in negotiations with neighboring communities, and in ritual occasions. The environmental and social sustainability of shepherding was indivisible under the traditional systems that prevailed in the Spanish Pyrenees until the 1940s. In this respect it exemplifies the way in which communal institutions are not only managed by a civil society but are sometimes virtually synonymous with it.

At the same time a number of important structural changes have served to separate *environmental* sustainability from its *social* concomitants, and to create a divorce between environmental and social sustainability. Among the most important changes is the development of commercial forestry and hydroelectric power generation, since the 1950s, throughout the Pyrenees.[6] During the last thirty years a third economic activity has transformed large parts of the Pyrenees: the establishment of ski-stations and associated hotel and chalet development. The mass popularity of skiing has led to extensive urbanization at very high altitudes, as hotels and chalets are built close to the ski slopes. This has served to increase the vulnerability of mountain slopes to erosion. It also led much of the flatter land to be developed on the valley floors;

in the case of the Val d'Aran, for example, this has almost displaced agriculture entirely.

These economic changes have shifted the control of resources away from local communities (comarcas) toward central and regional governments, and large, often multinational, companies. The preservation of distinct ecological zones throughout the Pyrenees, corresponding to high pasture, coniferous forest, meadows and cultivated valley bottoms, has been altered, if not destroyed, by all three activities. Although awareness of the ecological damage was late in developing, it is beginning to be included in future plans for the development of the region.

Second; Pyrenean pastoralism has been influenced by the changes that have occurred in agriculture in the region—the increasing emphasis on dairy cattle, and the dairy economy, and the intensification of agricultural production. This also has bearing on the ecological sustainability of the region. In many parts of the Pyrenees both sheep and goats, the traditional bulwarks of pastoralism, have disappeared, to be replaced by dairy cattle. These changes, it can be argued, need to be seen in terms of shifts in the Spanish diet generally, since the 1950s, toward a more global diet (at least in the developed world) emphasizing dairy produce and meat (Goodman and Redclift 1991; Lang 2003). It is important to add that more recently this homogenized international (or fordist) diet is itself being challenged by renewed interest in organic and natural foods, which is part of the new environmental consciousness among some consumers in the developed world (Remmers 1994; Murdoch and Miele 1999; Ekman 1999).

Third, a number of changes in the use made of the Pyrenean environment have laid the basis for a re-examination of development and modernization in the region. An increased interest in wilderness areas has accompanied the growth of mountain climbing, water rafting, and rambling. Footpaths that pass through the highest areas of the Pyrenees, notably GR 11, are now used regularly by international groups of walkers. Environmental groups have begun to appear in Spain, and notably between two national communities with significant land in the Pyrenees: Catalans and Basques. In both areas ethnic identity is closely linked, within separatist and mainstream groups, with environmental objectives (Barcena et al. 2000). The frontier in this case assumes a role in the recreation of identities, in cultural revival.

One manifestation of the close affinity between growing national and regional identities, and environmental consciousness, is the formation of local eco-museums throughout the Spanish Pyrenees, in villages and tourist centers. Tourist offices promote the wildlife and habitats of the region to visitors, and have raised awareness of traditional environmental practices, including shepherding (Ilbery and Kneafsey 1998). In some centers—such as Anso in Aragon—summer schools are organized for interested lay people. The rural crafts and practices of shepherds are prized as important facets of local material culture, together with vernacular house design and church architecture, despite the evident decline of the pastoral economy that supported these traditions (Bessiere 1998; Roige, Estrada, and Beltran 1997).

The development of alternative forms of employment, associated with ski-stations, tourism, and new "industrial" activities, such as forestry and energy, have reduced the amount of full-time employment in agriculture throughout the Pyrenees. Many local households are now part-time: combining work on small farms with seasonal employment in tourism and recreation. So-called pluri-activity has come to characterize employment in most communities, and the way in which villages have adapted to change has in turn stimulated interest in cultural survival (Ekman 1999). Changes in employment and labor migration undermined the effective management of common property resources. At the same time, as the social complexity of the Spanish Pyrenees has increased, the interest in traditional institutions, language dialects, and ways of life has acted like a magnet, bringing urban people to the area as visitors.

In regions that are marginal agriculturally, but important in terms of resources and politics, such as the Spanish Pyrenees, the speed of economic and social transformation has led to a re-examination of the goals of development itself, and an emphasis on sustainable development. Although research in Europe has often linked agriculture and rural depopulation to tourism, there has been relatively little published research to focus on the links between tourism and the capacity to retain, and utilize, environmental knowledge. This emphasis on postproductivist rural areas, in which agriculture has a limited role, buttressed by more attention to conservation of natural resources, and amenity concerns, is a central pillar of policy in the European Union (Gray 2000).

The significance of the transformation of rural areas is best understood within the broader European context, and especially that of upland Europe. By focusing on the specific case of pastoralism in the Pyrenees and the links between agriculture and environmental policy, this chapter has explored the different adaptation of place and regional/local cultures to the policy constraints and opportunities provided by the European Union. In later chapters the exploration of frontier locates these kinds of adaptation within an even wider, global, context, such as that of the Maya in chapter 7.

The future after productivism in Europe, as agricultural subsidies are withdrawn and farmers look for alternative sources of livelihood, requires attention to cultural practices and institutions that may be about to disappear. Many of these practices may paradoxically assume more importance in urban societies, where the preservation of social memory is valued as part of heritage. Research in mountain Europe has revealed that what sometimes appear as traditional ways of life can have enduring importance for new reasons, and for new generations of people. The Pyrenees provides an example of a region in which evolving systems of resource and land management were closely linked with more or less autonomous civil societies that were local in character and acknowledged that human populations depended on the maintenance of fragile ecosystems.

Common-pool resources formed an integral part of this system, as we have seen, and helped to underpin the individual's rights within the community, including that of private property. Later in this book the themes of common ownership and political rights are discussed further, in Ecuador and Mexico, within the very different context of societies founded on stark inequalities and the exploitation of indigenous minorities.

In the previous chapter we noted how grain production on the Great Plains of North America in the late nineteenth century shifted the commercial balance away from European producers and toward the areas of the New World that benefited from better resource endowments. The frontiers created in these new areas, by the global cereal market, had an enduring impact on grain producers in Europe. The Pyrenean region suffered analogously when areas with more specialized agriculture within Spain, used their comparative advantage and more specialized production to make gains in the second half of the twentieth century.

The production systems described in this chapter had facilitated labor migration from the Pyrenees in response to shortages elsewhere, especially in southern France, and also enabled the ecological balances within the Pyrenean region to be preserved. These areas were not strictly autarkic in that "relations with other areas . . . were essential for the reproduction of the [Pyrenean] model" (Collantes and Pinilla 2004, 154). They acted as a safety valve at a regional and international level.

But the ecological management that has characterized the Pyrenees is largely irrelevant to other parts of Spain and France. Wider national demands influenced the environment of the region. In the Pyrenees the traditional role of supplying labor and natural resources (especially energy) in the development of modern Spain was supplanted by new demands (Collantes and Pinilla 2004). These included bringing a new pole of attraction for consumers from outside the area, in pursuit of skiing facilities and recreation, and in pursuit of marginal zones rich in natural diversity and attractive to conservationists.

The old hegemonies established over areas like the Val d'Aran by the diocese of Comminges in France, and the Aragonese crown, and the remittances from migrants who worked outside the valley, were replaced by inward economic investment in the late 1960s and afterward. The "spatial practices," in Levebvre's terminology, that had ensured continuity were secularized and handed over to outside professionals. These new representations of space had their own hegemonic character, and increasingly specialization served to integrate the region at the cost of further undermining traditional civil institutions, most of which were no longer economically or socially viable.

However, partly as a result of the pursuit of diversity in an autonomous Catalonia, and the wider European Union, the symbolic importance of the frontier increased. Overlaying physical space, the social spaces of the Val D'Aran today have enabled the region to recreate itself, not merely in terms of economic activities, employment, and land use, but also in making symbolic use of its past and its memory. This reflexive, dialectical process, through which a frontier zone re-makes its history, for its own and external consumption, facilitates its economic and political survival in a global system where boundaries are drawn in quite different ways from those of the nineteenth century.

4

International Migration and European Settlement—Upper Canada

This chapter examines the effects of international migration on the Canadian Algonquins in the 1840s and 1850s. It examines what happens when international movements of populations breach national boundaries, and ideas of nature are extended culturally, through the incorporation of new lands and wilderness areas. In the midnineteenth century over one million people, most of them of British and Irish origin, settled in what was then known as Upper Canada, the area to the north and west of the Ottawa River.

Like other settler societies in the New World, British Canada was created out of the human raw material that arrived by boat or, in exile, overland from the United States. The native Indian population, which had already been subjected to the authority of the European settlers, was marginalized or destroyed, while the French colonist population of Lower Canada remained largely distinct and outside the purview of the English-speaking settlers. It was largely the British migrants, and their descendents, who occupied the previously unsettled areas of Canada and expanded westward.

These developments in empire formed the backcloth to a very different kind of overseas colony in which non-European labor played a major part, but by no means an exclusive one. In more temperate zones the momentum of colonization led to the large-scale settlement of European populations, many of which established family-run farms and gradually developed an economic orientation to both the global and the domestic market. In these settler societies the indigenous population was usually more sparsely distributed, and indigenous peoples were either exterminated or marginalized to so-called native reserves, as in the United States and Australia.

The people who arrived from Europe, in much of North America, the Antipodes, and the southern cone of South America, were often hungry for land, and their commitment to their new country was bound up with their close relationship with the natural environment. The existence of relatively open access to land and the fruits of forest clearance prompted demands for civil and political rights, still denied to the majority in the societies from which they had come. Bringing with them relatively little capital, their success in economic terms was heavily dependent on either the cohesion of their own cultural group or the establishment of new institutions and cultural forms more closely attuned to the environments they had settled in. In a sense a process of social learning was underway in such frontier societies from their inception: the challenge was to negotiate an identity for themselves that was distinctively different from their origins, and one based on a legitimate conception of social order.

At the same time it is questionable whether, as the Turner thesis demands, we should equate a nation's social and political institutions to the experience of the frontier alone. In other parts of the Americas, especially in the former Spanish colonies, the existence of frontiers populated by people of European origin (in Argentina, Southern Brazil, and parts of Colombia), far from acting as a seedbed for democracy, gave rise to national political cultures dominated by powerful *caudillo* leaders. In cases like that of coastal Ecuador discussed in the next chapter, the absence of representative, democratic institutions was linked to their fragility and their peripheral geographical position. The establishment of international frontiers, and new societies, suggests several new points of departure in which immigrants were very much defined by their class and ethnic origins. In some cases like that of the Scots, they sought cultural continuity in their adopted spaces and established settlements distinguished by a common Scottish ancestry.

This chapter charts the relationship that developed between these migrant populations and the wilderness that surrounded them. Many of the migrants from the British Isles who landed in Canada left at a time when their domestic agriculture was being "improved" and increasingly subject to market forces. The challenges of settlement, in what was seen as a wilderness, left its mark on the settler population and served to create a myth of the frontier that endures today. To establish their property rights and to survey the land, they had to follow in the wake of the lumbering community and cut down trees on a vast scale. In this context, as we will see, nature was invariably viewed as hostile to human development. With hindsight we observe in midnineteenth century Upper Canada the plunder of a relatively pristine, but rich, forest environment to make way for smallholding on land that was to prove of little agricultural value. But this could not be fully appreciated until the Great Plains were opened up, in Canada as in the United States, some decades later. The destruction of the forests was an inconclusive process, and the fact that much of the Algonquins were inappropriate for agriculture explains its status today as a conservation area where amenity is valued over agricultural land uses.

The Canadian frontier of the midnineteenth century was also one that only provided living space for one group of people—those of European descent. The rights of other human populations to their environment were denied, and the indigenous population was denied rights to nature through their denial of citizenship. The individuals who constituted the frontier in the Canada of 1847 need to be examined against the back-cloth of their own social and geographical mobility, but this history itself was used to undermine the claims of those who lived there as first nations. By forging their own history, British and Irish migrants buried that of others.

The social milieu experienced by the settler population provided individuals with both attachments and antagonisms toward the institutions of the British Isles, and often prompted attempts to break free of them. Revisiting the frontier then means examining frontier myths together within the context provided by everyday life. The spatial practices of the settler population ensured that the migrant populations were able to reproduce themselves; they were the engines of their own identities, providing them with everyday representational spaces in which they lived (Lefebvre 1991). At the same time this gave rise to new dialectical relations with nature, as both the concept of wilderness and that of the frontier were re-imagined, and handed on to posterity.

Upper Canada in the Midnineteenth Century: The European Legacy

Upper Canada came into being after 1784, when about one quarter of the Loyalist regiments that remained after the American Revolution moved northward, into British territory. The numbers arriving were small: only about seven thousand five hundred Loyalists, and about three thousand free blacks (Knowles 1992). On top of this modest base was constructed one of the largest immigrant populations of the early nineteenth century: by 1860 over one million new immigrants had arrived in Canada. Most of those who came to Canada, both from the United States and (more particularly) from Europe, were attracted by the promise of free land on the Ottawa River, where about ten thousand people had moved by 1812. Until that date most of the population of Canada was still "Yanqui," and made of three distinct waves: American merchants and New England planters, displaced Loyalists after the American War of Independence, and late Loyalists, land poor settlers who came in the 1790s and including some persecuted religious minorities (Buckner 1998, 6). Each of these groups led by free land was made up of "true pioneers" (Koch-Kraft 1992, 151).

There were now two administrative divisions to Canada. East of the Ottawa River was Lower Canada (Quebec), while to the west lay Upper Canada. Between 1791 and 1851 the population of (British) Upper Canada rose from about fourteen thousand (mainly Loyalists) to almost one million people. From the standpoint of the British government in the early nineteenth century, Upper Canada represented a bulwark against both the newly independent United States, to the south, and the French occupation of Lower Canada. John Graves Simcoe, the first lieutenant governor of the province, expressed the conventional Tory view when he stated that Upper Canada was "a successful colony on the British model." It was the objective of British policy to ensure that it remained so. In 1803 Thomas Talbot declared that Upper Canada remained a vital bastion, amid worries about "the growing tendency to insubordination and revolt" elsewhere in North America. It soon became official policy to encourage large-scale "British" (to include Irish) immigration.

Points of Embarkation: Emigrants to Upper Canada from Britain and Ireland

To fully appreciate the process through which Upper Canada was settled, and civil society developed, it is important to understand the experience of migration itself. Many of the ideas and responses with which recent immigrants to Canada evaluated the new society were formed from their own or their families' experiences and memory of their country of origin. These cultural legacies differed for migrants from England and Scotland, and those from Ireland. The social forces that prompted migration were different, and the social composition of the migrant groups differed also. The comparisons that settlers evoked with nature similarly expressed a different set of preoccupations. The immigrants from English rural areas were aware that *improvement* meant the introduction of new farming techniques, and accelerated enclosure of land. They compared what they saw in Upper Canada, in many cases, with the most modern English agricultural practices. For displaced Highland Scots, many of whom were the victims of the Clearances, settlement in Canada meant recapturing some of the social status and security that had been taken away from them by the forcible introduction of sheep farming in the far North and West of Scotland. For the Irish, especially after the appalling famine years between 1845 and 1850, their choice was an even more brutal one: they either emigrated (as nearly two million did in the decade after 1845) or they died, as another million did between 1845 and 1849.

By the end of the Napoleonic wars, in 1815, much of the English countryside was beset with growing displacement of population and impoverishment. As Cowan points out, this social distress occurred at a time when British North America offered work for settlers (Cowan 1968, 3). In the succeeding two generations the pattern of migration from England to Canada changed. Up until 1823 there was some limited assistance, but after that date even this was terminated. At the time of Confederation in 1867 most citizens of Canada were of British origin: they were descended from immigrants or had themselves immigrated without official support.

The pattern of emigration from England was interesting. The majority certainly paid their own way, and arrived singly or as married couples: "the human atom tore itself away from its parent root, and moved off to attach itself to a new base . . ." (Cowan 1968, 3). Even among the English the social composition of the migrant population was very varied; it included those who had advantages and those who had none. In essence the tide of humanity, at least in the first few decades of the nineteenth century, was linked to the existing patterns of trade, it formed part of the interchange of Empire. For the poorer people who went to Canada, the boats that brought timber and furs and corn to Britain, later took emigrants out in the same holds, on their return trips.

Much of the early migration that occurred between the mideighteenth century and the early nineteenth was undertaken by disbanded servicemen, who were sent to the colonies in the belief that they might need defending by the British army. In 1749, and again in 1763, Nova Scotia was settled in just this way. On the whole, though, assisted migration, of whatever form, was remarkably unsuccessful. After 1815 some British government assistance was again offered to servicemen suddenly made redundant by the end of hostilities in Europe. Each adult male was given one hundred acres, and an additional fifty acres was provided for each family member. These families were settled in border areas, between the Maritime Provinces in the east, and what was then thought of as "West" Canada, and thought to be vulnerable to invasion from the United States.

Subsidizing migrants was a short-term remedy and one that, in the case of Canada, did not prove really necessary. In July and August 1815 seven hundred Scots sailed from Glasgow. Plant (1951) also mentions the three hundred people helped by Lord Selkirk "from the Highlands of Scotland, and from the north of Ireland, (who were sent) to the Red River Valley, in what is now the province of Manitoba" (Plant 1951, 20). At first they lived in tents, but gradually they built shacks and log houses, their settlement attracting others from the south and from elsewhere in Europe. By 1833 there were over one thousand five hundred people in these settlements.

Poverty and distress also prompted British government intervention. Petitions from textile workers in 1820 and 1821, from Paisley in Glasgow, led the government to offer free land and small cash loans for the most needy. Three thousand people left for Rideau and Lanark settlements, just to the south of the town that became Ottawa. This movement of people was accelerated by the failure of the potato crop in Ireland, and approval was given for £15,000 and subsequently £30,000 toward the costs of Irish emigration. The first human settlement was to the Rideau area, and the second to Rice Lake, and the old district of Newcastle. "The publicity given these assisted settlers forced reconsideration of inducements for independent emigrants . . . they came in numbers so large, and at so small expense to themselves, and the Government, that such aid to emigrants was not repeated . . ." (Cowan 1968, 6).

Henceforth most emigration was unassisted, even if it was not always voluntary. The architect of this policy was Edward Gibbon Wakefield, an attractive figure on the contemporary scene, who formulated his ideas on emigration while he was in prison for abducting an heiress. In 1829 Wakefield propounded a plan for settlement in the Empire, which he believed would also contribute to its development. He suggested what amounted to early support for property-owning democracy that would extend British markets through emigration, relieve the pressure of population in the British Isles, and provide a new opportunity for capital investment. In Wakefield's view, land should be sold rather than given away, the land sales should be used to help set up an emigration fund to help further emigration, and preference should be given to young married couples rather than single men. "Wakefield argued . . . that paupers as a type were unsuited to pioneering, and that if settlers were to succeed, they must be carefully selected for the purpose, and must begin by gaining experience overseas as laborers" (Plant 1951, 34).

By 1831 an Emigration Bill had been introduced, and in 1832 emigration policy became part of the Foreign Office brief. Subsequently Wakefield visited Canada with Lord Durham, and they expressed surprise at the scale of existing migration. In 1838 Lord Durham's Report was published, which Wakefield influenced strongly. This argued that there was no need for stimulus to emigration to Canada, since "if free passages to Canada were made available, many of the emigrants might slip across the border into the United States after landing" (Plant 1951, 40). The other British colonies of the period, such as Australia, New

Zealand, and South Africa all received encouragement from the state, and state-aided emigration proved important throughout the nineteenth century. Canada was the exception—and it was not difficult to see why it was treated as such. Canada lay close to the United States, and closer to the British Isles than the other colonies. This meant that voyages were shorter and cheaper, and that any attempt to sell land would suffer adversely from the fact that, at this time, it was freely available in the United States.

In examining the characteristics of those who did migrate in the first half of the nineteenth century, it is particularly useful to distinguish between the three principal groups, the circumstances of whose departures for the New World were so different. The first group to consider are the Scots who, as we have seen, had settled in the Maritime Provinces in the early part of the century.

Emigration from Scotland has been described by Cowan as "early, persistent and hopeful" (1968, 5). The Highland Clearances had converted large parts of the north and west of the country into large estates for sheep farming. The displacement of peasant farmers from these areas, and changes in the kelp and fishing industries, left many Scots without work, and frequently without anywhere to live. "Why should we emigrate?" asked Donald Macdonald of Back of Keppoch, "There is plenty of waste land around us; for what is an extensive deer-forest in the heart of the most fertile part of our land but waste land?" It was not until the Crofting Act of 1886 that a measure of reform was brought to the Highlands, but it did little to halt the tide of Scottish emigration to Canada (Calder 2003, 15).

An influential pressure group, the Highland Society had, with the help of some Scottish landowners, passed through Parliament a law to regulate the passenger vessels that took emigrants to the colonies. It was designed to provide British emigrants with ships as safe as those for transporting slaves and, "incidentally, designed to decrease emigration by raising costs" (Cowan 1968, 6). The improvement of vessels was then a move to discourage, rather than encourage, emigration, since it was believed that Scotland needed to retain population rather than to lose it.

Among the twenty thousand Scots who set sail for Upper Canada between 1815 and 1821 about one quarter were small businessmen or property-owners. The removal to Canada was not exile for these Scots, as they were joining Scottish populations well established in Canada. They were seeking to reproduce the kind of thrifty, independent existence that had been more or less forcibly taken away from them by the combined effects of the industrial and agricultural revolutions in Scotland.

English emigrants to Upper Canada were rather more mixed than the Scots. Whereas the population of rural Scotland and Ireland was to fall during the nineteenth century, that of England rose. Between 1763, when the British first established a secure foothold in Canada, and 1820, the population of England had almost doubled, from seven to twelve million people. Nevertheless, the rise in employment did not take place with this rise in population, and the choice for most poor people, whether rural or urban, was the same stark one: win economic and political reforms at home, or emigrate somewhere else. As with some of the Scots, many of the English migrants left when they were able to pay their own way—using their savings, or selling their possessions, to fund the crossing. Many small business people and farmers wrote to the government in this period, requesting help from the colonies. There were usually professional families among the settlers, often the second, and third or fourth sons of clergymen, doctors, and lawyers.

The Irish migration sets itself apart from most of the experiences described above. It was prompted by a level of desolation that dwarfed even the social scars of the Highland Clearances. In 1815 some six million Irish people lived on about thirteen million acres of arable land, most of it devoted to cultivating the potato. Methods of farming were backward and unproductive, and most small farmers were tenants or smallholders, without capital, and only bound to the land by the most insecure of annual tenancies. Ireland had, by 1821, more mouths to feed per square mile than any country in Europe: Leinster supported 281 people per square mile, Connaught 411, and Ulster 414 people per square mile. These were to be the areas of greatest Irish migration to Upper Canada in the subsequent fifty years.

Since the end of the eighteenth century, land in Ireland had been subjected to the most damaging subdivisions, and people had been dispossessed in huge numbers. Small farmers answered advertisements from emigration agents in the newspapers, and often sold all their belongings and their crop within a matter of weeks in their desperation to leave. Most left on the ships that brought flaxseed to Ireland, together with tobacco and timber. They left from the ports of Londonderry, Cork, Dublin, and Belfast, returning westward with their holds full of new migrants: small farmers, trades-people, farmer-weavers from Ulster. In 1818 alone over eighteen thousand Irish arrived in British North America, many continuing on to the United States. The transport was difficult and cholera was a constant problem.

By 1847, when the ships started to take the thousands left destitute by the Potato Famine, emigration had become a prominent public issue in Britain and Ireland. There were two principal opinions: that the emigration of poor and destitute people would take the pressure off the population of Ireland (and parts of Scotland) and enable more of those who remained to make a decent livelihood. Others argued that those who left would in fact be among the best qualified to stay: the young and adventurous, rather than the old and dependent. These critics therefore opposed emigration just as vehemently. With hindsight it is clear that the industrial expansion, which characterized England and Wales in the nineteenth century, generated large numbers of jobs in the new urban centers—many of which were not available to the Irish or the Highland Scots. The population of England and Wales rose from twelve million in 1820 to twenty million in 1860. This increase was unimpeded by migration, which was in no way a brake on economic growth.

The situation in Ireland was, however, "catastrophic" in the midnineteenth century: "Five years of famine had caused a million to die from hunger and disease, and well over one million to emigrate . . . In many areas of the west and south of Ireland, the social and economic fabric of the country was in tatters" (Small 1998, 16).

The midnineteenth century was also an important period for the growth of Irish national consciousness. Daniel O'Connel, a brilliant Catholic lawyer from old Irish gentry stock, had weaned the small farmers (the so-called forty shilling freeholders) away from the control of landlords, and was campaigning for radical constitutional change. The English political leadership, such as Peel and Wellington, had been prepared to countenance Catholic emancipation in the British Isles; but the prospect of home rule for Ireland was, in their view, a step too far. "O'Connell, with the aid of local parish priests, broke this bond (between tenants and landlords) and in so doing undermined aristocratic control of elected representatives" (Small 1998, 16).

In the turbulent politics that followed Peel and Wellington eventually passed the Catholic Relief Bill, extending a number of important civil rights to Catholics but, critically, disenfranchising others. The social tensions in Ireland at the time were between the middle-class Catholic farmers and business classes and the poor Catholic tenants, rather than simply between English Protestants and Catholic Irish. However, the tithe war, under which tenants were expected to make contributions through their rents to the Protestant Church of Ireland, linked to the Anglo-Irish gentry served to increase the sectarian dimension. In the eyes of an increasing number of ordinary Irish people, even before the onslaught of the Potato Famine, the relatively impoverished Irish tenants were being asked to pay dues to the British state.

Between 1835 and 1840, some concessions were made to popular Irish opinion, for example, barring Orange Order members from the Irish police and (however inappropriately) extending the English Poor Law system to Ireland, with Boards of Guardians to administer the claimants. In 1841, a Tory administration came to power again in England, but O'Connell's attempts to repeal the Act of Union still failed. The livelihood options of the Irish rural masses were heavily circumscribed. "In Britain, the rural poor could migrate to the rapidly growing cities to find work: this was much more difficult to do in Ireland unless you wanted to emigrate" (Small 1998, 23).

For a few years the Tory administration in London sought comparatively humane solutions to the problems of Ireland, but in 1846 the Whigs came to power. They were much more firmly wedded to free market principles, and had a tendency to regard most forms of relief as an inefficient, and dangerous, interference with the marketplace. Their principal protagonist was Charles Edward Trevelyan, the assistant secretary to the Treasury, who has emerged, certainly in Irish political memory, as the *eminence grise* of the subsequent debacle. "In 1846, as the crisis (in Ireland) deepened, the Whigs under the new Prime Minister Lord Russell, decided against large-scale government intervention, and thought the burden should rest primarily on Irish landlords" (Small 1998, 24).

The British government reacted to the worsening crisis, in the potato harvests and trade, by cutting back on the very relief programs that had been recently introduced. Public works schemes were halted abruptly. From October 1846 people began dying from starvation in large numbers. Gradually the public works schemes were reintroduced but to little avail, since forcing starving, and poorly clothed men into hard physical labor during the winter was looked upon as barbaric rather than humane. It further soured relations between the British and Ireland for a century.

The collective memory of immigrants to Canada clearly reflected these diverse experiences of the forces that had prompted them to leave. As we have seen, these forces differed in England, Scotland, and Ireland. The collective memory, and experiences, of immigrants also extended to the journey itself—the exhausting and often brutal conditions of transit that eventually set the immigrants on North American shores.

The Emigration Committee of 1827 had recommended that an emigration board be established and be made up of emigration officers, or port officers, at all major points where migrants embarked and disembarked. In the colonies themselves, as well as in British ports, these officers soon became critical to the process through which huge numbers of "human cargo" arrived in Canada. They met emigrant vessels, which were often heavily infected with disease, looked over the passenger lists, and reported on the condition of the ship to the British emigration board. These officials also tried to advise newly arrived immigrants on the location of available lands and on the practical details of employment. As Cowan points out "[they also] sometimes struggled with the local charitable groups over the expense that ill-prepared emigrants imposed on their meager resources" (Cowan 1968, 11).

In the British and Irish ports of embarkation the emigrant officers, who were naval officers assigned on half pay and supplementary salary, had to deal not only with the prospective emigrants but also with the shipping companies whose vessels they had to inspect, to ensure conformity with the existing laws for passenger vessels. Cowan describes these controls vividly (Cowan 1968).

The conditions on board ship varied not only between ships but also between years. When emigration was at its peak, the battered hulks of the old Atlantic trade were brought into service, with hatches battened down, to carry too many passengers in appallingly cramped, and diseased, conditions. Cowan reminds us that in 1840, 1 percent of the "human cargo" died at sea; by 1849, this had risen, with the famine victims, to 16 percent. It was not until the passenger vessel act of 1855 that the passage rights of emigrants were formally recognized, and a real attempt to regulate conditions begun in earnest. During the mid-nineteenth century most emigrants survived very poor conditions on board, and only a minority experienced relatively comfortable passage. As Cowan puts it: "the cash-poor emigrant who survived the ocean crossing and managed to acquire land had taken a long step on the colonial road to the survival of the fittest" (Cowan 1968, 12).

Once they had arrived, the immigrants' experiences were transcribed into letters that, when they eventually arrived in the British Isles, became the raw material for future migrants. Families pored over correspondences that presented a picture, and gave advice, which in itself served to shape history. Sometimes too the letters contained money, and though it is impossible to know the full value of remittances sent back to Britain and Ireland, estimates put the figure at about one million pounds sterling. As Cowan says: "through remittances emigration was paying for itself" (Cowan 1968, 13).

It is clear that with the notable exception of Irish emigration after the Famine, the proportion of better-off emigrants increased as the century progressed. Between 1846 and 1859, the numbers of professional men, and experienced farmers, "some bringing £1000 and the family silver plate," began to increase (Cowan 1968, 14). This was the social class to which Francis Codd belonged, and the vantage point from which he saw Upper Canada.

The impact of the massive migrations to Canada in the forty years from 1815 to 1855 cannot be exaggerated. Within another thirty years Canada had become a confederation, and the population, which had grown to two million in 1850, stood at three and a half million. Most of Canada had been populated with British and Irish immigrants: from the maritime provinces to the vast empty spaces of western Canada

Figure 4.1
Alfred Stieglitz, *Steerage*

which, by the 1880s, were being settled by people of British or Irish descent.

Immigration and Social Cohesion

As we have seen, the British and Irish immigrant population that settled in Upper Canada in the 1840s and 1850s was propelled by processes of expulsion from the Old World as well as attraction toward the New. As Buckner demonstrates, parallels with other European colonies of settlement are "fundamentally misleading because the settlement of British North America took place later and in a context that was radically different [from that of other colonies in the Americas]" (Buckner 1993, 3). Settlement in British Canada took place after three centuries of rivalry among European powers, each determined to leave their mark through territorial expansion. At home these same European powers were involved in a series of wars with each other, and were gradually establishing strong centralized national states.

The British experience in North America was markedly different from that a century earlier in what became the United States. From the close of the Napoleonic Wars in 1815, until the scramble for Africa in the last two decades of the nineteenth century, Britain had no rivals overseas, while at home it was fast becoming the leading industrial power. In the century after 1815 Britain and Ireland contributed almost one quarter of the forty-four million emigrants who left Europe for the New World. Between 1815 and 1865 the cultural landscape of British North America was transformed by the impact of immigration, on a scale, and with a rapidity that was unprecedented.

In constructing a civil society in Canada, most immigrants sought to reproduce elements of social order with which they were already familiar at the level of communities and localities. The Protestant Irish introduced the Orange Order to Canada; by the end of the century about one-third of adult English-speaking men belonged to it (Buckner 1993, 15). On a much smaller scale the Gaelic-speaking people from the Scottish Highlands continued to form language communities for many years after settlement. Pamphlets printed in Gaelic included before and after pictures "to illustrate the transformation from frontier to ordered settlement that emigrants could expect" (Calder 2003, 17). But within a few decades the British immigrants had created the nucleus of a national community in Canada, and one that wanted to preserve strong links with the motherland. The volume of immigrants was such in this half century that they overwhelmed the small existing population. However, unlike other immigrant communities in Latin America and the United States, the British and Irish who settled in Canada created a new society from among themselves, and one that sought to retain cultural and economic ties with the British Isles.

The migrants to Canada were more socially homogeneous than the much larger migrant populations that flowed toward the United States in the same period. They settled in rural areas, rather than cities, and pursued their own ambitions of independence through the acquisition of land. In the process "the British North American frontier was transformed from a wilderness into a series of comparatively densely populated communities within the life-span of a single generation" (Buckner 1993, 10).

To many of the settlers in Upper Canada, the wilderness they settled was hostile; it lacked the appearance of the civilizations they had left behind. But, if nature was hostile, it was also bounteous, and its conquest became a condition for the successful advance of rural communities and embryonic civil institutions. In this respect there were parallels with other frontier societies populated by European immigrants in the nineteenth century, in parts of North, Central, and South America, in the Antipodes, and in southern Africa.

The effect of land policy in British Canada was not entirely satisfactory in the midnineteenth century. Macdonald notes that "the land policy . . . permitted free grants in a most lavish and improvident manner, with the result that most of the Crown lands in the most accessible parts had been alienated, though (they were) far from being developed, or even occupied" (Macdonald 1966, 11). The goal was to avoid speculation in land while, at the same time, encouraging its development, though by the mid-1840s most of the land that changed hands in Upper Canada was for speculative purposes. It was clear that—as in most frontier situations—development and speculation were intertwined.

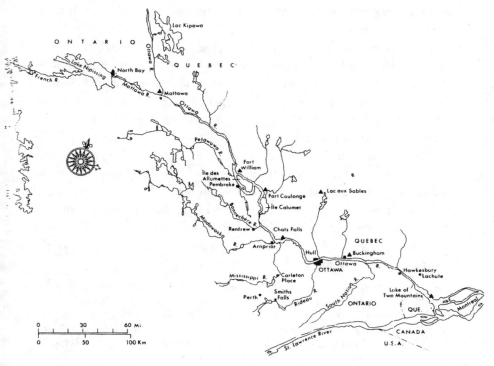

Figure 4.2
Map of the Ottawa valley, Canada, 1846

Settlement and the Frontier in Upper Canada

Upper Canada was not settled in the midnineteenth century by small farmers intent on a life of self-sufficiency, "gradually inching along the frontier" (Buckner 1998, 19). It was settled rapidly by people who wanted to own land and sell products to the market. By the late 1840s most of the good arable land had already been settled and cleared of trees. Roads were built, and by the 1850s canals and railroads linked the more settled areas of what is today Ontario. The newcomers turned to the production of two great staples—timber and wheat—since Canada was able to compete in both these products on the world market. The elements of subsistence agriculture that existed was supplementary income, designed to complement the livelihood provided by cash crops and wage-labor.

The speculation in land was encouraged by the building of roads. Between 1845 and 1878 sixteen roads were opened up in the region to the west of the Ottawa River. The chief beneficiaries were the lumber industries associated with land development on the Madawaska River, one of the tributaries of the Ottawa. It was the revenue derived from lumbering that influenced the government's road-building program rather than the settlement of farming populations. Markets for farmers were geographically remote from the new farming areas, and these farms were less well endowed than those in the areas to the south. Land speculation provided the incentive for opening up a wilderness, although as in other speculative activities, the destruction of forest brought farmers in its wake. The parallels are suggestive with settlement in the Amazon at the end of the twentieth century.

The government-assisted settlements had proved expensive, the land grant system unique; neither method brought in the income needed to relieve the mother country of the cost of colonial administration. With these results in mind, and one eye always on the rival land sale system of the United States, the government began to appeal to man's purely selfish instincts, by making his reward depend solely upon his own efforts. (Cowan 1961, 113)

By the 1840s the forested areas of Upper Canada were becoming distinguished from the more prosperous farming areas to the south. Careless (1967, 28) writes that "Canada West generally was so full of recent immigrants, and so much in the stage of extensive growth, rather than intensive growth, that its social structure was naturally ill-defined." On the Ottawa River a distinctive lumber community had developed, of whom some were farmer-lumbermen engaged on their own in logging during the winter, and farming during the summer. Many were shanty-men, hired hands of Irish or French descent, and an itinerant semi-proletarianized population increased in the 1840s.

Careless provides a vivid portrait of this lumber community on the Ottawa valley: "[The] community showed the contrasts and inequalities of the fast-growing forest frontier. It was opulent and powerful on the one hand, crude, ramshackle and unruly on the other. Bytown, its capital, was the scene of frequent riots and head-breakings between rival

Irish and Canadian lumbermen. In the early forties, in fact, a veritable 'Shiners' War' raged there, when the Irish element, known as shiners, sought to drive French Canadians out of the timber trade by force and intimidation, and met reprisals in turn. . . . And yet this rowdy lumber town, later to be re-christened Ottawa, was blithely urged by a local paper in February 1841, as a better choice than Kingston for the capital of Canada" (Careless 1967, 30–31).

This appearance of rough equality was probably something of an illusion. Those who had settled earlier, in the first few decades of the century, had already begun to benefit from the rise in land prices. The relative prosperity of those who came later was largely dependent on how much capital they arrived with. Buckner comments that "wealth was more evenly spread in British North America than in Britain but these were not egalitarian communities" (Buckner 1998, 19). The real beneficiaries were probably those people of British stock who had played a leading part as colonial lawyers, administrators, and merchants. The political economy of frontier life thus came to play a primary role in defining the social order, through the relentless expansion westward, and northward, and in the growing role of the market in early Upper Canada.

Unlike the French who had settled in Quebec, the frontiers people west of the Ottawa river were not, essentially, subsistence producers. They were much more sensitive to the market than the French settlers to the east. Cole Harris and Warkentin note:

As a whole they were little interested in conservation, or the long-term management of land, and sought to maximize short-term profits. . . . [S]ettlement was a by-product of nineteenth century dislocation, where the human landscape had emerged from the wilderness . . . [and] a great many gave the better part of their lives to clearing (the forest). (R.Cole Harris and John Warkentin 1991, 112–115)

Before large-scale settlement in Upper Canada in the 1840s the society— such as it was—had been Tory, highly stratified, and paternalistic, owing its allegiance to the British Crown. What transpired served to change these structures and, very much later, these allegiances. In many ways the midnineteenth-century settlers were behaving like classic liberals—seeking profits, chasing market opportunities, and amassing personal capital. Many of them became immersed in the business of land speculation. They had not come to Canada to settle into self-sufficiency; they had come to buy and sell land and farm products. They hoped to sell their labor, or to farm productively. To farm, they needed land, and the land needed to be connected "by a passable road or by navigable water to the local village" (Cole and Warkentin 1991, 119).

Consequently most early settlement in Canada west of the Ottawa was near the few roads that were built, where land was easier to clear and surface water provided. From its inception the settlement of land was tied to speculation in it. If the soils became exhausted in the space of a decade, the settlers were not deterred: their objective was to amass the capital they needed to move on, to prepare to colonize other frontiers. In this respect they resembled some of the early commercial settlers on the Ecuadorian coast, discussed in the next chapter. The endemic speculation in land, and the difficulty of much of the terrain, meant that the settlement pattern was highly irregular and dispersed, especially before the arrival of the railways in the 1860s.

The dispersed settlement, and the adventitious character of the population established around it, meant that the attachment to land ownership quickly assumed importance, even while land itself was changing hands. It would be a mistake to see the attachment to land on the frontier, a central core of "property-owning democracy," as bound up with subsistence or mixed farming, since as in tropical areas today land title follows from forest clearance. Settlers did not attempt to create a peasantry in Upper Canada, nor were they forced to do so, but they needed land titles to gain real independence. Much of their food was bought: there was a ready market for all and any goods, on the frontier.

In a sense dispersed settlement had been imposed on Upper Canada, and as a consequence the settlers who were highly critical of some aspects of government land policy, and the use of surveyors and land titles to establish freehold, were the strongest defenders of the principle that made it "virtually mandatory," in one commentator's view, to live on your own land (Cole Harris and Warkentin 1991). Land settlement was tied not only to ownership but to land occupation. Thus the clearing of forests, and the establishment of farming, became closely associated with the rights to private property and the civil institutions that could protect, or advance, these rights.

If we find the beginnings of civil society in the clearing of land, and the establishment of title and occupation, we find it too in the values that this clearance gave rise to. Clearing forest and, just as important, preventing re-growth, produced "an ingrained hostility to the forest. English gentlemen visiting Upper Canada, and witnessing the severe overclearing of the land in the early and midnineteenth centuries, "frequently contrasted their own sorrow with the settlers' exultation at the destruction of trees. For the one, trees were ingredients of a picturesque landscape; for the other (they were) a severe economic liability" (Cole Harris and Warkentin 1991, 135).

Forest was cleared to make way for a highly extensive system of agricultural production, and one which was adapted to the vulnerable market conditions that characterized much of Upper Canada. Land was cleared to cultivate wheat, and wheat was followed by fallow, the fallow period being followed by wheat. This wheat-fallow-wheat system was only replaced by more mixed farming, animal production and fodder crops, as communications with urban centers improved, and local markets developed for more varied agricultural products.

Farming in the 1840s and 1850s in this area was extensive, and market-orientated, in this respect acting as a precursor to the later Plains expansion. There was little emphasis on root crops or livestock production, although vegetable gardens and small-scale animal production were maintained for household use, in some cases. Any arguments about soil conservation techniques, or long-term, more sustainable planning of farming activities, like pleas for the conservation of the forest, when they were made at all "fell on deaf ears" (Cole Harris and Warkentin 1991, 142).

The material practices of the newly populated areas reflected both market opportunities, and vulnerabilities, not least in the difficulties and obstacles that the natural environment presented. This was to find expression at the time, and subsequently, in the way in which the frontier was conceptualized in the discourses about nature and society that accompanied the settlement experience in midcentury.

Figure 4.3
The Emigrants Welcome to Canada, British midnineteenth-century cartoon

Discourses of Nature

There are two discernible discourses about nature and the environment in the writings of visitors to Upper Canada in the midnineteenth century. The first is primarily concerned with the abundance of nature and the existence of plenty. This discourse might be termed "Nature is bountiful" (Thompson and Rayner 1998). The second discourse views nature as hostile to human beings, and asserts the need to "tame" nature, to bring it within the fold of human activity and management. Visitors, and settlers, describe nature as wild and treacherous, far removed from the settled landscape from which most British (and Irish) immigrants had come. The contrast is implicitly—and sometimes explicitly—with the British Isles.

These competing discourses provide contrasting accounts of early settlement, but they are also, in one sense, complementary. The implication is that by taming wilderness, and bringing it within the compass of human institutions, one is able to enjoy the bounty, the rich resources, of nature. The environment that the colonists encountered—whether seen as abundant or threatening—was one that was linked to the human condition on the frontier.

Gerald Craig, in his account of *Early Travellers in the Canadas* (1955), identifies many travelers for whom the beauty of Upper Canada was a surprise. They commented on the vivid autumn colors of the forests, and on the magnificence of the trees they found. They also commented on the ferocity with which most settlers attacked the forest. An unknown writer of the period comments: "In its present state in (Upper Canada) . . . should you wander a mile from a settlement, the face of man can hardly be viewed without an emotion of surprise, and every cultivated patch of ground is regarded as a trophy of his triumph over the desert" (Craig 1955, 38).

Isaac Fidler was one of a number of Anglican clergymen who went to the United States in this period, disillusioned with the condition in his own country. Eventually he moved north to Upper Canada, in the 1830s, and commented on the potential wealth which the land afforded:

So fertile is the soil of Canada, at its first cultivation after clearing, that an acre, upon which no more than one bushel is sown, will produce almost always between thirty and forty bushels. The first crop, with proper management, generally repays the purchase-money, the expense of clearing and fencing, the cost of seed, sowing and harrowing, and the expense of reaping, thrashing and carrying to the mill. In short, a prudent and industrious farmer may always calculate on being able to call the land he clears his own, by the first crop alone. . . . (Fidler in Craig, 1955, 91)

Another early account is that of John Howison, who spent two years in Upper Canada between 1818 and 1820 (Howison, in Craig 1955). Howison records that the forest was cleared for "improvement," a term that had clear connotations for British visitors with the agricultural changes taking place at that time in their own country, where the improvement of agricultural practices had come to mark the Agricultural Revolution. Howison commented that in Canada there was, however, little attention to improved tillage as in England. The principal objective of farming was to establish the right to settle—which was dissembled and equated with *agricultural* improvement:

The Canadians, in addition to their indolence, ignorance and want of ambition, are very bad farmers. They have no idea of the saving of labor that results from forcing land, by means of high cultivation, to yield the largest possible quantity of produce. Their object is, to have a great deal of land under *improvement*, as they call it: and, consequently, they go on cutting down the woods on their lots, and regularly transferring the crops to the soil last cleared, until they think they have sufficiently extended the bounds of their farms.... (Howison in Craig ed. 1955)

Another traveler was C. Weld, who visited Upper Canada in the 1850s. He commented extensively on the scale of deforestation, and the rapid advance of lumbering. If the principal objective of the farmer was to establish his title, and to see the land improve in value on the basis of high fertility, that of the lumbermen was to cut down the forest, in the knowledge that they would never be faced by a scarcity of timber resources:

The question naturally arises, how long will the Canadian forests continue to meet the enormous demand for timber.... A glance at the map of North America shows how small a portion of that vast country is included in this survey; so that although new channels of communication will be opened into the interior with the extension of commerce, it is not unreasonable to regard the supply of timber as almost inexhaustible.... (Weld in Craig 1955, 206)

The discourses of nature in the period are, not surprisingly, framed by the discourses of the home country, and the comparisons, either directly or indirectly, are usually with Britain and Ireland. In both these countries wild, uncultivated land was of poor quality, moor and mountain. Most of the cultivable land supported large populations of farmers—many of them very poor. The system of landholding was indistinguishable from the social structure of the society itself—with large, hereditary landholders at its head. For many of those who visited Upper Canada the most impressive sight was the apparently limitless extent of nature's bounty, which appeared to make few requirements of settlers, at least in the short term. For the settlers themselves the establishment of their holdings, and the clearing of the forest, were necessary preliminaries to new livelihoods, and they in turn made possible new civil and political rights, which remained only aspirations for most people in most of the British Isles.

Discourses of Frontier Society

As we have seen, the view settlers adopted of nature and the environment was inextricably linked with their concern to establish their own families and fortunes in a social milieu characterized by few formal civil structures. The letters and accounts written at this time maintain a tension between the promises of the unknown, and de-humanized, wilderness and the savagery of frontier society itself. What Anthony Trollope characterized as the "roughness" of the frontier, in his book *North America*, published in 1862, was contrasted unfavorably with the so-called civilized values of Europe and the eastern seaboard.

Just as there were several accounts of frontier nature, there were similarly several such accounts of frontier society. The first depicted the frontier of Upper Canada as one lacking in social refinement, coarse, and uncivilized. The other identified opportunities in the frontier that had not existed for the newly migrant population in their societies of origin. Upper Canada in the 1840s and 1850s demonstrated that in return for hard work people with modest means could survive and prosper.

These discourses on frontier society—like those on nature and the environment—took as their starting point a series of opposites: wilderness/settlement, violence/law and order, social refinement/uncouthness. However, in the text of these accounts we can also see evidence that the discourses on society and nature were assimilated into each other. The myth of civic virtues that develops to civilize nature itself also incorporates elements of the relationship *with* nature. This is expressed in terms such as the rough equality between individuals, the private ownership of land as a fundamental guarantee of civil rights, and the social mobility that came to characterize the frontier.

Craig comments on the way in which visitors to Upper Canada in this period emphasized "sound educational standards, honesty in the government service and respect for good manners" as just as important as clearing the forest, or laying down railway tracks:

Upper Canada . . . had everything in its favor. Here, in the heart of North America, the settler could enjoy the benefits of mild but orderly institutions, free of the high taxes, church tithes and harsh game laws that bore down so hard on the poor man at home. In Upper Canada there was an abundance of good land, available at nominal prices, and much more accessible than lands in far-off Illinois and Iowa." (Craig 1955, xxxix)

Similarly Thomas Fowler, who journeyed through Upper Canada in the 1820s contrasted it with life in Britain, with its low wages, where wealth:

... is drained in channels into the coffers of the great folks, as they are called, leaving the laboring classes and the agriculturist frequently without the necessaries of life [with British North America where] the farmers and the laboring class, all partake of, and have the wealth of the nation upon their hands. (Fowler 1955, 279)

If the Canadian frontier was one of opportunity for those without much capital, it also carried implications for those professional groups who arrived with the attributes of their own class. Looked at from the perspective of those who might lose social prestige by immigrating to Canada, the benefits of the frontier quickly become defects. John Bigsby, in 1850, commented that "the great defect in colonial life is the lower civilization which characterizes it" (Bigsby 1850, 130). For this reason writers at the time sometimes cautioned prospective immigrants to Canada that although the province was ideal for the lower orders, whose life was a misery at home, emigration to Canada was of dubious value for those of easier circumstances. Bigsby cautioned that members of the "better classes" who were "content with plain comfortable mediocrity" were advised to come to Canada, a country that he described as "a rude and rough place" that offered "real temptations to wildness," somewhere where "mental improvement is lost sight of" (Bigsby 1955).

Over twenty years earlier John Howison had noted that, among recent settlers, there were "absurd notions of independence and equality" (Howison 1955, 46). This was explained by another traveler, Professor Charles Daubeny, in terms of the shortage of labor, which led "to the tone of equality assumed by the lower class toward the higher" (Daubeny 1955, 192). A common reaction to the vulgarities of the frontier was that of Lieutenant Coke, who wrote that his English blood "almost boiled in his veins" when he was placed at table with two servant women, a situation he might have anticipated in the United States but had not expected in the British provinces (Coke 1955, 303).

These notable shifts in attitudes, and the removal of social deference from everyday life, were attributed not only to the absence of landlordism, and a rigid social hierarchy, but also to the reality of social mobility experienced by many of the migrants. John Howison commented that "nine-tenths of the inhabitants were extremely poor when they commenced their labors, but a few years' toil and perseverance has placed them beyond the reach of want." It was evident that the advantages to be derived from emigration to Upper Canada were not altogether "chimerical" in Howison' view:

No person, indeed, will pretend to say that the settlers, whose condition I have described, are in a way to grow rich; but most of them now enjoy abundant means of subsistence, with the earnest of increasing comforts; and what state of things can be more alluring and desirable than this to the unhappy peasantry of Europe? (Howison 1955, 61)

Isaac Fidler, another visitor to Upper Canada in this period, expressed a similar sentiment. He wrote:

Some of the advantages which emigrants of a lower order derive from change of country are the comparative ease of mind which they possess. They are not tantalized by the presence of luxury from which they are excluded; and they find labor is a capital which yields them numerous and daily increasing comfort. They cannot obtain, nor can they reasonably look for, sudden wealth. There is no region in the world, however fertile or well governed, that offers this to the generality of settlers . . . they see their flocks and herds increasing. They behold their families and houses supplied with more conveniences every day, and better furnished. They are not excluded, even at first, from the rights of citizenship, as in the States; nor from possessing real property, which immediately confers every political advantage, and which in most places can be cheaply purchased . . . They find that their children are more easily provided for than in England, and will fill a higher place in the grades of society . . . (Fidler 1955, 95)[1]

This chapter has examined the impact of European mass migration on the forests of Upper Canada in the midnineteenth century, and the beginnings of a civil society within these forest communities. It was suggested that the myth of civic virtues, and the establishment of civil institutions such as those of local justice and local government, represented an attempt to civilize nature, which in some respects was viewed as threatening and savage. Civil society developed through the settlers' relationship with nature, as they literally carved their way through the forests and lakes of the Algonquins, and the discourses surrounding social institutions came to reflect not only the social origins of settler societies but also their experiences of settlement itself. The Canadian frontier was an avenue of opportunity for people without capital, many of whom experienced changes in their social status as well as material improvement in their lifetimes. Nevertheless, the most lasting effects of the frontier experience were often societal rather than personal: providing a template for the new social institutions and a new geography of place.

Unlike the long established Pyrenean frontiers discussed in chapter 3, whose communities' relationship with nature had evolved slowly and in balance with population, the frontier in Upper Canada in the midnineteenth century marked the rapid transformation of the environment. Property rights could only be established when land had been cleared, and civil institutions were only developed when citizens possessed these rights. The civil society of Upper Canada was not equal, but nor was it hierarchical or feudal like those of England, Scotland, and Ireland at the time. British Canada, in the period we have been discussing, was tied to the apron strings of the mother country: space had not yet been fully commoditized but nor were economic markets subject to globalization. Already a cultural imaginary was opening up to fill the void left by forest destruction, under the heading of wilderness. This was to occupy succeeding generations of Canadians for whom the environment represented an area of loss as well as one of gain. This realization that nature could be seen as a negative utopia measured in the costs of its destruction was linked to the social and political realities of the frontier and its civilizing influence in the midnineteenth century.

5

Global Markets and Internal Frontiers on the Ecuadorian Coast

In this chapter the frontier that is being referred to is not one created by international migration, like British Canada in the midnineteenth century, but a frontier created by transnational commodities. In coastal Ecuador commodity frontiers were established from the early nineteenth century onward. The settlers in this area were not British or Irish immigrants, hoping for new opportunities in the New World, but poor peasant farmers from the Ecuadorian Andes or other areas of the coast. These migrants were of mixed race or largely indigenous, and they moved between different tropical cropping systems, following the fortunes of products such as cacao and bananas: global commodities on the world stage. The struggle of these people for land gave rise to some of the most violent peasant insurrections of the nineteenth and twentieth centuries, as we will see in later chapters.

The legacy of the changes introduced by world markets for tropical products is a civil society in coastal Ecuador that is still divided along ethnic and class lines but linked inexorably to global markets, and increasingly to the new frontiers of biotechnological research. These technological frontiers are discussed more fully in the Conclusion. In many respects, however, and despite advances in bioengineering, the politics and social structures of the Ecuadorian coast today are still contained within the world of patronage and clientalism that has characterized much of Latin America since the Colony.

Agricultural Frontiers, World Markets, and "Empty" Lands

The history of the frontier societies we are describing in the remaining chapters begins with the process through which European colonial states established their grip on the resources of other continents and peoples. As Europe industrialized, in the eighteenth and nineteenth centuries, so the material interest in non-European environments was extended, from trade and exchange of commodities (including indentured and slave labor) to the sourcing of food products, and raw materials for manufacturers and the growing urban populations. Land was the one factor of production that remained immobile as agriculture was internationalized, while capital and labor changed location.

Before the rise of industrial capitalism in Western Europe the international trade in agricultural products was centered on the East Indies and, in particular, on the island of Malacca. This trade was largely dominated by Arabs, Indians, and Chinese, and it had developed independently of the European maritime states (Crow and Thomas 1982). The object of the European powers in Asia—Britain, Holland, Portugal, and France—was to control the existing spice trade, as spices were an essential element in the preservation of food before refrigeration.

However, the conquest of the New World took this process one stage further. The Spanish and Portuguese had plundered Central and South America in a search for gold and silver: at first agriculture was largely confined to meeting the food needs of the labor force, much of it made up of indigenous people, slave or indentured workers of different kinds. Many of these workers in the Spanish and Portuguese colonies were only partially proletarianized, and were able to grow food and keep animals for their own use and consumption. Partly as a consequence the internal market for food crops was slow to develop. The products of the plantation were more important, and largely superseded precious metals as the main economic activity, in the late nineteenth century in the Americas.

Most plantation products were grown under conditions of slavery, or near slavery, as labor had been transported to the point of production. There was also a "return" exchange, of course: staples such as potatoes and corn were brought from the New World to the Old, and provided a stimulus for increased productivity, especially on the European periphery (Crosby 1986). The transfer of these food staples to the temperate zones of Europe played an essential part in the rise of industrial capitalism, and the environments from which they came were transformed as a consequence. In a sense the lifestyles of the rich industrialized nations were forged from the convergence of three factors in the imperial equation: the movement of biological species and crops, the control of trade in these materials, and the (often forcible) relocation of labor. Just as consumer preferences in the north help determine forms of resource exploitation today, and leave "ecological footprints" on the south, so, in the nineteenth century, the environment was being restructured around contemporary social practices in the north.

The Evolution of Coastal Society

The social institutions of highland Ecuador, and the *latifundia* (large estates), have their roots in the *encomienda* system established by the Spanish in the colonial period, and under this system the rights to use indigenous labor gave control of other natural resources. In contrast coastal social relations were the product primarily of nineteenth- and twentieth-century conditions, particularly the expansion of world trade, which led Ecuador to specialize in a succession of tropical crops. The result, as described in the reports on land tenure during the 1960s, was "successive agricultural frontiers, the oldest of which retain traditional qualities that we cannot observe in the more recent" (CIDA 1965, 140).

Until the export of bananas became important after the Second World War, the pattern of landholding associated with these successive export booms was similar to that elsewhere in Latin America. The banana boom, however, marked the beginning of what has been termed (misleadingly) a *democratization* process within the coastal society, as middle-class urban professionals came to own land on the newly established frontier. This frontier extended northward and eastward from the traditional cocoa estates of the Guayas basin. The evidence of agricultural censuses at the time was that this much-vaunted democratization made little difference to the concentration of land ownership on the coast as a whole. However, urban settlement undoubtedly had profound effects on rural labor markets, by accelerating migration from some areas and opening up new employment opportunities for the coastal (*montuvio*) population. The *campesino* on the coast had long enjoyed a reputation for independence and freedom from feudal forms of land-holding, which was often attributed to their participation in a succession of agricultural booms. However, in the 1950s and 1960s the coastal workers experienced even greater labor mobility than in the past: they were drawn to the coastal city of Guayaquil and began to colonize hitherto unsettled parts of the coastal hinterland. Soon the Ecuadorian coast came to represent a maelstrom of different crop systems and accompanying tenure arrangements.

The Liberal Revolution of 1896 and the Cocoa Boom

Cocoa had been exported from Guayaquil in the colonial period, and in the early nineteenth century it had a limited market in Europe (Humphreys 1940). Most early accounts of the Ecuadorian coast, however, suggest that cocoa was only one of a number of tropical crops in the region. In 1860 cotton, sugar cane, and tobacco were all widely grown in the provinces of Guayas and Los Rios (Villavicencio 1860). Later rubber was produced in commercial quantities, until the initiative passed to Brazil later in the century. Following the brief rubber boom, Ecuador began exporting *tagua* nuts from the province of Manabi, and a dye from the plant *orchilla colorante*. None of these products provided the basis for commercial consolidation, however, and the upturns in demand for them were short-lived.

In the 1880s the more settled areas of the Guayas basin, where cocoa and rice were later grown, were "little inhabited and little cultivated" (Wolf 1892, 115). The climate of the area was oppressive, particularly during the rainy season between December and March, when flooding made everything but the rearing of livestock difficult. Cocoa was already an important crop by the turn of the century, but its cultivation was confined to the drier areas and the riverbanks. Foreign travelers, like the mountaineer Edward Whymper in 1879, found that communications on the coast were primitive and deplored the difficulty with which muletrains journeyed from Guayaquil to Quito (Whymper 1972). The monsoon climate was suitable for the cultivation of rice, but little seems to have been grown. Of the forty-two estates in the Daule area in 1908 only two cultivated rice at all. The most important activities were cattle-raising, cocoa and coffee cultivation, as well as the production of *aguardiente* liquor, from sugar grown in the area.

Toward the end of the nineteenth century Ecuador began exporting considerable quantities of cocoa, and the amount of land devoted to this crop increased until the 1920s. Cocoa had been the mainstay of the coastal economy in colonial times. The Spanish had found the Indians cultivating cacao when they arrived in the sixteenth century, and it was first exported in 1740. However, the crop was almost wiped out by a fungal disease in the 1920s, and low world prices during the Great Depression further discouraged production. The cacao plantations were broken up and diversified into rice, sugar, corn, and bananas until after World War II increased prices for cocoa and new disease-resistant strains revitalized the industry once more.

The years of the cocoa boom were important for the establishment of frontier society in Ecuador. The country was the world's largest supplier for most of the period before disease struck the crop in the 1920s, when Brazil and the Gold Coast increased in importance. The cocoa boom differed from previous speculative adventures in providing the first real stimulus to the tropical colonization of the coastal region, which spread northward from Guayaquil to cover the central and southern parts of the Guayas basin by the 1920s (Hamerley 1970). It seems appropriate that cocoa, which was named the golden bean (*pepa de oro*) attracted labor into zones that had previously been only sparsely populated, almost in the style of a classic gold rush. It also summoned up entrepreneurial talents and energies in a way that had no precedent in Ecuadorian history. An Ecuadorian historian commented, "it was soon proposed to convert the coast (*zona montuvio*) into one immense cocoa farm, just as Cuba was being converted into an immense sugar factory" (De la Cuadra 1958, 872).

Except in the area known as the Arriba district, along the middle Babahoyo River and its tributaries, cocoa estates were widely dispersed and cocoa was usually grown in conjunction with other crops. The commercial potential that cocoa opened up acted as a magnet for absentee landlords, bringing them back to their estates, in some cases from overseas. This in turn stimulated the commercial and banking sector of Guayaquil, which rapidly became an important port and business center. Foreign observers who were otherwise critical of Ecuador's backwardness nevertheless conceded that Guayaquil had grown in economic importance. The American William Elroy Curtis remarked that Guayaquil was "the only town in Ecuador worth speaking of from a commercial point of view" (Curtis 1969, 303). Gradually the business interests associated with the export of cocoa developed a political and economic ideology inspired by laissez-faire, seeing in Ecuador's agricultural specialization the means to lucrative self-advancement. Such liberal sentiments drew popular support on the coast, and gave the region a political identity vis-à-vis the dominant conservative interests of the highlands.

The political culture of Ecuador was characterized by almost continuous *caudillismo*, in which government performance depended on the personal qualities of individual dictators and presidents. From the early 1860s Gabriel Garcia Moreno ruled Ecuador ruthlessly but was responsible for a number of notable achievements in the fields of communication and technology. The construction of the Guayaquil to Quito railway was begun, roads were built, and schools were founded (Reyes 1942). In the succeeding two decades that followed Garcia Moreno's death in 1875, the coastal business and landlord interests grew in strength. Under the leadership of Eloy Alfaro, liberalism became the political expression of this new commercial class and captured the support of the coastal masses as well as that of the export bourgeoisie. The rural population was made up *montoneras*, or popular militias, that supported Alfaro in the hope of receiving plots when the Liberal Revolution succeeded. This success came in 1896, and the Revolution was institutionalized under Alfaro's successor, Leonidas Plaza, during the period of commercial prosperity that marked the first two decades of the twentieth century.

In the early stages of the cocoa boom the export interests behind the Liberal Revolution of 1896 were indistinguishable from those of the landholding class on the coast. The period between 1900 and 1913, however, saw a fourfold increase in the provision of credit to cocoa producers and with it a growing specialization of functions within the commercial sector. This process of economic consolidation and political solidarity was only possible because the economic interests of the state and the *Banco Comercial* were looked upon as inseparable. Between 1913 and 1917, the bank increased its financial interest in external trade from 17 to 71 percent of total export credits. By the latter date the coastal export interests constituted the dominant social class and had achieved its objective, which was to "control external trade, monetary circulation, credit mechanisms and the budgetary apparatus of the state" (Moreno 1973, 148). From 1916 to 1925, the coastal interests representing the vast bulk of commercial activity in the country dominated national politics, through the controlling hand of the *Banco Comercial*.

The Cocoa Slump and the July Revolution of 1925

The period between 1880 and 1920 marked a rise in the fortunes of the coastal export interests, and the diminishing influence of highland landlords on national policy. It has been suggested that these years saw the transition from a predominantly feudal mode of production to a capitalist one, but such an interpretation is too sweeping (Moreno 1973). Detailed examination of coastal society in this period reveals important shifts in the balance of social forces, and the first stirrings of political consciousness among much of the rural population. The coastal population was acquiring a class physiognomy that drew on an earlier period of conflict (Cueva 1975).

Coastal workers had always exhibited more independence of the landlords than the largely indigenous population of the sierra. This sometimes gave rise to an exaggerated regional pride, marking out the *montuvio* as an independent and potentially rebellious individual (Quintana and Palacios 1937). However, this independence was closely linked to local labor markets, which were culturally specific to the coast. Since the abolition of labor services by the Indian population (*concertaje*), the demand for rural labor had peaked at critical periods—especially sowing and harvesting. This had given the coastal worker some leverage in their relations with the landlord. To attract labor from the highlands, it had been necessary to offer better conditions of work and wages in cash. Capitalist social relations had existed even when coastal exports consisted principally of forest products, like timber, furs, and rubber, but wage labor was not introduced until plantation owners growing coffee and cocoa needed labor to work for them. By the early 1960s an estimated 52 percent of the agricultural population of the coast consisted of wage laborers (Cueva 1975; CIDA 1965).

During the period of the cocoa boom, in the early decades of the twentieth century, wage laborers were not the only social class to make its appearance on the coast. Many small cocoa producers were tenants, called *finqueros*, operating systems of tenancy, like those for other crops of longer growing cycles, such as coffee and bananas. The sowing of the crop, and the care of the plants, were the primary responsibility of the tenant, who paid the landlord for the use of his land. Under these systems, however, the tenant did not market the crop himself. Instead, the landlord stepped in to "redeem" the crop (*redencion*) just prior to the harvest, paying the tenant a sum of money for each plant. The tenants, who took the risks, and witnessed the landlord making the profit, particularly disliked this system. The resentment that built up among the peasants was a factor in the peasants' movement that ensued in the 1970s, and which saw the rise of apparently collectivist action on the part of small farmers.

Tenancy and Landlords

The contradictions in the class position of tenants were obvious. Tenant cultivators, like the cocoa finqueros, often employed labor themselves, on a small scale, and this shaped their attitudes toward both the *rentier* landlords and the wage-laborers they employed. The cocoa tenants were an intermediate social class, providing the landlord with labor but at the same time taking entrepreneurial decisions. The finquero participated in this system in the hope of one day becoming a landowner himself. This was their ultimate ambition, and they were prepared to make almost any sacrifice to achieve it (De la Cuadra 1958). The landlord's patronage made an ally of the tenant—but it also alienated him from the largely landless seasonal workers who worked in coastal agriculture.

The cocoa boom was more protracted than previous periods of commercial prosperity. But eventually it came to an end, as a consequence of both a slump in world demand and crop diseases. Within a decade exports had dropped to only a third of the production peak in 1914 of forty-seven thousand tons exported. The change had come about partly as a result of the ravages of witch's broom and Monilla's diseases. Demand had contracted, and the population of cocoa estates drifted toward the city.

At the same time the interior of former cocoa estates were gradually converted to rice production. It became customary to allow tenants to make annual sowings of rice, often at excessively high rents (Quintana and Palacios 1937). The cocoa tenant and wage laborer were thus transformed, in many instances, to the even more onerous status of rice tenants, or *precaristas*. At the same time the highly labor-intensive nature of rice cultivation, under systems that transplanted seedlings, served to absorb much of the surplus labor unable to find work after the demise of cocoa.

The process, which began with the slump in cocoa production, did not lead immediately to a rapid expansion in rice production. The conversion of part of the labor force employed on cocoa estates into rice producers spanned several decades, and many former cocoa tenants migrated permanently to Guayaquil. Some large estates were bought by the banks, or passed on to them by the landlords' creditors. In other cases the tenants claimed the "abandoned" land as their own, in units of about ten hectares each, enough to provide a basic livelihood for a family. Sometimes the estates were simply left to disintegrate physically, eventually to fall into the hands of foreign companies. This decline gave an impetus to parcelization and served to stimulate both the demand for land and peasant entrepreneurship. The foreign-owned estates found it easier to attract labor than Ecuadorian-owned estates, since conditions were often better and wages higher. The economic slump also encouraged Ecuadorian landlords to live for more of the time on their estates, since land occupations were common, and they needed to prove that they were not absentees, unlike their predecessors in the 1880s and 1890s.

In the light of subsequent developments, one of the most significant effects of the cocoa slump on the coast was increased collective consciousness among peasant farmers, although, as we have seen, their class identity was confused. Landlords in the 1920s and 1930s often dismissed tenants from their estates, but even where they were able to hold on to land it was impossible for them to gain access to modern lines of bank credit. Many of these former tenants took up arms in the classic *montoneras*, against the landlords; a marked contrast with the Liberal Revolution at the end of the nineteenth century when tenants had supported commercial farmers. In response the government formed hunting brigades in the provinces of Guayas and Los Rios, in an attempt to contain the rural rebellion. Between 1908 and 1927 there were successive waves of discontent and strikes on the coast, particularly on the railroads and cocoa estates. At one time in 1922 Guayaquil was described as "paralyzed by street demonstrations . . . until it looked as if it was composed of nothing but the proletarian masses" (Reyes 1960, 727). There was a re-assertion of conservative interests, the army rebelled, and power passed away from the liberal banking elite and landlords toward the more conservative interests located in the sierra. This was to be a pattern repeated in Ecuador for the rest of the century—both coast and sierra sharing power, always with one eye on the barracks, where the officer class intervened politically whenever the consensus seemed to break down.

What is immediately relevant to our analysis is the way in which coastal society became fragmented and vulnerable following the demise of the cocoa estates. Foreign-owned estates began to increase in importance, national landlords being apparently unable to resist peasant pressures for land. The interior of estates was divided between different tenure groups, each with their own political agenda. Finally, the dispersal of much of the rural population, and the settlement of the new frontier opened up to banana cultivation, brought into play new political forces—those associated with a middle class made up of neither traditional landlords nor coastal tenants.

By the 1960s bananas were being cultivated in two areas of the coast: to the south in the province of El Oro, and in the new colonization frontier of Santo Domingo de los Colorados. Although almost half the land area under bananas was in the hands of relatively few families, cash tenants or smallholders often controlled the remaining half. The

CIDA Report in the 1960s commented that in the banana zones there were none of the systems of "precarious" tenure that characterized both the mountainous sierra and the former cocoa estates. In 1965 almost 90 percent of farm units under bananas were under a hundred hectares, and six years later the average size of a banana holding was as little as fifty hectares. Many of the owners were of urban origin, and the estates managed by a resident administrator. At the same time spontaneous colonization had attracted poorer people from Manabi and the sierra, and attracted middle-class professionals, as a form of investment at a time of high inflation. The new frontier represented by banana cultivation represented a break with the past, but it offered only limited employment—most former tenants and rural workers were still locked into class conflicts with landlords and, occasionally, foreign owners. There appeared no escape from either the poverty of the city or the land invasions and rebellions that characterized social relations on the coastal estates.

The rice tenants who occupied the former cocoa estates, on the other hand, were dependent on the landlords in a variety of ways that were not confined to the land itself. The tenant had paid the landlord in kind, usually about one-tenth of the total crop. Production was undertaken entirely by the tenant, who supplied the necessary tools and draught animals. The tenant leveled the land, removed the trees and bushes, and prepared the plot for sowing. This process was called the *desmonte* (after which the tenant was often described as a *desmontero*). This work was performed before the arrival of the rains in November or December. With the commencement of the wet season in January the crop was sown, and before the spring it was usually transplanted. During the growing season there was weeding to be done, and the crop was harvested in May and June after the rains had subsided. The labor-intensive nature of rice cultivation meant that all but the poorest tenant had need of wage labor to supplement that of his family during the spring and summer months.

A tenant who supplies the landlord with only one-tenth of the crop appears to have retained most of it for his own use and sale, but the landlord himself was often the means by which the crop reached the market. It was calculated during the 1960s that it took between one and three years for the landlord to receive the full value of his land in rents, such was the low valuation of land. At the same time it was clear to most rice tenants, like the cocoa producers before them, that since the landlord contributed nothing to the farming enterprise except the land, they were easily dispensable. They were aware that they had already paid for their land several times over in rent (Zuvekas 1976). Calculations undertaken at the time also demonstrated that it was cheaper for the landlords to employ tenants than to employ wage labor in the rice zone (Baraona and Delgado 1972). The decision-making and commitment shown by the tenants also "liberated the estate from the necessity to provide an administrative and supervisory apparatus" (Baraona and Delgado 1972, 5). Landlords were consequently often absentees.

The problems facing the tenant were made worse by the grip that landlords held on the market for rice. They owned most of the rice-husking mills, and landlords provided the only credit available to tenants, often on usurious terms. Tenants were prevented from receiving official credit by their lack of titles to land, and the need to renew their rental contracts with landlords who could easily employ somebody else in their

Figure 5.1
Members of a rice cooperative, Ecuadorian Coast, 1975

place. In commercializing their rice, tenants were dependent on money-lenders, rice mill-owners and landlords; there appeared to be no escape from their miserable economic and political status.

The State and Modernity

The key to unlocking the social aspirations of the rice tenants was sup-plied by the Ecuadorian state, although it took a form that was highly unequal, and favored those tenants who worked the best-endowed rice estates. Many of these tenants had already begun to acquire land title legally through their participation in a pioneering program, supported by the US Agency for International Development (USAID).

During the 1960s many landowners in the Guayas basin had begun converting their estates into "mixed" holdings, on which cattle were reared together with the cultivation of rice. After severe droughts in 1967 and 1968 the production of rice fell far short of what was required by the urban population, and the Ecuadorian government argued that it was justified in intervening to protect supplies of the nation's most important food crop. By early 1969, amid reports of speculation in rice by mill-owners and illicit exports, the government agreed to import the equivalent of a quarter of total rice production in the zone for the previous harvest. The government sought to reduce speculation and to control prices, commandeering trucks and promising more radical measures of agrarian reform to ensure that tenants were neither ejected from the land nor left it voluntarily. At the same time the prospect of increasingly recalcitrant tenants on their estates served to harden the attitudes of landlords, who met peasant resistance with further dismissals. Tenants, for their part, recognized all the signs of an impending land reform and exerted more pressure on the landlords.

The position of tenants had been buttressed by two processes, both of which came to symbolize the control exercised by the Ecuadorian state: the formation of marketing cooperatives on land where tenants had received land titles, and the technical control of irrigated land in the interests of "modernization" exercised by a technical agency dedi-cated to land evaluation and economic development, the Commission for the Development of the Guayas basin (CEDEGE).

Figure 5.2
Rice sacks, Ecuadorian coast, 1975

State Control and the Market

Rice cooperatives in coastal Ecuador were promoted by the US Agency for International Development (USAID) from the mid-1960s, to ensure that the rural protests were not further radicalized. These initiatives followed the 1964 Agrarian Reform Law, which led to an agreement between the Ecuadorian government and AID two years later. It was understood that the role of AID should be confined to providing technical assistance to producers, and to locating sources of finance to modernize production. By February 1969 there were six rice cooperatives in the Guayas basin.

There were several reasons why USAID became involved in the organization of rice cooperatives. First, it had calculated that the landlords in the region were unwilling to invest in improvements in infrastructure. Second, USAID recognized that improved levels of rice production required new rice varieties as well as improved methods of cultivation. Third, it was clear that tenants could not obtain credit from the banks, even those intended to help small producers, without possessing land titles. Finally, landlords, most of whom were uninterested in more efficient marketing and storage arrangements, controlled the commercialization of rice (Ojeda 1971). The recognition that coastal landlordism represented such a barrier to commercial modernization led USAID to press the case of the tenants, and the need for a liberal land reform.

The major contribution of USAID to such a land reform came in the form of a plan known as Land Sale Guaranty, which was launched officially in 1970. This proposal, far from being a radical political departure, was conceived as a way of avoiding large-scale land redistribution, and the formation of large cooperatives with radical, distributive objectives. Land Sale Guaranty enabled landlords who were threatened by land invasions, and lacked the capital to modernize to pass the title of the estate to a formally constituted "cooperative," without undue political disturbance. The cooperatives so formed would be tied into the system of state agricultural credit, and entitled to technical assistance. In return the Ecuadorian state would be able to control marketed production, assuring supplies, particularly to the urban market in Guayaquil.

The Land Sale Guaranty program was advocated in the belief that many landlords would be prepared to part with land if it were valued realistically. Currently low land values reflected political instability and the threat of land invasions by tenants. The authors of this scheme even calculated that if the formation of cooperatives served to inflate land prices, then the terms under which cooperative members paid for the land could be modified accordingly (Blankstein and Zuvekas 1973). The establishment of cooperatives under these arrangements was expected to reduce social tensions and provide an alternative avenue for the tenants' political energies. In evaluating the program, attention was paid to the commercial success of some of the cooperatives, and the fact that many of them employed rural wage labor. The cooperative movement, far from stimulating collectivism in coastal agriculture, was looked upon as an expression of individualism and private entrepreneurship.

The social processes through which land was transferred to former rice tenants were given an unexpected boost when one of those most involved with the development of cooperatives, Gustavo Riofrio, in 1970 formed a commercial organization, the National Federation of Rice Cooperatives (FENACOOPARR), which offered technical assistance to cooperatives in return for selling their rice. He later became undersecretary at the Ministry of Agriculture (Hurtado and Herudek 1974). In this position he was well placed to assist in the land reform program that was launched in December 1970 under a special decree (*Decreto 1001*) and under which traditional forms of tenancy (*precarismo*) were abolished on the Ecuadorian coast. At the same time this legislation did not redistribute land. Rather, it allocated land that was commercially viable to tenants who were already working it. It made provision for private sales of land, outside the terms of the decree, if tenants and landlords entered into these voluntarily. Even under the terms of the decree, the land was to be *paid for* by tenants, over a fixed period of years, and with assistance from the agricultural bank.

The second process that underpinned the apparent transfer of power to former tenants was one that shifted technical control over production from tenants and landlords to development professionals working for the state. Government intervention in the rice zone necessarily struck at the traditional landlords who controlled the commercialization of rice. The government was assisted in its resolve by the mounting evidence that the Guayas Basin had enormous potential for rice cultivation if the infrastructure of production, particularly irrigation, could be improved. The Commission for the Study of the Development of the Guayas basin (CEDEGE) issued a series of reports after 1967, all of which pointed to the need to invest in modern irrigated rice production (CEDEGE 1975).

The first study of CEDEGE's was financed through an Inter-American Development Bank grant. This was a pilot project to the east of the small town of Babahoyo, and considered the advantages of irrigating 11,500 hectares of land. The early investigations made it clear that if CEDEGE was to undertake development assistance in the area its role would need to be more than purely technical. To succeed technically there first needed to be social and legal changes in the ownership of land and other natural resources. The rights to irrigation water, for example, needed to be changed, not least because any technical improvements would increase land valuations, and these needed to be seen as public benefits that landlords could not capture. Modern irrigation systems needed changes in land title and a better use of natural resources. Traditional landlords were neither willing nor able to deliver these changes (CEDEGE 1970).

The studies of CEDEGE represented a new element in the prolonged discussions about Ecuadorian agrarian reform and land tenure. For the first time a prestigious organization, with considerable technical expertise and the considerable international reputation of the Inter-American Development Bank, was prepared to advocate sweeping changes in the system of land tenure. Progressive landlords could be won over by promising them significant improvements in productivity on the land they retained for their own use. They would be compensated for the loss of their land by agrarian reform bonds, and this would enable them to establish careers in more commercial agriculture, or in Guayaquil. At the same time radical voices were heard arguing that CEDEGE had not consulted with local tenants, or sought to gain their trust (Ojeda 1971). Like similar spectacles of modernity before and since, CEDEGE attracted the wrath of both sides in the conflict.

The activities of both AID and CEDEGE soon bore fruit in the rice zone. By 1975 there were twenty-four rice cooperatives, cultivating a total of 13,000 hectares of land, most of which was still being adjudicated under *Decreto 1001*. Although this only represented about 6 percent of the land under rice at the time, it attracted the lion's share of official agricultural credit for rice cultivation. They were also the cooperatives with greatest commercial potential, and best able to take advantage of sophisticated irrigation infrastructure and marketing.

Most of the cooperative members were made up of former tenants who cultivated nine or ten hectares of land and had ambitions to be modern rice producers. Many of those members whose livelihoods were based on rice cultivation had quite different ambitions—they cultivated perhaps one or two hectares of land or none at all. For them the only path was one of political resistance, and an ideology of collectivism that was totally estranged from that of USAID. This was the basis of peasant radicalism on the Ecuadorian coast.

Insurgent Collectivism and the Peasant Unions

The more radical cooperative members had little reason to put their faith in the Ecuadorian state, or organizations like AID, in the 1970s. They had little reason to believe that state investment in former estates, which were either largely unworked or entirely abandoned by their owners, would transform them into a new rural bourgeoisie. These radical peasants, and their organizations, put their faith in a more collectivist future, in which the land was owned and worked in common, and social differences based on class inequalities had disappeared.

Campesino unrest in the rice zone never found expression in a coordinated movement to take possession of the land from landlords. It largely consisted of more or less spontaneous and localized conflicts that varied in intensity and geographically. As we have seen, peasant uprisings had occurred when cocoa had been the principal coastal export. Since the 1920s there had been a number of isolated rural uprisings. In July 1955 the Federation of Coastal Agricultural Workers (FETAL), which was linked to the Ecuadorian Communist Party, had brought rural workers and railway workers together behind the demand for agrarian reform and the release of imprisoned activists. However, it was not until drought struck the coast, in 1968 and 1969, that peasant unrest reached regional proportions.

At the beginning of 1969 the press reported on the growing unease in agriculture. There had been invasions of land, estate managers had been kidnapped, and there were dire warnings about growing guerrilla activity, like that a decade earlier in Cuba. These manifestations of discontent were attributed not to individual grievances but to a general atmosphere of anarchy (*El Universo*, Guayaquil, January 20, 1969). In the province of Guayas there had been a gunfight between police and peasants working on Hacienda La Saiba, and six armed *campesinos* had kidnapped an estate manager near the town of Naranjal. Land invasions had increased and "huts made of branches, cardboard and tins had appeared suddenly on some estates" (*El Universo 1969*). It was recognized that the drought had contributed to this unrest, but it was alleged that behind the invasions there were also professional agitators and guerrillas who exploited the popular discontent. For the first time press reports were ominous, even despairing, for these land invasions were being used to mobilize the coastal peasantry on a massive scale.

Periods of discontent like this coincided with general anxiety about poor harvests, and the way in which commercial interests managed to hoard rice against an expected rise in price. From 1969 until the end of the 1970s there were regular accusations that the land reform body, IERAC, was giving assistance to recalcitrant peasants. For his part the director of IERAC argued that these land "invasions" could be described as peasant resistance to ejection from estates, moves that many of the landlords had initiated faced with what they saw as hostile agrarian reform legislation, especially the 1964 Agrarian Reform Law. It is interesting that the landowners claimed that until the land had actually been transferred to the peasants, the job of the government was to back them up. In a visit to the coastal town of Daule, the scene of much of the trouble, the Minister of Social Provision argued that the government supported the "peaceful" resistance of the *campesinos*.

Toward the end of 1970 the next wave of peasant militancy followed the decrees that abolished precarious tenancy. This time *campesino* activity was in support of the state, which was trying to implement the decree abolishing precarious tenure, *Decreto 1001*. Organizations that had come into being to help the peasants, by offering technical assistance and putting them in touch with sources of agricultural credit, such as the Christian Left (*Confederacion Ecuatoriana de Obreros Catolicos, CEDOC*) and the Ecuadorian Communist Party (*Partido Comunista Ecuatoriana, PCE*) sprang to the support of the organized resistance.

With the law on their side the position of rice tenants was a curious one. On some estates, like La Carmela, tenants were able to gain access to official lines of credit and pay off the debts that they incurred to the landlord, even before rice tenancy was officially abolished. In this case the landlord backed down from conflict, in fear that if the tenants did not take over his land the day laborers (*jornaleros*) would. In the view of the tenants on La Carmela, the laborers were anarchists and communists and not to be trusted. With the help of lawyers the tenants were able to challenge the landlord's claim to the estate, and by enlisting the support of the Agency for International Development (AID) and Riofrío's federation, FENACOOPARR, they went on to run the cooperative as an agricultural enterprise, in the name of the fifty families that constituted the cooperative. The cooperative in turn employed laborers, and their transition to commercial farmers seemed complete.

In other cases the tenants were forced into more radical political positions. On the estate called Urbino Jado, conflict between landlords and tenants had been particularly bitter and sustained. In this locality the landlords successfully resisted the attempts of USAID to intercede on behalf of the better-off tenants. After December 1970, when land began to be assigned to former tenants under the decree, this landlord unity broke down. One landlord, named Freire, even helped the peasants in their struggle with the dominant local family, the Trianas. Tenants had been thrown off their land, their houses had been burned and their livestock slaughtered. Organized armed bands, in the pay of the Trianas, terrorized the peasants and were held responsible for the death of one of their leaders, Arnulfo Castro, in June 1971. The landlords believed that if they terrorized the peasants enough they would back down. But in fact landlord resistance only provoked the tenants in their political resistance.

A third case, again distinctive, was that of the cooperatives formed near Daule, a small market town in the interior of the rice zone. Three landowning families, the Briones, Villegas, and Carchi families, wielded considerable power in the area. When the peasants began to form cooperatives, and to claim title to the land, the landlords in the area paid assassins to murder one of their leaders, Francisco Acosta, in late 1970. Three months later, after the decree, all the local leaders agreed to name their cooperative after the deceased, and Cooperative Francisco Acosta came into being in March 1971. This and other neighboring cooperatives affiliated to one of the organizations of former tenants, the *Asociacion de Cooperativas del Litoral (ACAL)*. Within two years ACAL owned its own rice mill to the north of Daule and most of the cooperatives in the area became affiliated, gaining technical assistance through another body that worked closely with ACAL, the *Central Ecuatoriana de Servicios Agricolas (CESA)*. This organization was made up of progressive agronomists, economists, and lawyers, many of them from the southern cone, who had come to Ecuador to advance the aspirations of the peasantry. They came to constitute a kind of expatriate intelligentsia, giving advice to the former tenants but at the same time remarkably aware of the complex social structure that was coming into being on the coast that bore little relationship to socialism and saw former tenants become freeholders, often at the expense of laborers as well as landlords.

It is possible to draw a number of conclusions from these examples and other similar ones (Redclift 1975, 1976). In the majority of cases conflicts were long drawn out, and third parties, offering technical assistance, only intervened after the tenants had already demonstrated their intention to resist. Often the dispute between the landlord and tenant began when the land was being sold, or the landlord was proposing to make substantial changes in the way that the estate was run, such as employing wage-laborers in place of tenants. There are very few confirmed cases in which tenants actually invaded land; generally they refused to be ejected from land they were already working. Once battle had been joined the landlords usually offered to sell at least part of the estate to the tenants, often at inflated prices. The carrot of a quick sale was attractive to tenants who despaired of waiting while the land reform institute (IERAC) transferred the land to them. Sometimes the time-consuming process of acquiring a title to land increased the tensions among tenants and played into the hands of landlords.

For their part the landlords were often adept at using force to secure their ends, while the police usually kept out of what they regarded as domestic disputes between landlords and tenants. Sometimes landlords hired laborers to eject the tenants, or resorted to threats on the lives of the peasant leaders. The roll call of deaths among peasant organizers in the Guayas basin after 1967 bears testimony to the reality of these threats. It has been suggested that like many peasant movements in Latin America, the struggles of the coastal tenants in Ecuador were uncoordinated and localized. This was certainly true in the early stages of the conflicts, and differences between *campesinos* militated against concerted action even after the peasant movements of the 1970s.

Peasant Movements and the Commons: The Case of Pancho Rule

The central importance of social differentiation not only militated against concerted action on the part of tenants and laborers in the rice zone, it also led both to prize communally owned land on many of the cooperatives that were coming into being. The case of a cooperative called Pancho Rule is a case in point (Redclift 1975, 1976).

Cooperative (Francisco) Pancho Rule is situated ninety kilometers north of Guayaquil. The nearest town, Balzar, is about five kilometers to the north, where the rice zone gives way to the commercial production of bananas and cacao. In the summer of 1975, when I lived on the cooperative, it was composed of one hundred and sixty members and their families, a population of about one thousand people all told. The members cultivated about four hundred hectares of irrigated rice land, within a total extension for the cooperative of two thousand hectares. One boundary of the cooperative follows the course of the river Daule, a tributary of the Guayas, for about thirteen kilometers. To reach Pancho Rule, you have to travel by road and canoe; to traverse it, you must travel on horseback. Even by the standards of other former estates in the area Pancho Rule is immense.

The present cooperative is composed of what were formerly three estates that were once owned and managed separately. Today their names designate the three administrative units into which it is divided: Naranjal, Javiera, and Perinado. The estate named Naranjal originally extended beyond the boundary of today's cooperative, onto land that is still owned privately, as the hacienda San Vicente.

Pancho Rule became a rice cooperative on October 4, 1971, by mutual agreement with the former owners, members of the Salecian order. The Salecians' decision to sell the estate to the tenants had been taken after mediation through one of the technical organizations in the zone, CESA, itself a Roman Catholic charity. The name was derived from the estate's former owner between 1946 and 1949, a Mexican with large landholdings in Ecuador. According to popular belief this man, Pancho Rule, had been the victim of a shipwreck at sea, from which he was the lone survivor. To mark his fateful escape he donated the estate to the Church, and so it came into the hands of the Salecians.

The Salecians seem to have administered the estate as enlightened despots might have done in eighteenth-century Europe. There were rarely more than five of them resident at any time, but their influence on the running of the *hacienda* was subtle, and they insisted on the peasant families practicing their Catholicism in a way that is uncommon on the coast. They particularly disapproved of couples not marrying in church and of men having several female partners in different towns, a common coastal practice.

The consensus on the cooperative is that the Salecians were ambivalent about leaving the entire estate to the former tenants. Along the river bank a significant amount of cacao and coffee was grown, and there was five thousand head of cattle on the inland pastures. It seems clear that the Salecians intended to transfer only the land under rice cultivation, at least to begin with. All the families on the estate had paid a proportion—about one-tenth—to the Salecians, although evidently the Order did not enforce this rent if the family were genuinely in need. Cooperative members also paid this tithe in 1975, although by then it was toward the freehold ownership rather than in tenancy. However, a small number of families clearly benefited from the patronage of the Salecians and were given the rank of *mayordomo*, or supervisor, and given authority over other poorer tenants. Some of these families had electricity in their houses when the Order installed a generator, and others even had concrete houses built for them. These elect families assisted the Salecians in religious rituals, their sons assisted as altar boys during the services. Even in 1975 they were marked out from others by their superior education, religiosity, and wealth.

Social inequality on Pancho Rule is partly dictated by the differentials in land ownership. Those families with a minimum of two or three hectares of rice land can, in a good year when rainfall is plentiful, double the amount under cultivation. The figures for land distribution are thus exaggerated during good times, when harvests are plentiful. Those families who own most land, less than a dozen in all, also own most of the cooperative's six hundred head of cattle. By grazing their cattle on the communal land owned by the whole cooperative, these families have a much greater access to an important common property resource than families with few or no cattle.

For the poorest families, those with only a couple of hectares of rice land, the communal land is important in a different way—as a way of guaranteeing work for the reserve labor from their own families, not all of which can be employed throughout the year on their own private plots. A family with seven or eight children, common among rice tenants, cannot employ all of them on a two-hectare plot throughout the year. For these people the communally owned land (*lote communal*) was an essential part of their livelihood strategies. In 1975 only about thirty hectares of rice land was worked collectively in this way, but the demand to increase the proportion of the communally owned land under rice came from several quarters. Better-off families looked upon the extension of the communal land as an essential step in a process to modernize the cooperative and attract the support of the government, credit banks, and marketing organizations.

Members could see that in other parts of the zone preference had been given to land that was farmed collectively, with official backing, and to much higher technical standards. Under this program the *Programa de Promocion de Empresas Agricolas (PPEA)* ninety-one elite cooperatives commanded the lion's share of agricultural credit. The cooperatives in the PPEA were endowed with better natural resources for the cultivation of rice—land that was regularly prone to floods and located close to transport networks. Beginning by authorizing credit for the rice crop, the technical managers in charge of the PPEA eventually consented to provide credit for infrastructure too. Most of these cooperatives had acquired land outside the terms of the official decree, *Decreto 1001* in December 1971. Many of these estates were very large—the average being over one thousand hectares of land, perhaps half of it under rice cultivation. The advantages of collectively worked land were apparent to technical personnel and former tenants alike. Officials argued that if land was worked communally, it could be leveled more easily and irrigated, and mechanized harvesting could take over from manual operations. The cooperatives could be managed remotely, from offices in Guayaquil, and to a much higher specification.

At the same time the advantages for members were also obvious. They had much better access to credit, a guaranteed market, and as much technical assistance as they needed. The potential for employing labor increased with collective production—both family labor, when it was in surplus, and casual labor when family labor was scarce. It was a condition of receiving land through the agrarian reform institute (IERAC) that labor other than that of cooperative members should only be employed exceptionally (although, of course, Pancho Rule was not subject to the strict dictates of the law). Members' families were paid a regular wage for working the *lote communal*, and this could be subtracted from the profits of the enterprise at the end of the season. It was thus a way of reversing indebtedness—by using communal resources to provide an advance income for the families whose labor was being employed. It was looked upon as a guarantee, at least to a limited extent, of a relatively stable livelihood.

For both the better-off and poorer members of the cooperative, then, there were clear attractions to increasing the amount of land under collective ownership and cultivation. It was recognized that the cooperative had come into existence primarily as a way of securing land ownership, rather than as part of a conscious social experiment. At the same time it was clearly understood that if the cooperative was to gain as much as some others, for example, those belonging to the PPEA scheme, then it would have to cede more and more control to outsiders. Although envious of other cooperatives that had taken the road to more collective management of resources, members of Pancho Rule could appreciate that successful cooperatives required restraint from members—they could not pay themselves more than they earned. Two expressions encapsulate what members believed: the first task was to "provide a livelihood for ourselves," and the other was "to struggle to control ourselves." There were real contradictions in meeting both objectives, of course, and as the process of modernization evolved, so these had to be resolved.

The Frontier Inheritance after 1970

Looking at the Ecuadorian agricultural sector as a whole since the 1970s, it is clear that political opposition slowed the implementation of the land reforms. IERAC received little government funding, largely because of the pressures mounted by landlords to discredit the organization, accusations that were not altogether without substance since bribery and corruption were widespread. Later amendments to the land reform legislation exempted all farms that were efficiently run. In the sierra much of the redistributed land was poor, and landlords kept the best quality land. Except for a few showcase examples farmers on small plots received no government assistance or services to help make their land more productive. By 1979 most planned expropriations had been completed, and only 20 percent of peasant families and 15 percent of agricultural land throughout Ecuador had been affected by agrarian reform.

It can be appreciated that structural changes in the rice zone, although not difficult for modern landlords to concede, were nonetheless exceptional. The situation in Ecuador as a whole was modest. By 1984 over seven hundred thousand hectares of land had been distributed under the land reform and, as we have seen, much more land under private arrangements, drawing on outside agencies such as the US Agency for International Development (AID).

Throughout the 1970s and 1980s the Ecuadorian government pinned most of its hopes for a relief of rural poverty not on land distribution but on colonization of the relatively underpopulated regions, especially the Amazon and the Oriente. By the late 1970s IERAC had awarded two and a half times more land in areas of new settlement than it had distributed in agricultural reform zones. Further most colonists in the Amazon received a forty- to fifty-hectare parcel of land under the reform: much more than in either of the other two regions of the country. In the Amazon the average holding was thirty hectares, and 65 percent of holdings were less than a hundred hectares, accounting for 83 percent of the agricultural land.

But the new frontiers opened up by the colonization of the Amazon were also the scene of bitter disputes and conflicts. Migrants, mainly men between the ages of twenty-five and forty, cleared as much land as they could, but as their savings were exhausted, and the support of their families dwindled, many migrants had recourse to wage labor, either for oil companies or for more established settlers. In the more heavily settled areas of the Amazon, houses stood beside roads that most often were unsurfaced and difficult to maintain. By the early 1980s most of Ecuador's colonists in the Amazon were at least six kilometers from the all-weather roads, a significant impediment in marketing their crops and improving their families' income. The tropical forests of the interior were a safety valve for much of the rural discontent, especially of the sierra, but the new frontiers that developed brought new handicaps: conflicts with the oil companies, the immiseration of many of the indigenous people who populated the Amazon basin, and a continuing dependence on export crops.

Reform in the rice zone had been a significant achievement against a background of only modest improvements. Production increased, from 330,000 metric tons in 1966 to 780,000 tons in 1987, to over a million metric tons in 1992. Rice production is very weather dependent, and annual harvests varied throughout the period since the early 1970s. In good years rice producers met domestic demand and managed to export a surplus. Rice was a strategically important food staple for the ever-expanding urban population that was continuing to flow into Guayaquil. However, during the 1990s the low international market prices for rice meant that the government sought to stabilize rice production at the level required to meet domestic needs, since, given its control of the industry, this was relatively easy to do. Government management of the rice economy was made easier by improved yields per hectare, which had increased consistently since the 1970s. It was this, rather than the political emancipation of the tenants, or the reduction in rural poverty that was arguably the greatest achievement of the coastal struggles.

Although initially struggles for land, social movements like those on the Ecuadorian coast became struggles for other resources too, for agricultural credit and technical assistance. In the transition from "feudal" agricultural regimes to technological modernity, which these frontiers signified, it is space itself that was transformed through capital employed to intensify yields and promote technological innovation.

While land itself is immobile, the biological resources that depend on land and constitute the ecosystems of other places—plant and animal life—increasingly became elements in international exchanges, in this respect not unlike capital and labor. Furthermore the technologies that had been developed to exploit land-based resources increasingly gave way to technologies that serve to alter the very nature of biotic resources and to transform environments. The biological materials that were subject to exchange, and that were increasingly removed from their place of origin, were becoming increasingly independent of physical space and spatially located environments. This has culminated in the development of bioengineering and genetic modification, on a global scale (Goodman, Sorj, and Wilkinson 1987; Goodman and Redclift 1991). In this sense, indeed, we can speak of some environments being divested of their "natural" quality, as their genetic component has been developed—a true extension of the industrial process to agriculture, and the environment. It is this dimension of the biological frontier to which we return in the concluding chapter of this book.

6
Chicle, and the Forest Frontier in Quintana Roo

The history of the eastern part of the Yucatán peninsula (the state of Quintana Roo) in Mexico contains elements of the frontier histories discussed in earlier chapters. Until late in the twentieth century much of the east of Yucatán (today's state of Quintana Roo) was a forest frontier settled by immigrants into the zone, in some respects not unlike midnineteenth-century British Canada. However, these settlers were from other parts of Mexico, and the impact of their settlement, as we will see, was to nationalize the new territories, forging closer links with the rest of Mexico. The forest clearing and establishment of agriculture and ranching came in the wake of an important, and potentially sustainable, extractive activity—the harvesting of *chicle* resin for making chewing gum.

Unlike the Ecuadorian coast, the population of Yucatán was largely made up of people native to the area (the Maya), so the effect of settlement was to displace them, pushing them further into the forests. White and mestizo groups dominated the formal economy of Yucatán, with roots in the Spanish colonial period. Mexican Independence in 1821 did not bring the freedom and justice that was promised to the indigenous populations of Yucatán, as elsewhere in Mexico. The social institutions of the Maya were both civil and religious, and their determination to resist the alienation of their land and labor led some of them into a prolonged struggle, the Caste War, which started in 1847, and has never been completely resolved.

In the case of the Yucatán, as in coastal Ecuador, foreign capital was employed in opening up land to exploitation for global markets: initially dyewoods, then *henequen* (a form of sisal or hemp), and ultimately

Figure 6.1
Indigenous woman, Valladolid, Mexico

chicle (the resin from which chewing gum was made). As we will see, the insertion of foreign capital and commercial interests even threatened the authority of the local state, and the white landowners in the region, and ultimately posed problems of authority and governance for the federal government in Mexico City. What distinguishes the frontier history of Yucatán, above all else, is the scale of the social resistance mounted by the indigenous Mayan people, and the extent to which it posed an alternative vision of the relations between society and nature, based on the religious and political beliefs of the Maya. This was the legacy of the Caste War.

The second important thread in this history of the frontier locates the Yucatán at the extremities of another social conflict, the Mexican Revolution, which began in 1910. Post-Revolutionary society brought people into the political process, especially peasant farmers, who had formerly been disenfranchised under the pre-Revolutionary rule of President Porfirio Díaz. Institutions grew up, particularly the *ejido* land unit, which acted to absorb labor and to provide for the minimum needs of rural households. At the same time their importance was clouded in rhetoric, enabling the Mexican state to appear to discharge its obligations to the revolutionary process, without threatening the interests of large landowners or foreign capital. The frontier regions of Yucatán, and the state of Quintana Roo, were seen as a blank canvas on which the Mexican state could extend its interests and control. As this chapter makes clear, in fact the canvas was far from blank, and the indigenous population that had resisted white domination survived around its own theocracy, its own ecological beliefs and practices, and religious rituals that bound them together. The *Cruzob*, or rebel Maya, present an alternative vision of their relationship with nature to that represented by the Mexican state after 1910. This was crystallized in the history of a natural product, chicle, which had always played a part in Mayan ritual but was to become an iconic product in twentieth-century America, chewing gum.

The Caste War in Yucatán was one of the most important movements of indigenous peasant resistance in the Americas. It began in 1847, and for most of the subsequent half century much of the Mayan population of the Yucatán peninsula was locked in conflict with the white population in a protracted struggle to defend their rights. The Caste War was an attempt by the Maya to recover control over their territories and to re-establish the rights they had not regained after Mexico's independence in 1821 (Reed 1964, 2001). Before the military victory of the whites under General Bravo in 1901, the rebel Maya fought on, retreating into the dense forests of what is today known as the Mayan zone (the southern part of Yucatán state and the northern part of Quintana Roo). These Cruzob Maya followed the Talking Cross, a millenarian cult that had given heart to the insurgents, and their ultimate victory, a belief that persists in a few isolated villages even today (Forero and Redclift 2004).

One of the most remarkable features of the Mayan rebellion, particularly in the later period between 1901 and the 1930s, was the role played by chicle, the raw material from which chewing gum was made, in helping to finance the rebel armies. During this period revenues from selling chicle helped to finance and support the rebel struggle. Later the chicle industry was able to achieve what the Mexican government was unable to do by force: the surrender of the Mayan chiefs.

The conventional account of these events pays little attention to the links between the rebel Maya and chicle, and draws a line under the Mayan resistance after the period of Lázaro Cárdenas's presidency (1934–40), when cooperatives were created for *chicleros* and the industry began to be regulated by an increasingly interventionist Mexican state. It is tacitly assumed that the enhanced role for the state, in mediating between chicle producers and the chewing gum companies based in the United States, effectively ended the period dominated by *coyotaje*, the illegal and exploitative activities of commercial intermediaries. The political project of President Cárdenas to create cooperatives as part of the land reform process on communal lands, called *ejidos*, that were given to chicleros has been celebrated in Mexico as a success for both the management of the forest and ethnic relations between whites and Maya. It linked the pacification of the Maya with the development of a national ideology, and the erosion of the forest frontier. This dominant discourse views modernity as at last catching up with the history of Yucatán and the Mayan people, leaving only isolated bodies of resistance in unreconstructed pre-modern zones.

However, more recent research puts this process in a different light. Earlier investigations in the areas from which chicle was sourced has underlined the important role that it played in helping to arm the Maya during the first decades of the twentieth century (Konrad 1991; Ramos Díaz 1999). New research also points to the continuing importance of paternalistic politics, *coyotaje*, and the marginalization of most Mayan peasant farmers from the institutions of the Mexican state (Forero and Redclift 2005).

Chicle and the Rebel Maya

It has been estimated that the population of independent (Cruzob) Maya was only about eighty-five thousand in 1850 (Reed 2001). During the next fifty years it declined further, some people moving into British Honduras to the south, others into the pacified areas of Yucatán to the north and west (where the Mayan population had always been subordinated within the agricultural estates). In most of the peninsula of Yucatán a new activity, the production of henequen (or sisal) made from the leaves of a local *agave* plant, brought prosperity to landlords and merchants. Technical developments, such as the development of steam-powered decorticating mills, enabled the coarse fiber to be removed from the fleshy leaves of the plant. In the days before artificial fibers, sisal had a number of essential uses, for rope making, carpets, and rugs. The technological breakthrough represented by henequen production, and the economic prosperity it brought to Yucatán, was similar to the role of the cotton gin in the southern United States. Soon the streets of Mérida were lined with carriages and exquisite fin-de-siecle mansions, like the Paseo de Montejo, which was modeled on the boulevards of Paris. In fact, in terms of culture and taste, Mérida was closer to Paris and London in some respects than to Mexico City. The wealth brought by the market for henequen in Europe and North America had served to develop and consolidate a new cosmopolitan spirit.

The development of the Yucatán peninsula continued during the transition from the nineteenth to twentieth century following the development of the new chicle industry. However, the chicle industry operated under very different conditions from those of henequen. The henequen industry operated entirely under the *hacienda* regime, a form of production with pre-capitalist roots in which indigenous people supplied labor and were often subject to violent coercion. To a large extent the labor conditions of henequen haciendas serve to explain the continued rebellion of the Maya (Reed 1964, 2001).

In contrast, the chicle industry could not be developed under an hacienda regime. The *chicozapote* trees (*Manilkara zapota*), from which chicle was extracted, did not grow in plantations as henequen did. Thus control over the labor force was exercised through a system of

Figure 6.2
Chiclero tapping *chicozapote* tree, 2004

debt-servitude (*enganche*). A contractor gave an advance to the chicle-tapper (*chiclero*) to enable him to begin his work in the forest. The advance was not generally given in cash but through supplying the tapper with the tools he needed to work, and the groceries he required to survive in the forest during the tapping season. At least in theory, then, the tapper would be obligated to work for the contractor until the value of extracted chicle covered the value of the credit initially given.

The system of indebtedness operated in other regions of Latin America where nonmonetary societies met with those of market relations, particularly those managed by European and American entrepreneurs. The system was used during the late nineteenth century to obtain rubber in northwest Amazonia, where it soon degenerated into a semi-slave system (Stanfield 1998).

In Yucatán the Maya already had a military structure and a supply of arms that gave them ample margin of negotiation with the Mexican authorities. Additionally numerous nonindigenous people coming from the Mexican state of Veracruz had been recruited into the labor force as well, since the early 1900s. Thus international entrepreneurs were forced to hire the services of local contractors, called *permisionarios*, who negotiated with Maya chiefs, providing the labor force for the exploitation of the forests where the tree was found.

The manufacturing and production of chicle was never a purely Mexican initiative, and it has always depended on international demand. At the end of the nineteenth century the president of Mexico, Porfirio Díaz, had established large forest concessions for the exploitation of woods to the British (mainly mahogany and cedar) and then of chicle to investors from the United States. In the south and east of the Yucatán peninsula, the followers of the Cruzob still controlled the forest and access to its resources. The legacy of the Caste War, and the geopolitics of the region, had created conditions that were very favorable for foreign commercial access to the region's resources. Already financial interests based in London had established a flourishing logwood and cabinet-wood business in Belize (British Honduras). By the midnineteenth century logwood extraction had penetrated farther north up the Caribbean coast of Quintana Roo. After logwood declined, the trade in mahogany and other valuable hardwoods expanded, and there were further incursions into the forest on the part of entrepreneurs and contractors.

The military conflicts in Yucatán, and the increasing involvement of the authorities in British Honduras to the south, provided both commercial and diplomatic possibilities for foreign capital. The forests of the Yucatán peninsula were no longer just a source of valuable timber extraction—they became the seat of a new commercial activity, which fed the tastes of consumers on the eastern seaboard of the United States.

The scale of the early chicle trade can be inferred from the annual Bluebooks that summarized the economic activities of British Honduras in this period. They show a gradual increase in the importance of chicle and other forest products, from slightly over 60 percent of export value in 1886 to about 80 percent by 1900. A little less than half of these exports were probably sourced from the territory of Quintana Roo. Within ten years the official value of chicle exports rose by 72 percent. As the forest resources of British Honduras became gradually depleted, further incursions were made into Quintana Roo and the territory controlled by the Cruzob in search of the *chicozapote* tree from which chicle resin was obtained. In fact, as most trade with what was formally Mexican territory was forbidden or discouraged, the statistics that exist almost certainly underestimate the importance of sourcing chicle from Quintana Roo.

These figures also give us some idea of the importance of foreign capital for the region in this period. Access to Quintana Roo's products was possible because for half a century the British had provided support to the rebel Maya, sometimes tacitly, less often overtly. At the same time London was anxious to maintain reasonably good relations with the government in Mexico City, precisely in order to gain access to southern Quintana Roo for its own commerce. British investment in Mexico had a long history, dating back to the early post-independence period. By the mid-1880s Mexico's external debt to Britain was twenty-three million pounds, which suggests very high levels of British investment, actively encouraged by the government of the dictator, Porfirio Diaz.

In the absence of Mexican capital every effort was made to develop the region with whatever foreign capital was available. In 1892 London companies established the Mexican Exploration Company to extract forest products in coastal areas near the Bay of Chetumal. This company was later declared bankrupt, but its concessions were taken over by another, based in Belize, in 1896. In the same year yet another enterprise, the East Coast of Yucatán Colonization Company, was formed in Mexico City, but financed by the Bank of London and Mexico. This company took over an earlier concession that gave it access to nearly three-quarters of a million hectares of forest.

These huge concessions, negotiated with British and other foreign companies, gave them access to forest resources that were effectively barred to the Mexican authorities before 1901. They positioned British capital to exploit almost the entire eastern seaboard of the Yucatán peninsula. In 1893 the Mexican and British governments had entered into a settlement known as the Mariscal–St. John Treaty, which made the Rio Hondo the southern border of Mexican territory with British Honduras. Via this strategic river system the British now had greater access to Quintana Roo, and consolidated their position with the Cruzob. At the same time the treaty undermined the rebel Maya in the longer term by introducing commercial relations. The Maya became increasingly drawn into this web, which dramatically transformed the culture as well as the economy of the region.

As early as 1894 the government of Díaz had passed comprehensive legislation regulating the exploitation of forest products and lands, which had increasingly fallen under the control of foreign commercial interests. This legislation would become the basis for future concessions to foreigners for which the Mexican federal government sought adequate compensation. The exploitation of Quintana Roo's forests had been further stimulated by the growth of trade with the United States in chicle. The rebel Maya had derived benefits from this trade and the Mexican government sought, through regulating trade, to cut off supplies of cash and arms to the Mayan rebels.

Queen Victoria, the British monarch at the time, was aware of the Mexican need to end the conflict with the rebel Maya and, wanting to recover the money owed to the Empire, acceded to the Mexican government's demands on two points: debt and the supply of arms. This left open the matter of boundaries. Later Porfirio Díaz conceded in giving a large extension of land from Blue Creek in Belize to Chetumal, in order to reach an agreement with the British that would help cut the supply of arms and ammunition to the Maya.

President Díaz approved the treaty in 1889, but before signing it, he had to negotiate with the Yucatecan elite; thus ratification would not occur until 1897. The British authorities, for their part, had to deal with the local interests in Belize, which were dubious about an agreement that was to injure what they saw as the friendly Maya. The British government offered a considerable amount of money for them to build a new navigation channel, which they hoped would settle things down (Reed 2001). Porfirio Díaz, for his part, made clear that settling the border did not mean commercial relations would stop between Belize and Mexico. On the contrary, in 1895 he gave the largest forest concession to the Belizean Plummer Company (Lapointe 1983, 1997).

The Mexican government initiated its military campaign from the sea, in an effort to strengthen communication with the rest of the country from the coast of Quintana Roo. A small naval force was sent to Cozumel and the Bay of Chetumal to the south, to provide bridgeheads for later expansion. As a condition of signing the Mariscal–St. John boundary Treaty the British government had agreed to prevent arms from reaching the Cruzob through Belize, and this new naval force helped to ensure compliance. This campaign began in 1898 with the patrolling of the Rio Hondo boundary by an armed naval customs vessel. The principal attack on the rebel Maya, however, would be overland from the west, using the town of Peto as the main point of departure.

In the short period between December 1899 and May 1901 the army of General Bravo gradually opened up the territory of Quintana Roo controlled by the Cruzob. In effect the role of the federal government's army consisted of protecting the work gangs that were constructing the rail link to Peto. Their superior munitions meant that they were able to defeat the Mayan forces in a series of skirmishes, which were understood at the time as battles of vital national importance. The losses were not great on either side, but General Bravo made it his business to keep the authorities informed of his progress, cabling both Mérida and Mexico City at different stages of the conflict. These were strategic victories rather than heroic military adventures, and more men were lost through fever, dysentery, and malnutrition than through battles.

The government's campaign highlighted the fact that the Cruzob were unable to prevent a serious military attack on their territory. The steam-driven railway, protected by guns and motivated by commercial gain, proved to be invincible. As one commentator put it, in an eloquent phrase, "the spikes of the commercial development were being driven into the heart of the *Cruzob* territory" (Reed 2001). The Maya's response following military defeat, however, did not finally put an end to their cultural resistance. It merely displaced it geographically, and the rebels guarded their Crosses with increased care.

That the rebel Maya were able to successfully resist cultural and political domination, even after the Mexican army's control was re-established in 1901, is largely explained by the role chicle came to play in the forest economy of the region. General Bravo had constructed fortresses, and made a prison of the Balam Na, the shrine of the Holy Cross. Such impositions on the Maya would continue until the defeat of President Porfirio Diaz, and the outbreak of the Mexican Revolution in 1910, when Bravo had to give up his command. Two years later, after Bravo's expulsion, General Alvarado as governor of Yucatán moved the capital to Chetumal (formerly Payo Obispo) and gave the town back to the Maya.

It comes as no surprise that the Cruzob wanted no business with the whites (*dzulob*). They cut the telegraph cables, destroyed the wells, and burned the railroad engines. The rebel Maya wanted autonomy and to re-establish theocratic rule. Witnessing and analyzing all this was a clever political mind, that of a Mayan sergeant, Francisco May, who rose to become head of the rebel forces (Villa Rojas 1945, 1978).

The Defeat of the Mayan Resistance

During the last few decades of the nineteenth century the rebel Maya were forced back into the jungle, but they were able to obtain arms by selling the chicle resin produced from their forests. This is shown in some of the documents collected in the state archives in Chetumal.

The company which I represent has done everything in its power to stop the selling of liquors, shotguns and ammunition. The company has been unsuccessful due to the presence of an Alvarado, who has settled in Yo Creek, few miles away from Agua Blanca. [He] has an aguardiente distillery, [the product of which] he trades with chicle, which is illegally and furtively extracted from the company terrains which [the company] I represent rents and from [terrains rented to] other persons. This Alvarado also supplies the Indians with arms and ammunitions, avoiding the vigilance that the manager of the company exercises and without this company having means to prevent such operations. These [operations] could be stopped [had the government] established an Army platoon in Agua Blanca which could patrol and prevent the illegal exploitation and export of chicle.

I am honored to transcribe to you the message for your knowledge and consideration, thus if you consider it convenient to make the appropriate recommendation to the Political Chief of the Territory of Q. Roo, in order for him to take the required measures to stop this commercial inconvenience. (From *Report of the Standford Manufacturing Company* 1906, AGN sect. 3a)

Strategically the large gum manufacturers in the United States, notably William Wrigley's, were dependent on *coyotes* (intermediaries and smugglers) for the transport of their supplies. One of the most important motives for seeking this solution was to avoid paying excise duty to the Mexican authorities. These political and economic ambitions, at the margin of legality, which were deeply resented by the Mexican state, served to cement links between some of the British banks—particularly the Bank of London and Mexico—American manufacturers, and the Mayan insurgents (Ramos Diaz 1999). At the same time Wrigley's was able to exert commercial power, entering into contracts with Mayan rebels whom the Mexican state still regarded as bitter enemies, and refused to meet with except as vanquished "indians."

On April 27, 1901, a soldier, who was looking for a missing mule, encountered an abandoned city. It was Chan Santa Cruz, the religious and political center of the *Cruzob*. With no resistance, Bravo, the general in command took the city on May 5, 1901, (Villa Rojas 1945, 1978). The Cruzob retreated further into the forest. General Bravo had medals cut in his honor, and the march of "progress" continued apace. Soon the telegraph wires that had spread widely with the Mexican army's advance sent the message out from the coast: the area had been "reconquered" and was now safe again for the whites.

Defeat for the rebel Maya was extremely painful. Many of them fled farther into the forest; for many there was nowhere else to go. Others crossed over into British Honduras, joined their compatriots there, and went on to found a refuge in the forests of northern Guatemala. Others stayed put, and were eventually discovered by the invading Mexican army. Their military tactics were useless against superior arms—they could fight with machetes against single-shot rifles but not against machine guns. Most of them were rounded up over the next few years and either killed on the spot or marched off to Peto, and from there handed over to large landowners to use as they wished. The "stated purpose was to free them from their savage habits, to open for them a civilized horizon" (Reed 2001, 302).

The Mexican forces of occupation then began to construct means of communication between Chan Santa Cruz (renamed Santa Cruz de Bravo after the Mexican general who took the capital) and the coast. President Diaz decreed from Mexico City that the new territory should be called the Federal Territory of Quintana Roo, named after a hero of the independence struggle. Yucatecans did not like it, since they considered the territory their backyard, and criticized the Mexican authorities for taking it from their jurisdiction. At the same time a smaller number of Yucatecans benefited from the new status, having been given both vast concessions to exploit the forests and a free hand with the native population.

Access to the forests was the first priority of the new regime, for which conquest itself had been little more than a construction project. It was decided that since Santa Cruz was only thirty-six miles from the sea, across mangrove swamps, against the ninety miles to the railhead at Peto, it would be better to build the railroad to the sea. A new site was chosen as a port, called Vigia Chico, which became the local entrepôt for lucrative forest products. In the first decade of the twentieth century Vigia Chico was a hated place, consisting of several whorehouses, a barracks, a hotel with a veranda, and an enormous pier. Indicative of the quality of life in Vigia Chico at the time is the suggestion that the interior design of some of the buildings came to reflect the lifestyles of most of the inhabitants in unorthodox ways. As Reed comments "the presence of glass floors in several of the buildings [were] made by pushing rum bottles upside down into the sand" (Reed 2001, 304).

Colonel Arelio Blanquete, an ally of General Huerta, the army leader who had ordered the execution of President Madero, was in charge of building the fifty-six kilometer Deauville railroad from Santa Cruz de Bravo to the Vigia Chico port. Political prisoners were forced to work as the laborers. If they were not affected by sickness, they were shot dead by Mayan snipers or by the Mexican army while attempting to escape. The railroad was to serve loggers and the new entrepreneurs of chicle. It was called *callejón de la muerte* (the passage to death) as it was claimed that each rail post was worth five lives (Turner 1965).[1] Platforms, drawn by mules and steam locomotives, were hauled along narrow-gauge tracks from the port through jungle and swamps. At the halfway point a guards' barracks was added to the installations, since recalcitrant Maya had been targeting members of the garrison. An army marksman, armed with telescopic sights, discovered them and managed to shoot the enemy with his Mauser field gun. The tree from which the Mayan rebels were dispatched was called *El Indio Triste* (the sad Indian) (Reed 2001).

Among the rebel Maya who took aim at the garrison and the workers on the railroad was a young man who was later to play an important role during the next thirty years, called Francisco May. May was the son of Damaso May and Maria Pech, but his father died when he was two years old, and his mother married another local Mayan leader, Felipe Yamá. Local accounts suggest that the bravery May displayed, in the charges he led against the tractor that transported chicle to the coast, was inspired by his stepfather. It marked him out as a potential leader, and accelerated his rise within the Mayan rebel army.

In 1910 the Mexican Revolution began, although it was two years before it arrived in Quintana Roo. A new revolutionary general, Manuel Sanchez Rivera, arrived in Santa Cruz from Vigia Chico with fifty soldiers. His mission was to explain to the aged General Bravo that his control was at an end. A banquet was served in the center of the rebel heartland, Chan Santa Cruz (de Bravo) under the orange trees. The political prisoners were freed and given passports, travel vouchers, and money. General Bravo fled to Vigia Chico and on to Mexico City, only concerned with saving his life.

The revolutionary forces tried to make contact with the Cruzob by hanging messages in bottles on trees, but to no avail. The mistrust between the Maya and the whites, even revolutionary whites, was too great to end overnight. Within two years, however, a new socialist governor of Yucatán ordered that the capital of Quintana Roo would be moved south to Chetumal, and the Indians were given definitive control of their own sacred place, No Cah Balaam Nah Santa Cruz, in 1917. Having been "liberated" by the Mexican Revolution, the remaining Mayan rebels were afflicted with smallpox, halving the population to about five thousand. However, the Talking Cross had survived, hidden from the excesses of General Bravo's army of occupation, which had desecrated the temple, the *Balaam Nah*.

After Santa Cruz was returned to the Maya, they separated themselves into two groups, one based at Yokdzonot, which claimed possession of the original Talking Cross, and another one at Chumpon. Both groups possessed a military structure for guarding their crosses. Sergeant Francisco May, who belonged to the former group, was especially gifted in warfare and was soon made general in the rebel Mayan army (Reed 1964, 2001).

The two groups realized that although loyal to their crosses, they could not fight each other. General May continued to gain power among his fellow brothers of the Cross. He had seen chicle and had acknowledged its importance, and thus he directed his military operations against the transport of the product. May knew that their ammunition supply depended on the smuggling of chicle to British Honduras to the south, but within the Cruzob territories he continued to negotiate with the railroad operators and foreign chicle resin extractors.

In 1917 a chicle entrepreneur achieved what no Mexican politician had done before. He obtained an agreement with General May in which the latter agreed to allow chicle operations on the land he controlled, in exchange for participation in the business. At last Octavio Solis, the governor of Quintana Roo, admitted that the negotiations employed by the British for over a century might be a better strategy than the brute force employed by the Mexican army. He invited the general to Chetumal and then advised President Carranza to follow this path. Subsequently May was invited to Mexico City, where the president made him a "general" in the Mexican army and put him in charge of pacifying the Maya. In return May received the railroad rights from Santa Cruz to Vigia Chico, (which the Maya would rebuild), a concession of over twenty thousand hectares of land, and the monopoly of *aguardiente* (sugar cane liquor) sales in the region.

The Chicle Concessionaries and the Decline of General May

By the beginning of the twentieth century the taste for both hardwoods and chewing gum, nurtured by consumers in Europe and the United States and funded partly by British capital in Mexico, had led an army of adventurers deep into the forests of Yucatán. Many of the *chicleros* who arrived in the first decade of the twentieth century were from other Mexican states, such as Veracruz and Chiapas, as well as Belize. By 1915 over three-quarters of the chicle imported into the United States came from Mexico. The Maya chiefs saw chicle as an opportunity to finance rebellion, and the chicle manufacturers in turn used them to guarantee security in the forests of their concessions and, if possible, the provision of a labor force.

The Maya often stole the mules and supplies from the adventurers who entered their forests, and most did not become chicleros themselves until the 1920s. Although they had effective control of their forests from 1914, harvesting chicle was not their primary economic activity and it would never be. It has been assumed that all the chicleros, whatever their ethnic affiliation, assumed a rough lifestyle in complete dependence on forest products, precious woods and chicle. But historical accounts, testimonies of contractors and of chicleros themselves, suggest that the main livelihood activities of the Mayan people were attached to the cultivation of their communal plots (*milpas*).

At the same time, however, chicle was becoming very important for the household economics of the Mayan population. After large-scale chicle contractor Julio Martin made the agreement with General May, other concessionaries arrived, including Wrigley's from the United States, La Compañia Mexicana from Mexico, and an influential intermediary, one Mr. Turton, based in Belize (Gonzalez Duran 1974). Casa Martin began to establish camps and collection points near Chan Santa Cruz, while in the north an important collection center was established inland from Puerto Morelos. The rebel Maya were poised to take advantage of the new commercial opportunities offered by chicle, and to do so without any significant concessions to the Mexican revolutionary government, which itself was largely distracted by events elsewhere in the republic.

The regime instituted by General May had all the hallmarks of Latin American *caciquismo*. Although virtually illiterate, May proved an effective businessman, an astuteness that he concealed behind an apparently simple exterior. It seems likely that he took great pains to disguise his real understanding of events, and their implications for the rebel Maya that he commanded. May exercised his authority through his command of a military force. He had twenty-five personal guards, and took overall command of the local population. People within his jurisdiction received lashes with a whip for any perceived wrongdoing, and were forced to enter the church and promise, after praying in Maya, not to re-offend. Foreigners living in the area were subject to similar treatment, and sexual abuses and marital infidelity were very severely sanctioned (Reed 1964, 2001).

The status and rights of the Mayan people was about to change, although only briefly. Very few Mexicans had attempted the desegregation of the indigenous peoples, a situation that had operated since the colonial times. Governor Felipe Carrillo Puerto was one of those rare leaders to have attempted to include the Maya as partners rather than as political subjects of the whites. In 1922 Carrillo Puerto helped General May to form a cooperative of chicle producers, in order to eliminate the exploitation of intermediaries. He also set up instructors in civil rights for the Indian population, in the hope of making the Maya full participants in the revolutionary project. President Carranza had already promised May that schools would be built in Quintana Roo, on May's insistence, and schools were built at Chancah, Dzula, Santa Maria, and Chumpon. But the *gente decente*, or *gente bien* (decent people) could not accept the Indians as equals. Unfortunately for the Maya, the governor of Yucatán, Felipe Carrillo, was assassinated in Merida, and Yucatán fell into a political void.

Stable government did not return until the governorship of Siurob, from 1927 to 1929. Siurob was a strategic organizer and was not willing to assume a paternalistic approach to the Indians. Instead, he joined the progressive forces of Yucatán that wanted to end the power of General May and the control exercised by the Maya over the forest and railroad. His principal objective was to eliminate once and for all any form of autonomous rule on the part of the rebel Maya.

The engine of progress was chicle. Although they did not always perceive it, the chicle tappers received few of the benefits from chicle extraction. Before them, and profiting from their work, were the foremen, the campsite chiefs, the *permisionarios* (national contractors), the international contractors, and the chewing gum brokers working for transnational companies. The system of indebtedness (*enganche*) operated from the top down. The brokers advanced money to contractors, who in turn lent money to their Mexican partners. The *permisionarios* gave the money to the central chiefs for them to hire the foremen and the chicleros. Each chiclero received tools and goods at prices established by the *permisionarios*. They were already in debt before they entered the campsite.

May was wise enough to know that taxing his own people would bring an end to his power. Besides, he did not need to impose taxes. He received money from the contractors, the renting of mules, the railroad fees, and the sale of *aguardiente*. Siurob, however, knew better. In his view the government and the "decent people" should be getting what the "Indian chief" was receiving. Representatives of the *gente decente*, like the Ramoneda brothers, embarked on a campaign to dismantle the rule of the Cruzob and give themselves a free hand in the chicle industry. Although governmental officials knew of the illegality of the Ramoneda maneuvers, they appear to have turned a blind eye to their maneuvers, perhaps reflecting their own political sympathies.

The Ramonedas's view prevailed and Governor Siurob continued his campaign in order to dismantle any institution that would allow the Maya to be participants in government. Everything from the civil register to education and economic development planning passed entirely to state control. In the name of modernity and "civilized values," power passed out of the hands of the Maya.

By the boom years of the late 1920s most of the chicle from northern Yucatán was transported by rail, from Peto to Mérida and from there to the northern coast. There were over fifteen hundred chicleros working at just one forest location in the north, Central Vallarta, during the harvest season, from September to January. In what was to be known as the Mayan zone (southern Yucatán and northern Quintana Roo), the chicle was transported from Chan Santa Cruz on the railway line to the port of Vigia Chico. The tractors used for transporting the gum carried four thousand six hundred kilos of chicle a day, twenty-seven thousand kilos a week.

Until a better arrangement could be made, the chewing gum manufacturers, and the contractors who employed chicleros, both American and Mexican in southern Quintana Roo, looked to the Mayan chiefs, May and Vega as their only source of protection. The platform and tractor for transporting the chicle belonged to General May, but Miguel Angel Ramoneda still managed to obtain the concession to run the railway. Much to May's disapproval, since his men had rebuilt the line and provided maintenance to the railroad, in 1924 Ramoneda had received the concession from the Mexican Ministry of War and Sea Defenses.

In a historic pact in 1929 the federal authorities dictated new terms of compliance to May. He was deprived of the power to punish offenders within his "own" jurisdiction, and civil registration and tax collection was handed over to the federal government. The Maya were also instructed not to fly the British Union Jack flag in their villages. Not for the first time they were told that henceforth they were a part of the Mexican federal state. On June 2, 1929, General Governor Siurob entered Chan Santa Cruz, and after a great fiesta, he and May publicly embraced. This represented the effective transfer of power from the fiefdom of a traditional *cacique* to the Mexican state.

Perhaps the most important factor in the downfall of General May was the fall in the world price for chicle, a consequence of the Great Crash in 1929, but for which he was blamed personally. Previously there had been limited opposition from within the ranks of the Maya themselves, who objected to the iron hand of his rule. In Chumpon, to the north of the area he controlled, the production of chicle was controlled by Mayan leaders other than General May, and other, independent contractors also penetrated the area. The Bank of London and Mexico directly controlled the zone of Kantunilkin. So, although General May was the leading chief of the Mayan zone, in other chicle-producing areas the control exercised on concessionaries was much looser.

Much of the chicle from the territory of General May found its way southwards, as we have seen, into British Honduras. To the north of

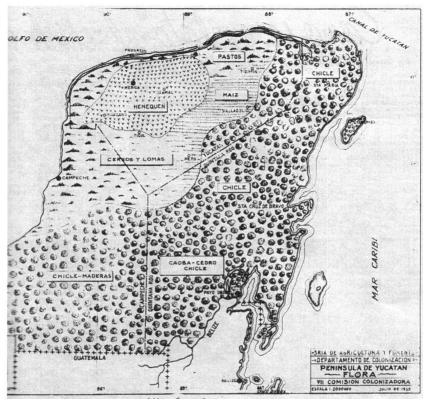

...ión territorial de Quinta-
s de 4.169,094 hectáreas y
...e poblada de bosques, de

...cción chiclera del Territo-
... a 1924, fué de 4.125,420 ki
con valor aproximado · d.
... a $0.86 el k. entregad.
H. B.
... de 1935 la producción d.
... de 37,500 quintales, o sea
...N SETECIENTOS VEINTI-
...L KILOS, habiendo paga-
...pañias extranjeras a $65.00
... de 46 kilos, o sea a UN
...ARENTA Y DOS CENTA-
...o, poco más o menos.

...l De V. Cruz, el 18 de junio
...ecibico en Vigía Chico.—Sr.
...cos de Sta. Cruz Bo.—Al-
...se a Progreso con muebles
...dmón. en Santa Cruz, dan-
...su llegada para darle ins-
...E. D. G. COSME HINO-

Producción
CHICLERA
Y MADERERA

De 1918 a 1924, el Territorio tuvo
ingresos por valor de $2.328,182.46 y
egresos por $8.900,745.19, o sea un dé-
ficit anual de UN MILLON DE PE-
SOS.

En 1935, el Gobierno del Gral Me..
gar tuvo un subsidio de CUARENTA
MIL PESOS, con los que el Territorio ha ganado más que con los mi
llones del subsidio de 1918 a 1924
En 1919 la exportación de caoba fu..
de 18 millones de pies cúbicos ..
442.000 kilogramos de chicle en 1920
Compárense los datos anteriores con
los siguientes:

EXPORTACION DE CAOBA Y CHICLE EN LA TEMPORADA 1935-36

	Cantidad exportada	Valor comercial	Impuestos territoriales
CAOBA	3.781,066 pies	$1.639,786.14	$81.989,25
CHICLE			
Exportado por Payo Obispo	382,579 kilos	$ 623,603.77	$ 31.188.6.
Exportado por Mérida, Yuc	610,788 ,,	,, 929,819.34	46.475.93
Exportado por Cozumel, Q. R	294,274 kilos	447,885.00	22,468.68
TOTALES	1.287,641 kilos	$ 2.001,108.11	$100.133.2.

Los datos anteriores fueron proporcionados por la Tesorería Ge
neral del Gobierno del Territorio de ... intana Roo.
        Payo Obispo, Quintana Roo, 25 de Junio de 1936.
Página 157

Figure 6.3
Map of the Yucatán peninsula, July 1935 showing area devoted to *chicle*

May's fiefdom the story was different—chicle found its way from the coast around Tulúm, to the offshore island of Cozumel. Around Tulúm, for almost twenty years production had been in the hands of the Cue brothers from Mérida. Chicle from these areas was exported northward, by rail to Puerto Morelos, which was only forty kilometers from Santa Maria, their estate. From Puerto Morelos the chicle went in small boats to Cozumel, where the vessels owned by the big chewing gum companies came to collect it. Cozumel became in fact the leading entrepot for the chicle trade in the region for many of the most important concessionaries. From Puerto Morelos cargo was also sent to Progreso, on the Gulf coast of Yucatán. An air service was even planned in 1929, at the height of the boom and before the crash, linking Yucatán with Cuba.

The 1920s saw the explosion of chicle production in Quintana Roo, with more than six thousand chicleros arriving from other parts of Mexico and Central America. During most of the 1920s chicleros earned about three hundred pesos a month, but by 1929 this had risen to one thousand eight hundred pesos. This was the period of relative affluence, when chicleros came down from the forests and spent their surpluses on jewellery in the shops of Valladolid. While they were in the forests chicleros were able to buy items that had not been available twenty years earlier: whisky and cigarettes as well as weapons. Indeed, the effect of alcoholism among forest workers was such that in 1929, echoing the United States, prohibition was declared in the territory, although this did little to prevent contraband liquor arriving from Belize.

In 1923 the first factories for manufacturing chewing gum were established in Mexico. Two years later over one million kilos of chicle was exported officially. By 1929 production reached its peak for the decade, of two million four hundred thousand kilos. The 1930s proved to be a decade of relative prosperity for most chicleros, despite the fall in price on the world market, since the workers themselves were better organized and won more support from the government (Marin and Gubler 1997). In 1933 production had dropped dramatically to under seven hundred thousand kilos, and only half that figure in the following year. However, this drop did not immediately affect livelihoods adversely, since a great deal of the trade via Belize was still illegal and much of the production was not accounted for in official Mexican statistics. Most of the profits from the chicle trade went to General May and the contractors with whom he worked, in the areas he commanded in the Mayan zone. Thus chicle played a key role in linking Cruzob local economy to international circuits of commerce (Konrad 1991).

General May, although a Mayan separatist, had all the hallmarks of a traditional cacique. Access to power, indeed to the authorities outside the region, was almost entirely in his hands. When the Mexican government was convinced that they could remove him from the scene, it was partially because Mayan authority was already divided. But General May's removal from the scene represented an advantage mainly for the permisionarios operating in the Mayan zone, whereas those in the northern zone, which Juan Bautista Vega controlled, had already begun to assert their rights and independence. The wealth that was being created around chicle was concentrated in the hands of a couple of dozen contractors and intermediaries, who competed with each other to sell to the chewing gum companies and to entrepreneurs in Cozumel (Ramos Díaz 1999).

In 1927 the Wrigley's company had made profits in the United States of thirty million dollars after tax. Almost half of the exports of chicle from Mexico came from Quintana Roo and much of the rest was from the state of Yucatán. Not without reason in 1930 the Mexican Consul at the border in British Honduras, Celso Perez Sandi, wrote, "the extraction of chicle was the only source of life for commerce in the region." He was referring to the physical and social infrastructure that the trade in gum was beginning to open up: towns, port facilities, schools, shops, and, with them, the arrival of new social groups without roots in the forest economy of the region (Ramos Díaz 1999; Konrad 1991). The social revolution in Yucatán and particularly the frontier region of Quintana Roo, which had been controlled by caciques like General May, gradually gave way to a society grounded in the politics of the post-Revolutionary Mexican state. However, the Maya continued to assert their cultural particularity, specifically with respect to the religious ceremonies that were linked to agroecosystems management.

The Cardenista Project: Ejidos and Cooperatives

During the great depression the demand for chicle diminished greatly. In December 1931 the Mexican President Pascual Ortiz Rubio ended the status of Quintana Roo as a federal territory, dividing the administrative jurisdiction between Campeche and Yucatán (Gonzalez Duran 1974). From then on and until 1935 the Mayan zone was once again, and to the dismay of the Maya, in the hands of Yucatecans. The chewing gum production diminished greatly as the Yucatecan permisionarios had to agree with the conditions imposed by the two companies that dominated the whole of the market, the Chicle Development and Wrigley's (Jaramillo Botero 1988).

In the Mexican presidential campaign of 1934 the PNR (Partido Nacional Revolucionario) candidate, General Lázaro Cárdenas visited Payo Obispo (Chetumal) and Cozumel. He promised to restore Quintana Roo as a federal territory if he were elected and kept his promise. This happened as early as January of 1935, when he had modified articles 43 and 45 of the Constitution resituating Quintana Roo as a federal territory.

As the Mexican state became more involved in the territory from which chicle was harvested, so the unrest, which had fueled the Cruzob resistance, became channeled into the progressive post-Revolutionary project. The state strategy was to gain control of the production process through the formation of chicle cooperatives, which were established throughout the peninsula from the mid-1930s (Beteta 1937, 1999).

The Mexican government began to establish cooperatives among chicleros with the idea of freeing them from intermediaries and enabling them to sell directly to agents and companies. Under President Cárdenas in the late 1930s the idea grew that chicleros should be more than itinerant workers with camps in the forest: they should be integrated into the land that provided their livelihood. This itself was a radical idea for forest communities, and particularly the Maya who had already abandoned cultivation of their lands. Many of the chicleros who had arrived in the region from outside, particularly the state of Veracruz, had little to do with the Mayan people and were uninterested in settling down in the Mayan zone.

On August 20, 1935, one of the first chicle cooperatives, Pucte, was founded with twenty-nine members (Encyclopedia de Quintana Roo 1998). The cooperative sold six tons of chicle directly to the Wrigley's company, increasing the income received by the chicleros threefold. The establishment of cooperatives had brought collective strength to the organization of workers in the industry. In the same year cooperatives were established in Carrillo Puerto, Xhazil, Yaactun, Dzula, Xpichil, Senor, and Chumpon, all lucrative areas for the chicle trade. The governor of Yucatán at the time, Rafael Melgar, made moves to expropriate large estates in the region, even bringing one of them before a new agrarian commission. The apparent economic and political success of the cooperatives was making inroads on the established landlord class.

Once started, the move toward "socialized production" was very rapid (Encyclopaedia de Quintana Roo 1998). Chicleros formed cooperatives because it enabled them to get both a better share and a better price for the resin through dealing directly with the buyers. That was the aim of the project. In practice, however, the process was more complex. Tappers had to rely on representatives from the cooperatives and the same institutional structure of foremen, subcontractors, permisionarios, and brokers continued to operate. Wrigley continued to rely on *coyotes* (intermediaries) and started to hire Mexican nationals in order to maintain the supply chain.

Under the governorship of Melgar an umbrella organization was established that took control of the sale and export of the cooperatives' chicle, using both Chetumal and British Honduras as the ports of embarkation. Forty-eight chicle cooperatives had been formed, and this second-level organization had offices in both Felipe Carrillo Puerto and Cozumel. Thus, although the Mayan rebellion had played such a central role in the fortunes of the chicle industry—especially near the border with British Honduras—by the 1930s the majority of chicleros who were not ethnically Mayan were now beholden to the Mexican state rather than Mayan generals like Francisco May.

At the beginning of the 1940s chicle production was given an additional boost by the entry of the United States into World War II. Within the space of a couple of years chicle resin had assumed strategic importance. It was part of the GI's rations, and demand for it from the United States, remained insatiable. The Mexican government authorized new concessions in the Yucatán peninsula, which led to widespread exploitation of the forest, creaming off many of the hardwoods, and using highly exploitative systems to remove the latex, which served to damage the remaining *chicozapote* trees.

In 1942 Mexico exported more chicle to the United States than at any time in its history: nearly four million kilos. This momentum in chicle production reached its apogee in June 1943 when a party of representatives of chicle cooperatives traveled to the United States, to meet government officials. Their object was "to discuss and defend the price of Mexican chicle, one of the most highly prized wartime materials in the United States." The American manufacturers who, in the view of the Mexican cooperatives, merely "added the flavor" to the gum, had refused to increase the price they paid for it, and the producers wanted to be paid for their gum in gold, rather than in US dollars, given the apparent precariousness of the wartime financial markets (Gonzalez Duran 1974). The economic relations governing chicle took negotiations to the highest levels of the wartime American and Mexican administrations, such was strategic importance of the product for both parties. The level of concentration in the gum industry had served to increase the companies' leverage over the US government, since just three American companies bought most of the chicle exported from Mexico.

The State Management of the Forests

The other principal objective of the Cárdenas reforms, the management of the forests in the national interest, also led to ambivalent outcomes. In their oral and written accounts both chicleros and permisionarios have acknowledged that there was considerable destruction of the forest, especially after Hurricane Janet on September 27, 1955. A former chiclero, Isidro Quiterio recalls:

What really changed chicle was the hurricane [Janet]. The south zone was completely devastated and the central zone or Maya zone, which did not suffer as much, was overworked. It became "repeladero" (overexploited) and chicleros went there to "poquitiar" (to take a few remains). When a chiclero worked in such conditions we called him "pichulero" (equivalent to rotten). But it was not that they were bad chicleros, it was that the forest was overworked and exploitation was excessive. In the lists available from those times, there were chicleros that managed to produce only one to three marquetas (blocks) of chicle, in three weeks.

Although there were problems, the cooperatives did help chicleros as labor conditions improved greatly for both Maya and non-Maya. Political representation of the Maya, however, was transferred to *presidentes ejidatales*; the Maya chiefs were dispossessed of their power and any trace of political autonomy was removed. They were left with the control over their own churches, and they continued their traditional agroforestry practices, which were never abandoned despite the increasing importance of chicle to their livelihoods.

Conclusion

Cárdenas has usually been regarded in Mexico as a genuine revolutionary and a true Mexican patriot. His unequaled charisma and commitment toward improvements in the conditions of the Mexican peasantry has made it difficult for Mexican historians to develop a critical assessment of his government's policies and their full implications. Some of the land reforms that Cárdenas carried out decisively helped Mexican peasants. However, state intervention through the cooperative movement failed to bring an end to the segregation of indigenous peoples; in some respects it can even be seen as institutionalizing Mayan separation. State interventionism facilitated paternalism in the first instance, and then widespread corruption prevented the creation of sustainable management of forest resources in the Yucatán peninsula. It is an ambivalent legacy, and one that needs to be understood if more sustainable forms of forest exploitation are to be developed in future.

The implications of the history of chicle for patterns of production and consumption are also interesting. There was great disparity between the commercial strategies of the United States and Mexico with respect to the chewing gum trade. While the Mexican government of Cárdenas was looking for economic stability through the control of production, in the United States they had already understood that capitalist power derived from the management of consumption. While, in Mexico, rural cooperativism was a way of managing cultural diversity in favor of the nation-state, and its political project of assimilating Indian populations, in the United States, consumerism was already being used to expand and strengthen the market.

The marketing strategy for chewing gum, as for many other products in the United States, was to appeal to the perpetually unsatisfied subject, the aim being to expand consumption by manipulating the consumer's desire as much as possible. It appeared that the consumption of chewing gum put the consumer in control. The Mexican state aimed at the opposite outcome; it sought ways to address social policy that were at once progressive and modern but often served to reduce the autonomy of the individual, and succeeded in tying the producer more closely to the increasingly ubiquitous state.

The history of chicle and the rebel Maya in Yucatán reminds us that frontiers are often defended, as well as settled. The Cruzob fought to defend their space and their culture against the modernizing mission of the Mexican state, both before and after the Revolution. It is difficult, however, to conceptualize the world of the Cruzob as a civil society, since the syncretic religious beliefs that inspired them brought together both a military and a religious hierarchy.

The Mayan relationship with nature was also significantly different from that of the whites and mestizos who dominated Mexico and eventually the whole of the Yucatán peninsula. The product that helped sustain the Mayan rebellion, chicle, was of ceremonial importance to the ancient Maya and had been tapped from a tree, the *chicozapote*, that the Maya continued to hold in high regard, ritually and in economic terms. Ancient Mayan sites bear witness to this importance, as they were invariably surrounded by stands of *chicozapote*, a fact commented on by archaeologists today. But the Mayan relationship with the forest, and its role in their cosmology, was transformed by the commercial chewing gum industry. This was a forest resource that helped arm the rebels but also eventually helped undermine them—leaving them at the mercy of dramatic shifts in world markets for the product that many of them had come to rely on for their livelihoods. The dependence on chicle served to undermine the traditional authority of Mayan leaders in the longer term, and to lay the basis for the patronage of the Mexican state and its secular institutions. Civil society in post-Revolutionary Mexico was writ large, in the Constitution, the existence of ejidos, and (despite assurances to the contrary) the devaluation of indigenous beliefs and cultures.

The post-Revolutionary period also ushered in dramatic change in land use, by encouraging settlers into lands first penetrated by chicleros and loggers. Forests were cleared for *milpa*, community ejidos were formed, and cattle ranching was established. Foreign capital came to dominate the least protected parts of the Yucatán peninsula, especially the Caribbean coast. The fortunes of chicle might have been defined internationally, but many of the costs of its decline were borne locally.

The history of chicle in Yucatán also demonstrates the way in which myths surrounding space and culture are created and recreated to meet different purposes. For many years after its demise the history of chicle was all but lost to the political and public discourse of Mexican politics. Fortunately it was not lost to memory, and local people continued to invest their past with value and significance, as the research literature has demonstrated. In exploring the role of space and the dialectical character of social space, we are necessarily concerned with the way space is constructed culturally and understood discursively. This chapter has demonstrated that social memory is linked with the wider economic currents that define the relationships of space over time. In examining the rebel Maya, and their links with chicle, it provided an example of the way commodities become embedded in labor processes and cultural practices. The frontier between Quintana Roo and the outside was cultural as well as spatial. The erosion of this frontier led to the opening up of the territory of today's Quintana Roo, initially through primary extractive industries, later through agriculture and livestock holding, and finally through tourism.

The possession of a new resource, in the form of a Caribbean beach environment almost without equal in the region, led eventually to the development of Cancun and the so-called Mayan Riviera to the south. As we will see, this development, which continues to proceed southward today, has itself contributed toward new forms of cultural construction of identity and place that encompass the consumption habits of global consumers. It has also led to a remaking of the frontier, as part of identity and place. Today these frontiers of the mind are an important element in the transformations currently underway on the Mexican Caribbean, and suggest a new relationship between space and consumption linked to the tourist economy.

7

Symbolic Frontiers: Nature as Commodity

Introduction

We have seen how successive frontiers became established on the Mexican Caribbean through close links with global markets. The chicle frontier reinvigorated a peasant rebellion, which had led the rebel Mayan armies to challenge the supremacy of the whites and to establish their own civil and military institutions in the south and east of the Yucatán peninsula. Chewing gum was one among many consumer products that led tropical forests to be cleared and served to transform indigenous societies: bananas and coffee have similar histories (Tucker 2002). This process, through which commodities were generated for global markets, was initiated as early as the sixteenth century. Beginning with dye-woods, the resource frontiers of the Yucatán peninsula moved to mahogany and copra (made from coconut shells) in the eighteenth century, and eventually to henequen and chicle in the nineteenth and early twentieth centuries. In the case of chicle the developing consumer markets in the north led to a weakening of local control over resources.

These were all commodities destined for global markets, but this chapter takes the discussion further by examining what happens when the market, in this case tourism, converts space into a commodity. Again, the geographical focus is the coast of the Mexican Caribbean, the state of Quintana Roo. During much of Yucatecan history the people who acted as mediators between local resources and global markets on this coast often became wealthy, and acted as entrepreneurs in new businesses. In some respects their personal career trajectories paralleled those of the social groups opposed to the region's incorporation within a new national identity. What the rebel Maya (Cruzob) saw as extraneous secular forces, to be resisted politically, were seen by the new entrepreneurial "pioneers" of tourism, as business opportunities. This in turn led these developers to change direction when large-scale national and foreign capital identified new sources of profit on the Mexican Caribbean coast. Indeed, some of the chicle entrepreneurs referred to in the last chapter, became early "tourist pioneers" on the Mexican Caribbean coast.

This chapter examines the growth of a new tourist frontier as linked to consumer tastes in the developed world, in the same way as mahogany and chicle, but defined in terms of spaces of recreation, amenity, and conservation. It also compares the frontier that developed under chicle extraction with the tourist frontiers that have developed since the middle of the last century, and that have brought new global influences to bear on the area. The tourist frontier on the Mexican Caribbean occupies spaces left by other resource activities, but in this case the product is the location itself—space has become an object of consumption. It is soon clear that the process by which space becomes commoditized requires a re-creation of cultural meanings for local people as well as visitors. Tourist frontiers are a hybrid of the material and the symbolic that exists not only in geographical space but also in cultural and cognitive discourses. As global tourism relocates consumers, it also reconfigures geographical spaces. As we will see, these processes of cultural reconfiguration help to create frontiers of the mind, which, unlike material spaces, can be recaptured and re-imagined by successive generations.

The "active," transitive conceptualization of space carries implications for the way in which we view resource peripheries, particularly within the context of globalization. It is a process that is increasingly seen as pre-dating modernity rather than an outcome of it (Hayter, Barnes, and Bradshaw 2003). Geographical frontiers are ascribed figuratively, temporally and spatially in ways that serve to influence succeeding events. Their "discovery" and "invention" are acknowledged as part of powerful myths that are worked and re-worked by human agents, serving to create environmental histories as real as the material worlds that they describe.

As we saw in chapter 2, recent research in geography and in history has benefited from a more reflective view of space and an active search for its properties and significance over time (Lefebvre 1991). Space is no longer a given in intellectual history, the blank parchment on which human purposes are written. Some writers even argue that space should be seen as enactments or performances: as constructions of the human imagination, as well as materiality. In the view of Nicholas Blomley, for example, "space (is present) in both property's discursive and material enactments. Space like property, is active, not static. (And) spaces of violence must be recognized as social achievements, rather than as social facts" (Blomley 2003). Space thus assumes a position previously denied it, and performs a much more central role in the making of historical events.

Tropical Paradises and Abandoned Places

These frontier imaginaries rely on repeating histories of discovery and rediscovery. Today a myth has developed around the Mexican Caribbean that probably explains why so much of its history is still unwritten. One of the foremost tourist guides to the area says:

Cancun, until very recently, was an unknown area. Formerly it was a fishing town but over a period of thirty years it evolved into a place that has become famous worldwide. It is located in the south-east of Mexico with no more "body" to it than the living spirit of the Mayas, a race that mysteriously disappeared and who were one of the great pre-Columbian cultures in Mexico. The only thing that remained was the land transformed into a paradise on earth. (*Everest Tour Guides* 2002)

This extract reveals all the major myths about the area. Cancun was uninhabited when it was first "discovered", it embodied the spirit of the ancient Maya (who had mysteriously disappeared), and those who survived contact had the good fortune to be in possession of "paradise." These three myths guide much of the "Maya World" tourist discourse today: space was devoid of culture, Indians were devoid of ancestors, and paradise was only waiting to be "discovered" by affluent visitors.

However, if we examine these claims closely, it is possible to distinguish ways in which the metaphorical grounding of tourist expansion borrows from earlier travel writing, such as the use of pioneer succession as an organic process, the preference for the natural sublime over human landscapes, and the utilization of so-called virgin resources (Jones 2003; Martins 2000; Salvatore 1996). Each of these discourses provides a different construction of space and, in the Mexican Caribbean, is associated with such distinctive pioneer generations of settlers. In charting the resource histories of places, and the histories of the visitors and tourists who have claimed discovery of them, we are continually re-working a narrative. In effect the social processes by which we come to identify space over time resemble a series of successions (Cronon 1996) that can be understood as possessing a discursive chronology as well as an historical one.

The creation of existential spaces as part of the fabric of environmental history is seen clearly in the successive accounts of the Caribbean coast of Mexico. Over time we view a "wilderness," discovered by archaeologists, a "wild forest" full of exotic stands of trees ripe for

Figure 7.1
Beach scene, Playa Del Carmen, Quintana Roo, Mexico.

commercial exploitation, an "abandoned space" utilized by pioneer hoteliers and, today, a "tropical paradise" promising escape to international tourists. In this chapter we follow this progression in its later phases and suggest that the history of a specific location can illuminate wider spatial dimensions and the social construction of spatial identities.

The coastal resort of Playa del Carmen is today a case in point. Playa is one of the most rapidly growing urban centers in Latin America, but it was not "discovered" until the summer of 1966, according to one account in a tourist magazine:

Playa was discovered by a sixteen year old boy, in the summer of 1966. A momentous event, which changed forever the face of history for this small fishing village. . . . In 1966 Fernando Barbachano Herrero, born of a family of pioneers, arrived there and found it inhabited by about eighty people, with a single pier made of local (chico) zapote wood. Fernando befriended the local landowner, Roman Xian Lopez, and spent the next two years trying to talk him into relinquishing some of his land. . . . (Playa Magazine 1999).

Two years later, in 1968, Fernando Barbachano bought twenty-seven hectares of this land adjacent to the beach for just over $13,000 (US), or six cents a square meter. In 2003 it was worth about $400 (US) a square metre, an increase of over 6,000 percent (*Playa Magazine* 1999).

Today this piece of coastal real estate constitutes less than 10 percent of Playa's prime tourist development. As Playa developed, piers were built for the increasing number of tourist craft, and game fishers, hotels and bars were constructed fronting the "virgin" beach, and clubs were opened a short way from the shoreline. The first hotel to be constructed was Hotel Molcas, in the 1970s, next to the little ferry terminal to Cozumel. Gradually more people were attracted to the tourist potential of Playa, and the list of celebrated pioneers grew longer. The local newspaper, *Por Esto!*, recently celebrated the fact that a plaque had been laid in the center of the town, commemorating "the founding families." The report noted that few of the one hundred thousand people living in Playa today had any idea of its origins, since it had been a fishing village until the early 1970s. However, Playa had been mentioned on November 14, 1902, when a local chicle contractor had gained permission for the construction of a road to the coast (*Por Esto!*, November 16, 2003).

Today the town possesses shopping malls, selling designer clothes and global brands. International gourmet restaurants compete for the lucrative tourist business; twenty million tourists visited Mexico in 2002. Today the beaches draw migrants from all over Mexico to work in the tourist informal economy, particularly the poorer states such as Chiapas, and the town's hinterland contains squatter settlements as large as many in urban Latin America. These areas have names that sometimes suggest wider political struggles: like Donaldo Colosio, a squatter area named after a prominent politician in the PRI (Party of the Institutional Revolution) and the hand-picked successor to President Salinas, who was murdered in 1994 under mysterious circumstances.

Early pioneers of tourism had taken an interest in the Mexican Caribbean coast even before Fernando Barbachano stumbled upon the resort potential of Playa Del Carmen. In the longer view tourist expansion on the coast of Quintana Roo can be compared with the trade in dyewood three hundred years ago, or of mahogany, copra, and chicle more recently. As we have seen, all these products were milestones in the development of the region, and linked it with global markets and consumers (Dachary and Arnais Burne 1998). Each possessed their own pioneers, like Fernando Barbachano, who discovered a land of rich natural resources unworked by human hand. To some extent, however, these timber and gum pioneers paved the way for tourism and re-enter the story at a later date as pioneers of tourism. It is worth recalling that the account of Playa's discovery in the passage above refers to a "single pier made of local *zapote* wood." This is the *chicozapote* tree from which chicle was tapped, which also served as a valuable building material, especially for wharfs and jetties. Clearly, the publicists for Playa had failed to spot the evidence of prior economic activity in what was still regarded as an abandoned space.

The island of Cozumel was one of the first pioneer tourist zones on the coast. The Grand Hotel Louvre on Cozumel, owned by Refugio Granados, had been constructed in the 1920s. Advertised in the *Revista de Quintana Roo*, in 1929, the owners publicized its merits in the following terms:

Tourists, tourist, tourists, travelers and travel agents! If you want a well-ventilated room and are demanding of the very best in attention, come to the

Grand Hotel Louvre. In addition it has a magnificent restaurant attached. Set meals and a la carte meals are available in a constantly changing menu. Expert chef. Calle Juarez with Zaragoza. Proprietor Refugio Granados. (Dachary and Arnaiz Burne 1998, 217)

Between the late 1920s and 1940s two other hotels were built on Cozumel, the Yuri and Playa, but at this time most visitors to what are today major Mayan archaeological sites on the mainland still slept in improvised cabins. The majority of tourists still left Cozumel by boat, landed on the mainland coast at Tankah, stayed briefly at the most important copra estate nearby, and then either cut a path in the jungle to Tulum or took a boat along the coast.

In taking this route, they were beating a track that had been followed by earlier pioneers, the most famous of whom were John Stephens and Frederick Catherwood, the giants of Mayan archaeology in the mid-nineteenth century. Stephens and Catherwood had already explored the major Mayan sites of northern Yucatán, such as Chichen Itza and Uxmal, and arrived in Valladolid at the end of March 1841. They made inquiries about getting to the Caribbean coast, no mean feat at the time since there were no roads. "It is almost impossible to conceive what difficulty we had in learning anything definite concerning the road we ought to take," Stephens reported to his diary (Stephens 1988, 316).

The coastal location that they aimed for was the settlement of Tankah, where a pirate named Molas had sought to evade the authorities in Mérida, where he had been convicted of smuggling. Since there was no road, they had to journey to the northern (Gulf) coast and take a "canoa" down the Caribbean, past today's Cancun and Isla Mujeres, to the Mayan fortress of Tulum. The journey took them two weeks, and it was accomplished despite every privation known to explorers of the time: no wind, no protection against the sun, so much provisioning that there was no space for the human occupants, and little idea of where they were headed. Stephens says their objective was "in following the track of the Spaniards along this coast, to discover vestiges or remains of the great (Mayan) buildings of lime and stone (that had been reported)" (Stephens 1988, 318).

They sailed first past Isla Mujeres, or "Mugeres" as Stephens described it, an island notorious as the resort of Lafitte, another pirate who (rather like Molas) was well regarded by the Mayan fishing communities of the coast, and "paid them well for all he took from them." Next was Cancun, or Kancune, as Stephens described it, which left a very poor impression on the travelers. It was nothing but "a barren strip of land, with sand hills, where the water was so salt we could barely drink it" (Stephens 1988, 323). Whenever they landed, usually in search of water, they were pursued by hordes of "moschetoes." The mosquitoes made life difficult, and would continue to have done so one hundred and thirty years later if the Mexican government had not intervened and sprayed them into oblivion.

They went on to land on Cozumel, at the only inhabited spot, the ranch of San Miguel where they record that "our act of taking posses-sion was unusually exciting." Here they stopped to feast on turtle and fresh water, strolled along the shoreline picking up shells, and went to sleep in their hammocks, "as piratical a group as ever scuttled a ship at sea."

The island of Cozumel had been "discovered" several times before, once by accident, it is said, when Juan de Grijalva caught sight of it in March 1518. He had set sail from Cuba (Andrews and Jones 2001). Unlike Grijalva, three centuries earlier, John Stephens knew where he was in 1841 and noted for the benefit of the *modern traveller* that they alone had proprietorship of "this desolate island" (Stephens 1988, 323).

It was another century before modern tourism arrived in Cozumel, with the construction of Hotel Playa and the patronage of an influential American William Chamberlain. From about 1952 Chamberlain enticed numerous foreigners to the area, and constructed the first tourist *cabanas*, which he named Hotel Mayalum. This was also the first recorded attempt to link the region and its coastal tourist attractions to the cultural life of the Maya, the historical antecedents of the Maya World, the brand name for most of this zone today.

In the mythology of pioneer coastal tourism, the main protagonists in Cozumel were adventurous Americans and a medley of rather unusual Mexican businessmen. On February 13, 1948, a Panamanian merchant vessel, the *Narwhal*, under Captain J. Wilson Berringer, with a crew of ten, transporting bananas from Guatemala to Mobile, Alabama, was cast onto the reefs off the island. The owner of the boat, Charlie Fair traveled from New York to Cozumel to take charge of the rescue and supervise the paperwork. Here he soon made contact with Carlos Namur, one of the few local people to speak English. Namur, who is now celebrated in the museum of Cozumel as a "founder and tourist pioneer," booked the American into the Hotel Playa, and Charlie Fair was so entranced with the island, and his stay there, that he almost forgot the circumstances of his arrival and wrote to his friends recommending they join him.

By 1957 an article on the island had appeared in the American glossy magazine, *Holiday*, and the first eight tourists arrived on a new flight from Merida to Cozumel. Unfortunately, their host, the indefatigable Carlos Namur, was himself in the United States at the time, and the tourists had to be put up with local families, some of them on the second floor of the building occupied by the harbormaster. Sharing this accommodation only excited their interest more, and since several of the tourists were journalists, they soon made good copy of their visit to tropical Mexico. Soon afterward, in the 1960s, the French filmmaker Jacques Cousteau discovered the reefs nearby and attracted more international attention to the island.

In Mexico Cozumel had blazed a modest trail, as a tourist destination, followed by Islas Mujeres, where relatively small hotels and guesthouses began to cluster around the modest central square, and provided important facilities for discriminating groups of Mexicans and Americans anxious to avoid large-scale tourism. By 1975 ninety thousand tourists were visiting Islas Mujeres annually (Antonchiw and Dachary 2001). Behind much of this growth were powerful new political interests, later to play a part in the development of Cancun, and linked to the person of President Luis Echevarria, whose godfather was a leading businessman on the island.

During the 1960s fourteen new hotels were built in Cozumel, with a total of four hundred beds, an apparently modest figure in light of subsequent developments. But by the end of the decade, fifty-seven thousand tourists had visited the island and two-thirds of them were foreigners. This remarkable commercial success prompted some of the inhabitants to examine their own histories more carefully. It was soon revealed that almost the entire population was made up of pioneers, or founders (*forjadores*).

Most citizens of Cozumel had a claim to foundation status. Refugees from the Caste War had in fact repopulated the island in the midnineteenth century, contrary to the prevailing view, "created by global tourism that the Mexican Caribbean lacked any identity of its own." The islanders had not entered an empty space, even if they had begun an improbably distinctive journey of their own. Unlike the rebel Maya who held the mainland, the twenty-two families of refugees who arrived in Cozumel in 1848 felt themselves to be the only surviving Mexicans on the peninsula (Vivas Valdes 2001; Antochiw and Dachary 1991). This view was endorsed during President Cárdenas's visit to Cozumel on November 29, 1939.

Cozumel had played an important advance role in tourist development because, apart from its roster of former chicle entrepreneurs who were interested in putting their capital into a profitable new business, it also boasted an international airport, originally built during the Second World War for US airport reconnaissance. Cozumel had traditionally been a staging post for the natural resources of the region, but it had become transformed into a natural watering hole for foreign tourists moving in the opposite direction. Unlike Cancun, however, the pioneers and founders of Cozumel had been its own indigenous bourgeoisie (Antonchiw and Dachary 2001; Connolly 1994).

Cancun: The "Abandoned Space"

The development of Cancun, beginning in the 1970s, made earlier tourist incursions seem very modest indeed. In the view of some observers, Cancun was chosen because the Mexican Caribbean was like a political tinderbox, liable to explode at any time (Dachary and Arnaiz 1998). Cancun was not simply a gigantic tourist playground, in this view, it was an "abandoned space" on the frontier that needed to be "settled, employed and occupied." Even in 1970 almost half of the population of Cancun was from outside the state of Quintana Roo, and as the zone developed, it pulled in people from all over southeast Mexico and even further afield. Indeed, a major concern for local government was attracting enough settlers to achieve statehood, which coincided with the "opening" of Cancun in 1974.

Before work started on the vast physical infrastructure of Cancun, the Mexican Fund for Tourist Infrastructure (*Infratur*) and the *Banco de Mexico* completed an unusually complete feasibility study of the tourist potential of the region. The study reported that the withdrawal of Castro's Cuba from the tourist scene had left a vacuum that Mexico was in a weak position to exploit, since so much of its Caribbean coast was undeveloped. The danger was that other places such as the Bahamas, Puerto Rico, Jamaica, and the Virgin Islands, would fill the vacuum left by Cuba. The study suggested that two sites should be given priority for Mexican investment: Cancun, in the Caribbean, and Ixtapa-Zihuatanejo on the Pacific. The early development of Cozumel gave the development of Cancun an advantage, and the reasons why the Yucatán peninsula should be favored were spelled out in the document. The Mexican Caribbean possessed an army of underemployed or irregularly employed workers, since the demise of henequen and chicle, and these workers lived close to some of the most beautiful marine environments in the Caribbean. Rapid tourist development would bring the labor force together with the undeveloped reserves of natural beauty.

Cancun could only be developed if all the available land was acquired by the project. The task of land acquisition, much of it is the form of lakes and marine lagoons, proved to be a mammoth operation. Unfortunately, the man who was its guiding light, Carlos Nadir, died before his work could be completed (Dachary and Arnaiz Burne 1998). The project was divided into five subprojects that served to separate the tourist zone from the new city. A bridge was built connecting the island of Cancun with the mainland, and the harbor of Puerto Juarez. At the same time an international airport was constructed that could handle incoming flights from Europe and North America, as well as from Mexico.

The second part of the project involved a massive drive to sanitize the zone, eradicating mosquitoes like those that had bothered Stephens and Catherwood (and most other forms of wildlife) and providing a secure supply of fresh water by the construction of twenty enormous holes in the porous rocks. These lakes had to be constructed since the Yucatán peninsula has no rivers. This was followed by the electrification of the new zone, linking it with the national grid and opening up a vast new telecommunications network. Finally the whole area was subjected to building and construction on a scale hitherto unknown in the region.

About two-thirds of the capital for the development of Cancun, initially one hundred and forty two million dollars, was provided by the Mexican state, with help from Inter-American Development Bank loans. The scale of this investment, and the risks borne by the Mexican government, virtually assured complementary private investment of a similar magnitude. Cancun began to function as a tourist resort in 1974 with fewer than two hundred hotel beds. By 1980, when the project's first phase was completed, there were forty-seven hotels, four thousand beds, and almost three hundred thousand tourists staying in Cancun. The coast was passing from a forest enclave, producing tropical forest products for markets in Europe and the United States, to a tourist economy, bringing people from these same areas to the Mexican Caribbean coast.

The collapse of oil prices in 1981 forced a massive devaluation of the Mexican currency the following year, and as a consequence more efforts were made throughout the 1980s and 1990s to earn additional foreign exchange from tourism. Environmental concerns, although frequently voiced, did little to hold back the pace of tourism on the Caribbean coast, nor the gradual destruction of the coastal habitat. Pollution became a growing problem, and Cancun spawned slums that spread northwards and sewage that turned the lagoon on which the city was constructed into a diseased sewer, alive with algal blooms and exuding a terrible stench. The environmental externalities of large-scale development began to be experienced negatively by the tourist industry itself. Ecological problems were mirrored by a growth in criminal activity, including the large-scale laundering of drug money through inflated resort development. Drug barons moved into Cancun in the late 1980s, and one of them, Rafael Aguilar Guajardo, was famously gunned down in Cancun in April 1993.

By the early 1990s Cancun had lost much of its initial appeal, even to tourists. It had developed too quickly, and at too much cost, and the developers feared that however much lip service was paid to the environment, it was evident that mass tourism, especially from the United States and Europe (which was increasingly the market for Cancun's resort owners), was moving elsewhere. As Cancun lost its glitter, so the tourists began moving south, in a quest for the unspoiled beach and the living reef. Cancun had been the principal example of an archipelago of artificial paradises in tropical Mexico (like Loreto and Cabo San Lucas in Baja California, Ixtapa near Acapulco, Puerto Escondido on the coast of Oaxaca), but Cancun was still the jewel in the Mexican tourist crown (Simon 1997, 190).

Gradually foreign tourists began to follow the Mexican tourists, the backpackers, and beachcombers south of Cancun to the coastal area opposite Cozumel, where local tourist pioneers established themselves in the 1970s, in places like Akumal. Most of the tourists, however, did not travel so far south, and they arrived eventually at Playa del Carmen. As we have seen, here the developers were of more recent provenance. One of them claimed to have initiated a different kind of tourism: Ted Rhodes was quoted in a tourist magazine:

Ted Rhodes is a local developer and pioneer for ecologically sound technologies, who is attempting to combine state-of-the-art technology, while enjoying the benefits of eco-tourism. He's only been in the Playa area since 1995, but is in the process of planning and developing six major projects . . . carrying disdain for the use of the word "eco," which he feels has been an over-abused term for a less than fully understood concept. Ted describes his ventures as "raw jungle converted with the hand of Mother Nature, to create a positive impact, using Mother Nature's rules." He works with the natural elements of the land, employing natural building materials from agriculture to culture, including water treatment which respects the composition and inhabitants of the land. . . . (*Playa Magazine* 1999)

Comments like those of Ted Rhodes are worth our attention because they encapsulate the ambivalence toward sustainability that lies at the heart of the tourist industry. It is clear that much of the development of Mexico's Caribbean coast has been at the expense of conservation objectives—whether it be conservation of marine turtles, mangroves, or coral reefs. The natural environment is fragile and needs protection. Nevertheless, the economy of the region is highly dependent on tourism, and any suggestion that the environment is under threat rebounds against tourism. The response has been to provide a new "eco-tourist" discourse that appears to pay attention to the concerns of both the environmentalist and the concerned tourist. Coastal development has been re-branded as "eco-friendly," "natural," and "sustainable." However, these new ways of repackaging development pay scant attention to the history of the area, which shows every sign of social and political conflict and little consideration for long-term sustainable development. Like earlier forays into public relations on behalf of the Mexican nation, this re-packaging of place was largely for external (tourist) consumption.[1]

Southern Frontiers: Reinventing Tradition as "Heritage"

The journey south from Tulum, beyond the Mayan Riviera, reveals a darker, stranger history and one that promises to color the future development of tourism on the coast. The Xian Ka'an Biosphere Reserve is, in legal terms, one of the most comprehensively protected environments in Mexico. So successfully "protected" has it become that most local people are only barely aware of its existence as a "reserve" at all. It extends over 530,000 hectares, a huge area of almost uninhabited lagoon, reef, mangroves, lakes, tropical forest and savannah. As the guide books record:

> [A] feature of Sian Ka'an is that conservation has generally been given precedence over tourism. There are few roads, none of them paved: the one from Tulum to Punta Allen, a very little-used road from Felipe Carrillo Puerto to Vigia Chico on the coast, and one from Mahahual to the south, . . . it is very difficult to find your way around. (Rider 2002, 217)

There are several reasons why it is difficult to orientate oneself in southern Quintana Roo, south of Tulum and the Mayan Riviera. First, there are fewer brand names to guide and interest the tourist, and partly because of that, there are fewer tourists. The road to Vigia Chico is a case in point. Even armed with a good guidebook the tourist would be hard pressed to say exactly what Vigia Chico represents today. It takes about three hours to get there through the forest and mangroves, on a very rough road, and is not recommended in a hired car. When you arrive all you see is a small Mexican military base, manned by tired conscript soldiers, and one vestige of the past, a lighthouse. There is nothing much to see at Vigia Chico, but with luck a boatman will take you to Punta Allen, a small resort town that does possess a few hotels and guides to the reserve of Xian Ka'an. Today this part of the coast is valued for its future, as the location of much of the remaining ecological wealth, rather than for the part it played in the conflicts discussed in chapter 6.

When General May first landed at Vigia Chico, he had just met with the Mexican President Carranza in Mexico City and had been feted as a natural ally of the revolutionary government. He had also acquired a new lady friend there and had difficulties persuading her to go ashore at Vigia Chico, where he was met by assembled Mayan warriors. As we have seen the governor of Yucatán, Siurob, tried to negotiate with May in 1926 and, in return for limited favors, to effectively surrender his power to the Mexican authorities.

The hard-core Cruzob followers, who refused to surrender, took what remained of their Talking Cross and carried it to their villages, deep in the jungle. Some of their grandchildren still patrol these villages today, to the north of their old capital No Cah Balam Na Santa Cruz. However, they too have just entered the tourist vernaculars, in a bizarre move that illustrates the ability of mass markets and discourses to refashion even modernity's own antithesis. One tourist guide to the state of Quintana Roo now recommends a drive to one of these Cruzob villages, Tixcacal Guardia, as part of a "traces of the Caste War" tour, one of several recommended routes to the past (Quintana Roo 2001). This tourist excursion takes visitors to Tihosuco, which was important in the early stages of the Caste War and where the local museum serves as a vibrant source of local memory. This museum has initiated local people into new activities: bringing the local Mayan children together with their past, through exhibitions, plays, music, oral history, and the encouragement of traditional artisan skills. Their mission is to work for and with the local Mayan population.

The paradoxes of development and modernity do not end at Vigia Chico, or the Cruzob villages. In other Cruzob villages tourists are unwelcome unless they have come to pay respect to the Talking Cross, and only a few years ago visitors, like the distinguished historian Nelson Reed, were asked for money to buy arms (Reed 2001).[2] Such villages cannot easily be incorporated into the tourist heritage. The solution is partly to construct the heritage in front of the tourists. A new chiclero village is being built at Chacchoben so that tourists to the southern coast can spend some time admiring the region's history. Chacchoben is also a "real" village, and it was once a settlement founded by chicleros for their extended tapping seasons in the forest. The interesting thing about Chacchoben is that the local ejido, which is affiliated to the regional Plan Piloto Forestal and has a strong interest in community forestry, was able to negotiate a concession from the state government. The ejido was thus able to develop its own community-based ecotourism enterprise. It now promises to become very different from the theme parks that line the coast to the north, which were once pristine lagoons. These new so-called eco-parks, in locations like Xell-Ha, Xcaret, and Tres Rios, were areas freely accessible to everyone even in the 1980s, before they were turned into commercial resorts for tourists.

The location of Chacchoben is important because it signals the development of one of the most ambitious tourist frontiers in Latin America. A six-lane highway is being built, linking the existing road south to the largely undeveloped coast, to Mahahual and on to Xcalak, almost one hundred miles. Here a new generation of tourist pioneers is establishing itself, around diving and game fishing. Some of them are considering leaving when mass tourism arrives, as it is predicted to do. The electric grid is about to arrive, bringing with it a new impulse to larger scale development. Meanwhile fishing communities like Xcalak, which has already been destroyed once by Hurricane Janet in 1955, is preparing to meet the arrival of civilization, bars, clubs, and nightlife.

Hybridized Nature

The accounts of eco-tourist development, from brochures and tourist magazines, suggest that words such as "nature," "natural," and "sustainable" can be used to good effect in a number of ways. By throwing a cordon around part of the coast and enclosing a saltwater lagoon, the developers of Xell-Ha, one of the resorts south of Playa, were able to brand "nature" with a company name, to privatize it. Each of these parks provides a variety of tourist facilities, including restaurants and shops, that sell a product that is both a natural and a social construction. They promise a safe recreational experience, complete with limestone sinkholes, or *cenotes,* that are developed for kayaking, swimming, and snorkeling.

The line between the natural and the human-made is also blurred in other ways. Many of the local staff are ethnically Mayan, but the restaurants and cafes that sell Mayan cuisine, and the bands that play Mayan music, are an embellishment, if not a counterfeit, of the Mayan culture. At one level it appears to work: people signing the visitors' book, thank the resort for offering them the chance "to live among the Mayan people." Reality and illusion are indistinguishable at this point. The *ethnic* label Maya is the exact complement of the *eco* labels, such as nature, natural, and sustainable, which describe almost every activity that visitors are invited to undertake.

In contrast to the global eco-parks, the coast also boasts a major UNESCO designated Biosphere Reserve, called Xian Ka'an, to the south of the major resort areas. The Mexican government created this reserve, with an extension of 1.3 million acres, in 1986. The following year it was designated as a World Heritage Site, and ten years later another two hundred thousand acres were added. Today the reserve accounts for 10 percent of the land area of the state of Quintana Roo, and over one hundred kilometers of coast is within its boundaries. It includes a population of several thousand local Mayan people, and twenty-seven archaeological ruins.

Before declaring this reserve a more authentic example of environmental protection than the global eco-parks, we might reflect upon the meaning of nature in this hybridized context. The Biosphere Reserve of Xian Ka'an is as much an artificial creation as the resorts of Xcaret or Xell-Ha, although its claims to conserve nature might sound more worthy of attention. It is intended to be free from development, and it provides limited access to visitors with a serious interest in conservation ecology. These claims need to be placed in context, however. Most tourists who come to the Mexican Caribbean do not visit Xian-Ka'an, nor could it withstand mass tourism. Xian-Ka'an is able to fulfill this role because of the existence of more commercial resorts that meet the needs of mass tourism. To fully appreciate the contribution of reserves like Xian-Ka'an, one needs also to consider the objects of mass appeal, like

Xcaret, Xell-Ha, and Xpu-Ha, that have transformed the natural environment into something that can be more readily consumed.

Like the descriptions of eco-friendly hotels in Playa del Carmen, which are a manifestation of the environmental consciousness of the tourist developers, Xian-Ka'an is a case of pre-emptive environmentalism, designed to disarm the environmental critic and to demonstrate that coastal developers have learned hard lessons from the bad publicity over Cancun. At the same time it can be argued that the eco-parks absorb increasing numbers of global tourists, many of whom would visit the Yucatán peninsula whether or not they existed. They may act as honeypots by attracting tourists away from areas of ecological interest that would otherwise be under threat.

Behind the rhetoric of eco-tourism lie other conflicts of interest over the environment of which most tourists remain oblivious. One example is the opposition being mounted by local peasant families (*ejidatarios*) to the Mexican electricity utility (CFE), which, they claim, has deforested their land. Rallies to condemn these activities have been an almost daily occurrence in the region in the last few years. Similarly there has been much public criticism of the dangers and risks inherent in speculative development, notably in the construction of substandard hotels. In some of these hotels electric cables run dangerously through hotel swimming pools, and visitors are exposed to numerous avoidable hazards, denounced in the local press. These ecological disasters, which might affect tourist safety, like the destruction of reefs, mangroves, and turtle breeding grounds, now form part of the daily currency of political discussion on the coast. They serve to increase the efforts of some developers, and to convince skeptical publics, that their products are free from the taint of ecological risk or damage. The presence of tourism in these locations has moved the environmental debate toward greater consideration of their risk and security, as elements of wider environmental vulnerability. These new consumer concerns parallel the ecological vulnerabilities that drew some of the visitors to the area in the first place.

To fully understand what is happening on the Mayan Riviera, we need look no further than the way in which towns themselves have been rebranded. Until 1999 the principal administrative unit (*municipio*) to the south of Cancun was called *Solidaridad* (solidarity), a name suggestive of the Mexican Revolution. Enthusiasts for the Mayan World then suggested that it should be renamed Xiamen H'a, its original name in Maya but one that is rarely used locally. (Most of the ethnically Mayan population has only a superficial knowledge of the language.) A third, and dominant view, supported by developers was that the name Playa Del Carmen should continue to be employed, since it was well known in tourist brochures and was good for promotional reasons.

In effect the same place was being accorded three separate identities: one administrative and linked to the Mexican state, another conferring an ethnic identity, and the third exploiting the familiarity of the tourist connection. One view of the resurgence of interest in Mayan culture, especially among intellectuals and middle-class well-wishers, places these historical oppositions firmly within the camp of contemporary protest over environmental/ethnic abuses in the region. Others caution that both ethnic and environmental struggles in contemporary Latin America have failed to deliver a viable political platform and that there are dangers in associating Mayan identity with nature, and oppositional politics.

Throughout the coastal zone dedicated to tourism, we find evidence of the way the tourist economy has structurally transformed the environment. This is apparent from the pivotal economic role that nature affords in both tourism development and the local subsistence economy. The relatively buoyant labor market in areas like Playa Del Carmen has attracted people to work in the tourist sector, and served to reduce local peoples' cyclical dependence on subsistence agriculture and the village *milpa* (maize) zone. Tourism has created what is, in effect, a parallel economy, based on the tourist dollar and the vicissitudes of the North American and European vacation seasons. In terms of the natural environment, the extraordinary invasive capacity of tourism has privatized the shoreline, giving local people little access to the beaches that under Mexican Federal Law are everybody's property. At the same time as the shoreline has been effectively privatized, access to the marine environment, through dive centers, cruise ships, and offshore facilities, has also been partially privatized. This was once an open access resource, accessible to fishing communities and local people, but today it has become much more socially differentiated according to peoples' ability to pay.

The emergence of global resorts and eco-parks, all claiming to be concerned with environmental protection, forces us to examine some of the fundamental distinctions that are made between nature as pristine wilderness and the managed nature of environmental protection.

First, it is unclear whether a clear distinction can be made between human-*produced* nature, in forms such as eco-parks, and protected natural areas. As we saw earlier in this chapter, to the south of the Mayan Riviera lies a large Global Biosphere Reserve, Xian Ka'an. There are only two ways of visiting this reserve: by a poor quality dirt road (which very few people take) or via a guided tour, organized by a travel company based at one of the resorts. These guided tours, though of restricted size, provide many of the same activities as those of the eco-parks: snorkeling, floating in the cenotes, and the night observation of marine turtles. There is also considerable illegal development within the reserve, and few effective planning controls. Although the environmental space occupied by the Biosphere Reserve has not been so thoroughly transformed as that of Xel-Ha and the other parks, it can be argued that Xel-Ha's existence makes it better able to repel further development. It can be argued that the eco-parks have become natural heritage sites in themselves, capable of withstanding saturation tourism without repelling the more adventurous prospective visitors from visiting areas like Xian Ka'an.

Second, the use of terms like sustainability is entirely dependent on the context in which it is employed. Much of the impetus for environmental protection on the coast comes from the perceived need to internalize environmental costs, and to minimize the negative environmental effects of development. The interest of a minority of tourist entrepreneurs in cleaner, "greener" tourist facilities is distinguishable from the wider questions of nature protection in the region. We do not know whether the tourists who visit the coast, and express an interest in the environment, are more concerned with the environmental standards in their hotels and swimming pools or with the welfare of the colonies of dolphins and marine turtles. It is likely that eco-tourists come in various guises, and that the policy discourses surrounding sustainability and nature have appeal to different types of tourist. In addition the way in which Mayan culture is invoked in many of the new tourist discourses is beginning to lead to a third discourse about nature. This seeks to identify traditional forms of sustainable livelihood practiced by the Maya, and associates them with Mayan views of nature.

It is clear that the different temporal dimensions in which these policy discourses are employed are paralleled by spatial dimensions. The domain of human choice and consumption is heavily contested, and eco-tourism, however rhetorical, is a convenient label on which to hang contrary messages. Nature can be used by economists to suggest something that the market might help preserve as well as something that is destroyed. This is the logic of tourist eco-parks. Other approaches to environmental management seek to regulate and manage the environment in ways that control access to "natural" areas. This is the logic of the Biosphere Reserve. In practice, of course, the two currents often converge. The only person patrolling the principal beach, on which marine turtles lay their eggs at Xcacel, is an employee of the tourist company developing Xpu-Ha, a hotel complex just a few hundred meters down the coast. It has fallen to commercial developers to provide the policing needed by conservationists, making it difficult to distinguish among their respective interests.

This chapter has argued that in the face of global eco-tourist development, we cannot easily draw a line under produced nature that separates it from the "natural" since this kind of development is designed to blur this very distinction. Discourses of the natural increasingly incorporate human concerns with public access and recreation, as well as conservation goals, and need to be understood in terms of the structural processes that affect individual choices and lifestyles. From the demand side these processes include the ambiguously defined eco-tourism, and they have served to underline the importance of different spatial and temporal perspectives on the meaning of nature. The nature to which tourists are attracted on the Mexican Caribbean is rarely the more formal scientific accounts of ecological systems in the specialist literature.

The meanings of Mayan and nature are no longer, if they ever were, of local or parochial significance alone: they are now part of a global lexicon. They also carry messages across time, from the Caste War and the era of Talking Crosses, and across space, from North America and Europe, the sources of most tourism to Mexico. The search for discovery in the era of global tourism is not confined to wilderness areas, or wild-life expeditions. It takes the form of new kinds of consumption, includ-ing tourist recreation, that in the process of transforming nature also transforms peoples' lives.

New Forms of Ecological Politics

Eco-tourism in Yucatán has been led by the need to generate foreign exchange earnings. In the case of Mexico the state possesses impressive powers to control and regulate the impact of industries, including tourism, and to protect the environment. In discussing the history of state regulation of the chicle industry, we have seen these powers dis-played in a different context, in the support given to the export of gum and the patronage afforded the chicle cooperatives. In the case of tourism such regulatory powers are only weakly implemented in practice, partly because of the political sensitivities to the benefits that flow from tourism, including employment and the growth of personal incomes. As Simonian points out:

Mexico must first generate revenues and raise living standards through rapid economic development before it can afford to redress environmental problems. Ironically, such a strategy would put Mexico in the position of destroying its environment first in order to save it later. (Simonian 1995, 220)

The concept of eco-tourism gained currency following the interest generated by the 1992 Earth Summit in Rio de Janeiro. Subsequently the concept was woven into many of the deliberations and discourses surrounding sustainability, and it was seen as part of a burgeoning new market that linked the environment with lifestyle and personal con-sumption. The World Wide Fund for Nature has defined eco-tourism as "tourism to protected natural areas, as a means of economic gain through natural resource preservation" and as "a merger of recreation and responsibility" (Kallan 1990; Wahab and Pigram 1997). More recently, however, the term has been used more widely, to include quite disparate forms of sustainable tourism. The growing literature on natural reserves, partly promoted by tourism, within the eco-tourist literature, places emphasis on the extent to which such areas provide an authentic experience of local cultures, and nature.

Eco-tourism in the Mexican Caribbean serves to illustrate the contradictions inherent in attempts to achieve both development and conservation goals, in projects that seek to combine both. Plans to conserve natural eco-systems, even in protected areas such as Biosphere Reserves, are mixed up with essentially developmental objectives. An uneasy line is drawn between conservation areas free from human incursion and tourist enclaves, where tourists have easy access to nature.

Given the speed and level of urban expansion and tourist development on the Mexican Caribbean coast, it is not surprising that it has given rise to different forms of environmental protests and political resistance. The construction of eco-parks and extensive hotel developments has helped to foment an ecological opposition dedicated to preserving nature, and centered on the conservation of marine turtles and their habitats, the beaches and reefs. Protestors have drawn attention to the way in which marine ecology acts as a "positional good," losing value precisely because these environments attract more people (Hirsch 1976). Much of this opposition has been galvanized through new forms of networked activism, especially the World Wide Web.

Other social protests have focused on the social exclusion of much of the Mayan population whose cultural identity is exploited by the developers. These protests have drawn attention to the way in which Mayan peasant families, living on ejidos, have had their land alienated from them by electricity utilities and hotel developers. In the view of these protestors, the development of global tourism has been prejudicial to the ideals and objectives of the Mexican Revolution that sought to protect the peasantry and their cultural inheritance. They draw attention to the example of the masked zapatistas in Chiapas who have proved highly effective in challenging the Mexican state and have provided a platform for other indigenous peoples in the country. The zapatista rebellion, which was mounted on behalf of local, ethnically Mayan people, has mobilized international opinion and the global media, culminating in caravans of protestors converging on Mexico City and demanding restitution of their rights from the president.

For most foreigners who visit the Mexican Caribbean, the most obvious manifestation of ecological politics is that represented by the public face of eco-tourism. Other environmental protests, linked to

Mayan identity and the machinations of the Mexican state and property developers, are largely unknown to them and only reported in the local Spanish-language press.

It is not surprising that the qualities of Mayan culture that are prized by developers are those that can be accommodated within the idea of the Mayan Riviera, a term that designates both place and culture and that lays emphasis on the value of tourism to the local and regional economy. In this use of ecology and ethnicity, progress is represented as the progressive integration of Mayan culture within the wider objectives of the global economy. Invisible to all but a very few visitors are traditions of civil unrest and organized social opposition that have important historical antecedents in the nineteenth century and that carry their own ecological resonance. The history of chewing gum can be looked upon as a lost thread in this tradition.

The re-constitution of the Maya as a cultural and historical force has also led to a reappraisal of their achievements. There has been considerable debate about the ecological practices of the ancient Maya, and whether or not these were responsible for the eventual downfall of Mayan civilization. Until the 1920s the prevailing view was that the Mayan dependence on slash and burn agriculture had exhausted the fertility of the soil. The milpa (corn fields) could only be worked for two or three consecutive years before the land began to lose its fertility. In the two most important areas of Mayan settlement, the Peten and Yucatán, between four and seven years was needed for the fallow land to recover its fertility. The conventional argument was that this fallow period was shortened in the face of population pressure, and that it contributed toward soil erosion, crop failure, and starvation (Coe 1973).

Difficulties arise, however, when the proponents of this theory project this view of carrying capacity onto the modern Maya, whose conditions of existence are radically different from those of their ancestors because of forces that have undermined Mayan identity itself, including growing links with international markets, and the Mexican state. At the same time archaeological evidence that the ancient Maya were dependent on slash and burn agriculture has been challenged. There is now substantial evidence that the Maya, "developed a diverse system of agricultural production (which included) kitchen gardens for the production of vegetables and fruit trees, and raised fields" consisting of soil and organic waste (Simonian 1995, 21). This diverse system spread throughout the Americas, during different periods, and is known as raised-bed cultivation.

The interest in raised-bed agriculture, which the Maya used, has convinced most archaeologists that they were well aware of what we refer to today as sustainable agronomic practices. The use of milpa land, for the production of the staple, and of kitchen gardens and raised beds, helped to ensure that the forests were not subjected to undue pressure. Far from seeing the forest as an unlimited resource, or free good, the Maya regarded the survival of forestlands as central to their own survival. The Maya successfully adapted to the exigencies of a tropical environment by achieving a balance between shifting and permanent agriculture, an adaptation that is frequently cited today.

In the Yucatán, as elsewhere, the environmental credentials of indigenous peoples have been questioned on the basis of historical evidence from areas in which they traditionally lived. This is a curious juxtaposition, if we stop to consider whether populations in the developed world would be equally prepared to be judged by the behavior of their ancestors. At the same time, however, indigenous peoples' access to modern technologies and means of communication is sometimes cited as evidence that they have lost their authentic voice. History has displaced many millions of indigenous people whose survival is no longer necessarily connected with their place of origin. People like the Maya are frequently subject to romantic generalizations that overlook their own ambivalence to the environment, and their own history of mobility and adaptation to change.

It is clearly impossible to develop an objective stance on the contemporary Maya or the social movements in which they are involved. Mayan political action is closely linked with other forms of global action. Writing about the Chipko movement in India Rangan argues:

Perhaps it is because we live in a world that is rife with debates over impending ecological catastrophes emerging from deforestation, global warming, desertification, and floods that so many people are drawn to the Chipko movement with such faith and hope. Chipko as myth touches all these problems in some way. . . . It provides the symbolic weapons, the small ammunition, that fires the spirits of those who hope to save the earth, and who, perhaps, also nurture the romantic desire to see the meek inherit the earth one day. (Rangan 2000, 2)

The example of the Chipko people, who sought to protect the forest, has immediate appeal to the developed world, and to environmental activists, in much the same way as refashioning of the Mayan legacy and identity. In the case of the Maya, much of the identification with their concept of nature, and their cultural practices, is based on imaginative links, and the supposed lessons for the developed Northern economies. The political resistance of the Maya, as depicted in Maya World imagery, is confined to the pre-colonial and colonial periods when the Maya are seen as sorcerers and warriors. The forest struggles of the nineteenth and twentieth century, in which the Maya were often mingled with non-Mayan groups, have largely been overlooked, and they fit rather awkwardly into the myths that have been built up about Mayan affinity for nature. As Goldmann writes:

Is all knowledge common, generalizable and universally accessible, as the global discourse assumes? Are heritages, histories and interests necessarily common? Are the dynamics of ecosystems, and natural-social relations embedded in a commons site, really transferable, replicable or generalizable? In discovering or inventing the global *ecological commons* and its fragile future, elite Northern scientists and policymakers also gave birth to the appropriate method for their understanding (i.e., *global science*) and the character of its inhabitants (i.e., *global citizen*). (Goldmann 1984, 4)

The Mayan political resistance in Yucatán during the last century suggests that the contemporary construction placed on the Maya and their environment is misleading. Tourists who visit the sacred wells, or cenotes, of the Maya, do so for sport and recreation rather than in admiration of their spiritual value to the Maya. They are presented with a sanitized and unthreatening view of Mayan culture.

Similarly the Mayan calendar is sold to tourists, copied in stone, and sold as a Mayan artifact. Increasingly tourists are even discovering a Mayan cuisine to enlarge their appetites, although most of the dishes were invented by relatively expensive restaurants within the last decade. (Interestingly the existence of a specific Yucatecan cuisine, which has much more claim to authenticity, is largely ignored by the tourist industry.) The traditional dress of Mayan women, the *huipil*, is used to dress not only Mayan women but also Barbie dolls and other products of the global consumer market. Indeed, there is evidence that the huipil, as worn today, is an evolutionary form of dress, like many others, and modeled in part on nineteenth-century costume. In this sense it resembles the Scottish tartan kilt, a creation of Victorian times.

It is not only the material culture of the Mayan World that needs to be treated with caution. The management of nature is sometimes undertaken in the name of the Maya but not necessarily by the Maya. Few members of local communities are involved in the decision-making of important Biosphere Reserves like Xian Ka'an, to the south of the Mexican Caribbean coast. There, as in other parts of the Yucatán peninsula, international nongovernment organizations have forged few links with local Mayan people (Carballo Sandoval 1999).

Meanwhile much of the environmental politics of the Mexican Caribbean coast, like that of other parts of Mexico, is taken up with campaigns and protests over such mundane things as sewage disposal, electricity supply, and land titles. These conflicts are implicit in the scale and rapidity of urbanization, and the conflicts of interest between private developers, migrants, and government. They are also of major concern to the Maya, the hundreds of thousands of people from the region who labor on building sites and in restaurants and bars, both in Mexico and in the United States.

Resource Histories and the Nature of Space

How might we begin to analyze these successive histories of resource frontiers on the Mexican Caribbean? One attempt would be to make use of categories derived from research undertaken against a larger historical canvas.

It has been suggested, by the Swiss philosopher Aurel Schmidt that existential space in the Western world has been occupied by three distinct epochs: the analogue, the digital, and the virtual (Schmidt 1998; Merk and Muller 2000). In using these terms Schmidt was thinking of broad historical epochs, but the metaphors work quite well for exploring specific resource and tourist histories and the utilization of space. The tourist pioneers described above fit conveniently into the first category:

analogue space means the discovery of place and its initial advertisement to others, usually a limited coterie of cognoscenti. Digital space, on the other hand, is associated with the consolidation of resource use, with the commercialization of place and its economic development. Digital space is exemplified by the way in which peripheries are transformed, and increasingly integrated within global models of production and consumption. The histories of these spaces are inscribed in the minds of people as necessary and inevitable, as chicle production was seen as inevitable and almost timeless during most of the twentieth century. Last, virtual space describes the creation or re-creation of "place" regardless of where it is located: Disneyworld and Center Parcs, in many geographical locations in Europe and North America, and perhaps also Xel-Ha or Chacchoben, as described above.

We might, however, choose to push the metaphor a lot further, and examine the lack of spatial and temporal continuities in the real world, which these ideal types fail to capture.[3] If we look closely, we find that places are discovered and rediscovered over time, and by different groups of people. Successive generations of pioneers and their resource histories are not located in black boxes, in time or space, that can be taken out and understood. They are in fact full of ambiguities. First, there is the ambiguity of abandoned spaces that open the door, as it were, to new discovery, settlement, and occupation. These discoveries erase some histories just as they illuminate others.

Second, it is clear that the other in these discoveries is an invention of the human imagination rather than a form of geopolitical mapping. Tourist histories are about what people aspire to *be* as much as who they are. This problem of identity is a central concern when resource histories are being transformed and host communities feel threatened. An example is the alleged response of the fishing community of Xcalak to outside entrepreneurs who were interested in recruiting them for tourist development. The fishing communities wanted to be left alone to fish.

Finally, where—and at what distance—are these discourses of space and their histories *created?* As we peel back the layers of the onion, we invariably find somebody has already been there before the histories we are examining. In the case of the Mexican Caribbean the paradoxes offered suggest an engagement with nature complicated by myth and location, and probably only comprehensible in the long view.

Trajectories of Consumption and Space: Chicle and Tourism Compared

This chapter has placed the history of tourist development in Quintana Roo against the background of resource histories in the area, and examined the historical narrative within which spatial relationships are established—in this case between the Mexican Caribbean and the United States and Europe. In some cases the individual entrepreneurs who were involved in the chicle trade later became involved in tourist activities. In other cases they, like the chicleros themselves, merged into the landscape of Quintana Roo, finding employment wherever they could find it.

At one level the similarities between chicle/chewing gum and mass tourism appear superficial. It seems no more than a coincidence that these very different activities have taken place sequentially in the same geographical space. However, in exploring the role that societies play in transforming the environment, and the way that they construct nature in this process, we can take the analysis much further. Table 7.1 suggests ways in which we can usefully compare the role of chicle and mass tourism in the development of the frontier, and the way in which the epithet "nature" is utilized. It also brings together several of the most salient aspects of environmental transformations discussed in this book. These include the social construction of nature, the degree of integration of production and consumption in resource systems, their branding and marketing, the substitution of human-made for natural capital, and the effects of environmental externalities.

As the table shows, both chewing gum (commercialized chicle) and tourism are commodities with global appeal, so international linkages are central to their importance. In addition they both involve the transformation of nature in some form. In the case of gum this is a material transformation, taking something from the wild and making it into a product, traded on the market. Nature is involved in these processes in another way too, since the body acts as the medium through which

Table 7.1
Environmental impacts of chicle and tourism compared

	Chicle/chewing gum	Tourism
Construction of nature	Largely through embodiment, with the body as a medium—ingestion and waste disposal	Largely evokes nature through imagery and marketing, with place as a medium for evoking the natural
Production/ consumption links	Consumption of chewing gum geographically and culturally remote from (original) natural source	Highly integrated, tourist production and consumption almost impossible to separate
Marketing/branding	Brand names to create loyalty to product	Place, through branding, made more identifiable and marketable
Capital/nature substitution	High degree of substitution of synthetic gum for natural capital	Substitution of built environment for nature but subject to limits (*hybridity*)
Environmental costs/benefits	Environmental costs externalized through forest destruction/land alienation from peasant farmers	Externalized environmental costs through losses (reefs, mangroves, species); problem of positional goods; internalization in some eco-tourist products

chewing gum is ingested and egested. Nature clearly involves the embodiment of the product through its consumption as well as its source. In the case of tourism the product involves a repackaging of nature, drawing on climate, terrain, and the natural features of "place", but combining these with cultural elements designed to appeal to visitors and creating identity partly by utilizing the identities of local people. The key element in the part nature plays in tourist economies is through imagery and association—linking the individual visitor with the location.

In considering the linkages between production and consumption, however, we enter a new domain. Although in both cases the product is linked to global markets, the production–consumption chain is very different. It matters little to most consumers of gum where their product was sourced, and the production of chicle remains both geographically and culturally remote from its consumption. The links between production and consumption are much closer in the case of tourism, however, where it is impossible to identify the consumed good apart from the environment in which it is consumed. In the case of tourism consumption and production are almost indissoluble.

Another important dimension is that of product branding. In the case of chewing gum it was the creation of brands, and variety within the brands, although the product existed before brands, that created product loyalty and led to commercial success. Some of these brands exist even today: Wrigley's Spearmint, Orbit, even the chicle-based "Yucatan." The natural environment of the Mexican Caribbean, however, has also been branded to attract tourists and to help develop consumer identification. This usually takes the form of labeling places—the Mayan Riviera, the Turquoise Coast (around Cancun). It also takes the form of manufacturing identifiable cultural artifacts such as the food, clothes, and music that come to be associated with place. This process, which is already well advanced on the Mexican Caribbean, still has a long way to go.

In evaluating the environment there is another dimension that needs to be considered. This is the extent to which human made capital can successfully be substituted for nature, or natural capital. Chewing gum was a product for which synthetic substitutes could be found relatively easily. Even in the 1930s experiments had been undertaken to use hydrocarbons in producing synthetic gum, particularly bubble gum (Redclift 2004). From about 1950 synthetic chewing gum had taken over the bulk of the market from the natural product, although various forms of natural chewing gum continue to be produced commercially in countries like Greece and Turkey. The substitution of the built environment for the natural environment has proved much more problematic in the case of tourism, where the debates are often concerned with the authenticity or otherwise of attempts to recreate natural phenomena in an artificial form, whether as eco-parks or Biosphere Reserves. Some would argue that there are limits to the successful merger of produced nature, and the natural environment: swimming with dolphins has great appeal for some tourists visiting the Mexican Caribbean, but the dolphins have been abstracted from their own environment. In what sense is it in their nature to want to swim with tourists?

Finally we can examine the environmental costs of both kinds of resource development. In the case of chicle, the measures to control the production and marketing of the product within Mexico contributed to the opening up of the frontier, to the clearing of forest, and the conversion of land to other uses, both for subsistence agriculture and cash crops. Some of these externalized costs were passed on to poor land users, particularly Mayan peasants dependent on their corn fields (milpa) as land that was valuable for other purposes was taken from them. During the chicle "boom" in the first half of the twentieth century, however, it is possible to argue that chewing gum brought advantages, at least to those people involved in its trade. As we have seen most of these benefits were short-lived.

The environmental externalities associated with tourism are in many ways easier to appreciate. Tourist locations, including those on the Mexican Caribbean, tend to be what Hirsch called "positional goods"; that is, their value derives from their position, and they tend to lose value as their use increases. Tourists come to the Caribbean to swim near the reefs and to watch the marine turtles lay their eggs. However, tourist densities are increasing all the time, and with these increased numbers comes the destruction of live reefs. As people use sandy beaches for their own amusement, it puts in jeopardy the nesting places that marine turtles have traditionally used. Eco-tourism can make use of turtle breeding grounds to attract certain types of interested tourist, of course, but the commercial pressures associated with coastal development, bright lights and noise, tend to deter the turtles from nesting. Some environmental costs can be reduced, or even internalized, in tourist amenities that make use of conservation principles, but the grain of history still appears to push development in the other direction.

8

Conclusion: Civil Societies and the Frontiers of Nature

Each of the case studies in this book has considered the relationship between civil society and nature, although the experiences vary widely historically and the meaning of civil society employed reflects very different kinds of social organization. As we saw in chapter 2, civil society is understood as a product of the increasing importance given to individualism and private property under modernity. At the same time it also coveys a sense of common social norms, the existence of social capital. This book has explored some of the ways in which the transformation of nature, under frontier conditions, is both the outcome of social capital and a source of problems for modernity. The idea of civil society is as complex and multifaceted as the term nature.

In this chapter we visit each of these studies in turn but do so with a different object in mind. The intention is to provide general and comparative conclusions that illuminate process rather than merely analyze events and histories. The concept of frontier has been employed in a number of ways, some of which have heuristic value in exploring aspects of space and nature. This relationship between nature and society, encapsulated in the frontier, has been explored as a metaphor and a point of departure for examining the contradictions of modernity.

Frontiers and Empires: Exclusionary and Inclusionary Tendencies

One of the points to have emerged from the case material is that frontiers provide an illuminating example of how nature is employed to mark out the social boundaries of inclusion and exclusion. In a fascinating and iconoclastic essay Bill Schwartz has written about the uncomfortable fact that black West Indians discovered a frontier when they arrived in the United Kingdom from the Caribbean in the late 1950s. He writes that:

Frontiers have functioned not only as sociological facts but as symbolic systems. Frontiers demarcate not only nation states but also moments of danger. (They frequently represent) cultural formations emanating from the margins . . . which have created new possibilities for the metropolis as a whole. (Schwartz 1999, 270)

These remarks were made in the context of comparative urban systems and their manifestation in different imperial forms, which were not always immediately evident to those who did not choose to see them. In Schwartz's case people from the margin (black West Indians) had arrived at the center (London) and, together with other immigrants, helped make the metropolis what it is today. Reviewing Hardt and Negri's (2000) work on "empire," Frederick Cooper makes a similar point. He notes that Hardt and Negri's *Empire* is "not only borderless within itself, but it has no 'outside.' There are no areas of the world that are not part of the global circuits of capitalism and the networks by which biopower is asserted" (Cooper 2004, 252).

The histories in this book trace a set of robust relationships between distinctive societies and their relations with the outside. All of them had become part of the inexorable circuits of capital that define modernity, or were well advanced to that end. In many of the cases discussed we see evidence of processes of inclusion and exclusion at work, through which empires extended their power and influence, and natural resources came to serve wider, global interests. The term "biopower" employed by Hardt and Negri (2000) had not been invented when European settlers occupied Ecuador, or the Yucatán Peninsula, or Upper Canada, processes of settlement that were separated by centuries, but if we examine the position of indigenous people in each of these societies it is clear that what marked their "defeat" was not their military inferiority alone but also their models of nature, which were difficult to accommodate to modernity. With hindsight, it is easier to appreciate that indigenous views of nature that might have fallen victim to history are still of considerable importance to posterity. As David Lowenthal has observed: "Settlers generally judge indigenous impacts as slight compared with their own, but time has reversed the conclusion once drawn from this difference" (Lowenthal 2004, 233–34). In most cases our own societies have been forced to re-examine the complexities of indigenous epistemologies only when they posed threats to our stability, or when we wanted to extract their bio-resources.

At the same time social exclusion is not a choice made by everyone caught up in the throes of ecological transformations. It is possible to distinguish in these historical narratives those who "were trying to get into a capitalistic system of production, or a state system of citizenship, from (those) trying to get out" (Cooper 2004, 253). Indeed, this distinction marks the collapse of some systems of resource management (Pyrenees) and the continuing conflicts in others (coastal Ecuador). Some groups, like the Cruzob in Quintana Roo, have tried to remain outside modernity and have found that to do so, they needed to retreat behind the frontiers that separate them from dominant white society. The choice seems to be between token status as props on the stage of the newly convened Maya World, or self-imposed exile in communities of fellow believers. Migratory histories frequently illustrate processes of exclusion as well as inclusion, and only occasionally do they reveal nature and society co-evolving together (Norgaard 1993). Frontiers, then, are often contested zones and the spaces of rival imaginaries.

Frontiers, Land, and Citizenship

This book has also examined several specific historical and geographical cases where the exploitation of natural resources within land frontiers has been associated with new claims to citizenship. In each of these cases civil societies have developed either to manage common property resources or to legitimize private landholding. Social groups have employed their efforts to introduce forms of environmental management that create local legitimacy for civil institutions, whether land reform bodies or private farms. The definition of nature has, in each case, been closely bound up with these civil transformations.

In the first case (Spanish Pyrenees) the development of common property helped maintain the ecological balance between forests, pastures, and the human population. Traditionally this balance had been institutionalized through transhumance, enabling communities either to derive rental income from other resource users or to pool natural resources while conserving the collectively maintained mountain pastures.

By the middle of the last century, however, the management of communally owned resources was no longer effectively in the hands of the communities themselves. The state Forestry Commission (*Comision Forestal*) managed the woods in the Spanish Pyrenees, the valuable water resources were in the hands of a hydroelectric company, and the mountain slopes were being developed for tourism, especially ski installations. Control of resources had passed from the community, under the system of corvee, to the central government. At the same time, as the twentieth century came to a close, many of the natural resources of the region were subjected to re-evaluation, and the burgeoning tourist industry stimulated a revival in local heritage industries, such as food, vernacular architecture, and mountaineering. The mountains and valleys became part of one of Spain's National Parks, "Aigues Tortes," and subsequently designated a global Biosphere Reserve. The management of nature and space was still centralized, but the rise of Catalan nationalism and pride ushered in greater concern for conservation objectives, and the Val d'Aran was re-branded to reflect latter-day Catalan concern for sustainability and the irrevocable ties of a people to the land. Increasingly it is wildlife conservation and the impulse toward conserving local identity that have displaced traditional civil institutions.

In the case of Upper Canada in the midnineteenth century, discussed in chapter 4, the private property rights in land were established as a consequence of colonial conquest. Land settlement was undertaken by immigrants from Britain and Ireland, on territory that had been alienated from local, indigenous people. In the accounts of most migrants in this period, the Indian population was barely visible, and there is no suggestion that indigenous people possessed rights that needed to be respected. Instead, natural resources were drawn into the vortex of modernity, and the creation of new civil institutions took precedence over long-term environmental considerations. In midnineteenth century Canada the forests represented an apparently inexhaustible supply depot of wood for the international market. The plunder of the forest released this resource, but succeeding generations are still engaged in conflicts over its management and conservation.

In Upper Canada the clearing of land was a necessary step toward establishing land titles, itself a step toward settlers achieving full citizenship. The families that cleared the forest and established homesteads were among the first generation to vote in elections and to help chart Canada's political future. However, from an agricultural viewpoint, the quality of the land in the Algonquins left much to be desired, and today (rather as in the Val d'Aran) the region is principally important for its amenity value, as a location for tourism and recreation under the protective management of outside conservation bodies. Frontier society has come to occupy mythic status in Canadian history. Those who settled the frontier are frequently depicted as pioneers, but the existence of apparently endless natural resources bred attitudes that contributed to their destruction. "Green" Canada is an outcome of the early plunder of nature as well as the efforts to create a civil society on the part of its pioneers.

Coastal Ecuador provides a different history in which the development of civil society was contested between distinct social classes, each with a different interest in land. The frontiers that were established on the Ecuadorian coast followed the ebbs and flows in world markets for primary commodities. Most of the tenants and sharecroppers, like the rice precaristas, discussed in chapter 5, struggled to secure the freehold of the land they worked against the interests of the landlords. For many, their civil obligations and rights could only be secured through land reform and through a radical redistribution of resources, including access to irrigated land that was potentially highly productive.

In the Ecuadorian case the population engaged in land conflicts was also made up of migrants, but unlike the immigrant population of Upper Canada, these were people of indigenous or mestizo background, many of whom had been forcibly expelled from the Ecuadorian Highlands. In some respects they bore more similarity to the native Canadians marginalized by the immigrant population of Upper Canada a century earlier. For these people collective organization on the Ecuadorian coast was both a way of maintaining their livelihoods and a means to secure their civil rights, aspects of civil society that had appeared natural to

Hobbes and Locke in another context. The cultural footprint and political legacy of these ideas has found partial expression today in the social movements that have come to characterize conflicts over land in Latin America, in which rural producers often gain land but lose market power. The rice sharecroppers of coastal Ecuador pursued a quest to join modernity, rather than resist it, and in this sense their struggles have followed, unevenly, the grain of history.

In some respects the last frontier discussed, that of the Yucatán peninsula and particularly the eastern state of Quintana Roo bears some resemblance to the Ecuadorian coast. However, in the case of the rebel Maya in the Yucatán the line of demarcation that separated them from the whites did not represent a global frontier of primary commodity production, but a circle of exclusion. The rebel Maya sought to redress their grievances with the Mexican state soon after Mexican Independence in 1821 and by the middle of the nineteenth century was in open revolt. Their objectives included ridding themselves of obligations to landlords and the Catholic church. By the 1930s they had fought successfully to protect their own lands, but they had been effectively excluded from political and economic power. For over half a century the conflict between the rebel Maya and the whites was a stalemate and the Maya withdrew into their forests, retreating behind the frontier that separated the rule of Mexican law from that of the Cruzob.

The history of chicle production, from which chewing gum was manufactured commercially, provided the rebel Maya with a source of income, with which to buy arms, and a way of prolonging the conflict. Many of the chicleros were not ethnically Mayan, however, and their penetration of the region, together with new lines of communication, schools, and civil institutions, opened up under President Cárdenas and during the 1950s, ultimately sounded the death knell for Mayan independence. Civil society in Quintana Roo spread from the north and the west, in the social and political transformations undertaken by the Mexican state. The society of Mayan separatists may have been more of a theocracy than a civil society, but it could not stand up to the hegemony of cultural and political Mexicanization unleashed on the area. Private property replaced collective ownership and postrevolutionary institutions dominated those of traditional communities.

Today in the Mexican Caribbean there is a re-packaging of regional and ethnic identity, designed to encourage tourists from other countries, just as there is in the Spanish Pyrenees. There is also a wider interest in preserving nature as the cornerstone of the Mayan World: the limestone sinks (cenotes) and coral reefs, as well as the manatees and marine turtles that inhabit them. The Mexican Caribbean has been transformed from a supply depot for global extractive markets (chicle and hard-woods) into the locus for new mass markets represented by global tourism. The conflicts between protecting nature and the rights of peoples have resulted in vain attempts to contain illegal development in the Biosphere Reserve of Xian Ka'an. The frontiers that are delineated today, including those that describe protected areas, are re-presenting the past and its geographies to audiences in the present and, in the process, changing our view of nature. Despite the clear evidence of a popular Mayan cultural revival, in Quintana Roo today the most excluded citizens are precisely those who are most attached to their own cultural heritage but effectively on the other side of the cultural divide. The frontier has extended citizenship to some groups, but individual gains need to be set against market-induced losses. The historical narratives in this volume clearly demonstrate that frontiers are re-negotiated in ways that often reduce the importance of land title in favor of effective market power. Frontiers are spaces in which tenure acquires additional fragility in the face of globalization, especially in consumer markets.

Globalization and the Environment

It is at this point that the cases discussed in this book help illuminate wider issues for policy and international relations. Global environmental management, particularly addressing the problems associated with global warming, has involved a scaling up of the environmental management practices that were developed to meet the local and regional externalities associated with economic growth. There is no global environmental agenda without local struggles and practices.

At the same time the traditions of resource management and nature conservation, which are embedded in many of the social institutions discussed in this book, are part of a different circuit from the technical instruments beloved by planners and international organizations. These traditions help define the responsibilities of civil societies to their members, and the citizen's responsibilities to the wider society. Many of the problems confronted by local groups in the face of globalization make the management of nature more difficult. Global processes and institutions appear to annihilate space, jeopardizing local cooperative efforts to conserve nature. Together with culture and history, the management of space seems to have been forfeited to the expansion of global markets. In the process it is difficult to invoke personal responsibility for the environment, since these responsibilities work most effectively as part of the institutional framework of civil societies that preceded globalization, like the comarcas of the Spanish Pyrenees.

One example of the difficulty in re-establishing communal rights, considered in several of the chapters, is that of forests. As we saw, forest resources have often been alienated from local communities and subjected to increased market pressures. In some cases, such as the Pyrenees and the Yucatán, these moves were taken without serious consideration being given to the interests of local people. In other cases, of which Upper Canada is an example, the felling of the forests was viewed at the time as a necessary step toward achieving civilization, and the achievement of an ordered civil society. The destruction of the forests, in both cases, was one of the central ways in which civil societies have entered history. This leaves us with a paradox, however, for environmental policy today. Many of the global environmental agreements that are entered into today demand the conservation of what is left of the forests as a condition for giving financial support to those who work and live there. This can be described as "Green conditionality" (Horta Duarte 2004). People are being offered citizenship in return for handing over the management of nature to outside agencies rather than as a means of securing their own control over it.

Frontiers and Ideologies of Nature

It is clear that the discussion of civil society and nature, as a dialectical process, has taken us a long way from the discussion of sources in chapter 1. This consisted of three different accounts of events in 1847 from three different sources: the American philosopher, Henry Thoreau; a migrant to British Canada, Francis Codd; and evidence from the Caste War, which had just started between rebel Maya and the Mexican government. It was suggested that taking a synchronic approach, observing one point in time, rather than the recourse to historical accounts utilized elsewhere, might facilitate our understanding of nature/society linkages in these cases.

Each of these accounts represents a distinct approach to the pervasive definitions and debates surrounding the environment at the beginning of the twenty-first century. Thoreau's thinking provides, in graphic form, an example of the traditions of self-sufficiency and economy that underpin much Green thinking today. His emphasis on the "use values" of objects rather than their market value, prefigures today's concerns with consumption and consumer fetishism. Similarly in *Walden* Thoreau sets out his program for living within physical and environmental limits while valuing nature as the source of human livelihood. In Thoreau's view frugality bought independence through applying labor in ways that were satisfying and also socially useful. His pursuit of simplicity, at the age of twenty-seven, was prompted by a need to "transact private business with the fewest obstacles," almost a textbook objective of sustainable individualism.

Francis Codd, by contrast, entered the Canadian frontier in 1847 in a quite different state of mind. The ideological tradition to which he belonged is the dominant spirit of our times as well as his. His was an instrumental approach to natural resources and a Promethean insistence that human purposes demand the transformation of nature. Frontiers, on this account, are where nature as wilderness gradually gives way to landscape, and the beneficial impact of the human hand. If Thoreau's views came to be associated with self-imposed frugality and conservation in the First World, Francis Codd's views represent the optimistic, modernizing impulse of much of the subsequent century. Francis Codd eventually saw that he needed to break with many social conventions that had traveled with him from the Old World to survive successfully in the *déclassé* New World. He came to see that his own indebtedness as a form of credit that bound him to his "clodhopping" neighbors in ties of mutual exchange and resourcefulness, essential for successful frontier life.

The account of the Mayan rebellion of 1847 introduces a third element that is also present in the discourses of environment and development today. The Mayan view of the relations between humans and nature was essentialist and uncompromising. Their cosmology demanded the recognition that humans were part of nature. The cultural exchanges that took place when societies positioned themselves inside nature rather than apart from it were often considered antiquated and reactionary at the time, in the white heat of the nineteenth century scientific revolutions. With hindsight, however, the indigenous vision of human relations with nature seems more prescient than anachronistic. In the Yucatán peninsula the rebel Maya were engaged in a military conflict to defend their identity and their culture. Many would argue that this kind of struggle, however anachronistic it might have seemed a century ago, has much broader appeal to those interested in sustainability today.

Three ideological positions that influenced the intervening centuries grew from embryonic sources like these. The first of these places emphasis on reducing the burden our consumption places on the environment (*Green sufficiency*). The second position is that of the mainstream: the environment exists primarily to source economic growth and development (*weak sustainable development*). The third position argues for a more holistic approach to the environment that clearly locates humans within, rather than outside, nature (*biocentrism*). Today each of these positions has its advocates and defenders. At the same time these ideological currents have created myths that still lie beyond scientific method to dissemble. A lowered "ecological footprint" (Thoreau) has mythical as well as programmatic importance today, and it is invoked by churchmen and ecological activists alike. Carving civilization out of a hostile wilderness not only appealed to Francis Codd in 1847, it also appeals today to adventurers and oilmen in their search for new material resources and sources of energy. These are the frontiers that increasingly determine the viability of our economies. Finally, the myth that guided the rebel Maya was not merely the Talking Cross, it was the idea of indigenous invincibility.

These ideological positions, even in their most mythological forms, are all dependent on spatial models of nature and society that take us to the frontiers of science and history. They each provide versions of space that have clear material dimensions and prioritize human subjectivity. The frontiers in each case are frontiers of the mind as well as of materiality. Self-sufficiency and the idea of achieving gains in welfare from recycling and repairing are necessities in many parts of the world, but they represent part of the wealth ecology of the North, filling the void left by materialism. The distance between the two worlds of the developed and the developing can be calculated by examining the ecological footprint of the North on the South. But even here it is important to recognize the existence of obstacles. The reflexive individual is able to relocate himself, through his beliefs, in the space occupied by others in the South who are less responsible for global pollution and waste, but he is unable to take their place physically. There are limits to political empathy.

The Frontier in the United States Today

It will be clear from previous chapters of this book that whatever the merits of the Turner thesis in provoking discussion about democracy of the late nineteenth and early twentieth centuries for the United States, it has only limited heuristic value for other societies and times. However, in the view of some contemporary commentators, the frontier is still a useful concept with which to view American society. After the 1980 population census in the United States, Frank Popper, today a professor of land use at Harvard University, began publishing a series of papers and books that refuted the Turner thesis and set out the basis for considering the American west in different terms. These have culminated in a series of recent papers that have argued for an enduring sense of frontier in the United States, but one linked much more closely to indexes of social marginality and exclusion (Popper 1995, 1997, 1999, 2002). Popper observed that large tracts of land in the American west were still underpopulated and geographically remote from most urban services. This suggests that more than half the land area of the United

States could still be considered frontier and, indeed, that there had been a growth in the number of frontier communities.

The characteristics of these contemporary American frontier communities, in Popper's view, require us to look beyond the boundaries of human settlement, since these communities have long histories apart from their continuing significance to Native Americans. Much of the contemporary frontier consists of native reservations and trusts. The US government, the military, forest services, national parks, the bureau of land management, and similar agencies, control other areas of frontier. The American frontier today is as diverse geographically as it is demographically and socially.

In 1997 the Frontier Education Center convened a group of frontier providers and policy experts to develop an acceptable and empirically adequate definition of frontier. After six months of work they were able to agree on a definition based on a series of variables, including population density, distance, and travel time, which were put together to form a matrix (Frontier Education Center 2005). Employing the matrix that they developed suggests a population of about nine million people in the United States living on the frontier, and occupying more than half of the land area of the country. Each of the forty states with frontier characteristics received information and maps to enable them to identify which of their counties was part of the frontier. Only one state, Vermont, decided that proximity to larger urban communities disqualified it from frontier status. Within the other thirty-nine states there were 940 counties that met the criteria, one of which, Alaska, was so remote that much of it was re-classified as wilderness.

The US federal government is unable to meet many of its obligations to some of these frontier states, especially in the west of the United States. The federal government owns from 27 percent to almost 80 percent of the land in the twelve western frontier states of Montana, Washington, New Mexico, Colorado, Arizona, California, Alaska, Wyoming, Oregon, and Idaho. This reduces the tax base, and therefore federal income. The scale of public land ownership has created a permanent barrier to the development of private sector infrastructure, and at the same time underlines the needs that only frontier areas can provide: for natural resource conservation, wildlife and watershed management, and the preservation of historical open space. These environmental services are all seriously underfunded.

At the same time the labor markets of these frontier states have shifted in ways that make the conservation of natural resources even more fragile, as they are put under new pressures. Rural areas in the United States have experienced considerable economic restructuring in recent years, and employment has moved away from resource-based industries toward more service-based economies. Unlike much of the rest of rural America however, the designated frontier areas offer little diversity in employment and few opportunities other than farming. They tend to be overly dependent on a single economic activity and only one or two employers, making them extremely vulnerable to economic fluctuations. In this respect, at least, areas of the American frontier today resemble some of the zones described in earlier chapters of this book such as coastal Ecuador and the Yucatán, whose fate was decided by the demand for commodities on global markets.

The frontier has become a category in health and social policy, and the geography of the frontier in the United States has attracted renewed interest. As social deprivation in some areas of the Deep South increases, they in turn qualify for frontier status based on their social isolation and lack of health and educational services. It is interesting to reflect, pace Turner, that although the debate that was waged about the frontier a century ago was largely about social inclusion, with the expanding frontier seen as a guarantee of freedom and social mobility, today the situation is reversed. In the United States today the frontier is largely conceptualized in terms of social *exclusion*.

A Frontier Dialectic

In conclusion, it is important to reconsider the frontier from a theoretical standpoint as well as from the perspective of current policy. The processes described in this book can be understood in terms of a frontier dialectic, seen as an evolving process of understanding as well as of scientific advance that applies to human sensation as well as materiality and yields knowledge of the natural, phenomenal world. This use of the dialectic places it closer to Hegel and to Marx, than to Kant, who saw the dialectic as a logic of reasoning rather than understanding, and largely independent of experience (Popper 1969).

Following Hegel the argument of this book is that we cannot separate dialectical understanding from other features of the natural world in which this understanding is firmly located. From a Marxist standpoint, in contrast, it is suggested that in frontier situations dialectical change comes about through the clash of contradictory systems, which came to be called the forces of production and the relations of production. Departing from a Marxist position, however, it is suggested that the engine of the dialectic can be seen as cultural and phenomenological as much as material, and the relations of production (ideology, governance, taste) can have a determining influence on the outcome of social changes. Nor is the dialectic employed here seen as progressive in the Marxist sense, since historical advances are neither inevitable nor necessarily beneficial, and do not follow in any recognizable grain or patterns that can be determined in advance. Frontiers do not follow a discernible modernist chronology.

The frontier then is a canvas for a kind of revisionist understanding of the dialectic, loosely associated with the work of Hegel and Marx. At the same time, if we examine the relations between civil societies and nature explored in this book, it is clear that the frontier is more than simply a canvas. It is more like a painting or a camera lens through which modernity is drawn and refashioned, bringing together opposing and incompatible tendencies, some of which favor living within sustainable natural limits and others favor defying these limits. The frontier is a constantly refashioned space, ideologically and culturally as much as geographically, in which competing definitions of sustainability and progress meet and collide.

The histories described in this book provide examples of the way in which conflicting models can be transcended, in a dialectical form. The rebirth of interest in pastoralism today in the Pyrenees, for nature conservation rather than rural livelihoods, and the Mayan cultural renaissance in Yucatán, both emerged from conflicting models and struggles over the governance of resources and territory. Canadian concepts of frontier, and the contradictions behind Canada's commitment to Green policies internationally, have similarly emerged from the struggle between a pioneering individualism similar to that lauded in most settler societies and a "hostile" environment of almost limitless natural endowments.

Ecuadorian land conflicts between landlords and tenants took place against a background of technological modernization that has marginalized them both and created an intensive frontier of agricultural products that feed international exchange and global trade. The biological ingredients of this technological frontier have served to recombine nature in new genetic materials that increasingly defy physical boundaries and spatially located conflicts. The frontier dialectic, while located in our world of images and identities, is also a substantive process with a materiality and physicality of its own.

The argument sustained in this book is that we can understand the interconnections between nature and civil society by comparing civil societies that came into being to manage the *balance* between population and resource (Pyrenees) and those that took resource exploitation, settlement, and extraction as primary activities and developed civil societies out of the conflicts they produced in remote and "empty" lands (Canada, Ecuador, Mexico). It has also been suggested that the first and second versions of frontiers have in effect given rise to a third version, in which hybridized frontiers reflect growing reflexivity in societies and across them. However, this process does not follow a uniform historical sequence. Indeed, civil societies are evolving continually that question the process through which material transformations are made—in the Val d'Aran as much as on the Mexican Caribbean coast. In each of these societies, although a historical identity has been lost another has been re-imagined within different cultural and economic contexts.

As suggested at the beginning of chapter 2, identifying cultural processes across societies is not a purely discursive activity, devoid of political consequences, but an invitation to view human societies and their environments as part of a wider dialectical process. This book has viewed the frontier as a locus of exchange between nature and culture, and as such, its employment enables us to transcend the choice between a materialist and a social constructivist epistemology. The frontier can be invoked for many purposes, as history, territory, and myth, but ultimately its heuristic value derives from the way it illuminates processes in both nature and society.

Frontiers are not simply existing physical and social boundaries, they are increasingly located at the outer reaches of modernity, in cyberspace as well as real space, in new genetic materials as well as in embodied cultural forms. Frontiers are also the product of peoples' imaginations, of geography, culture, and space. In this sense frontiers can be consumed much as products are consumed, emitting clues to identity and difference within the increasingly homogeneous contours of global society. From this perspective, too, frontiers are far from immutable. They are constantly changing, and our engagement with them, whether as consumers, travelers, or Web surfers, is a form of displacement available both physically and virtually. Perhaps we now begin to live our dreams of the frontier *before* we experience it, unlike most of the individuals whose histories are described in this book.

Notes

Chapter 2

1. This discussion is linked to an even broader concern—the relationship between nature and culture in Western thought, analyzed by Clarence Glacken in his 1973 epic study, *Traces on the Rhodian Shore*. Glacken begins by suggesting that there were three views of this relationship: it was part of the Grand Design (God), that the environment determined human adaptation, and that humans can be seen as geographic agents. "Although the idea of environmental influences and that of man as a geographic agent may not be contradictory— many geographers in modern times have tried to work out theories of reciprocal influences—the adoption by thinkers of one of these ideas to the exclusion of the other has been characteristic of both ancient and modern times" (Glacken 1973, viii).

Glacken reviews these ideas exhaustively, adding to scholarship as well as our knowledge of the centrality of thinking about nature. However, particularly as an historian, his task was not to provide a conceptual position of his own, well illustrated by the words with which he ends his historical *tour de force*:

The design argument explaining the nature of earthly environment really looked upward to the creativity and activity of God; the idea of environmental influence to the force and strength of natural conditions; the idea of man as modifier of nature, to the creativity and activity of man. (Glacken 1973, 713)

2. One indication of the growth of interest in frontiers, both conceptually and historically, is the growth of scholarship in this field across the humanities and social sciences. As Elliot Young points out:

The veritable explosion in recent years of books with the words "border" or *frontera* in the title indicates that the "border," at least as a concept, has gone from a marginal field of specialization to the center of academic debate across several disciplines. There is, however, an important analytical distinction to be made between the border as a concept on the one hand, and as a physical place on the other. (Young 2004, 6)

Later he adds that he hopes to show "the dialectical relationship between metaphysical and physical borders without allowing one to stand in for the other" (Young 2004, 6). This sentiment is similar to my own, although the use of "dialectic" appears serendipitous.

3. The problem lay partly in the audacity of European colonists, and partly in their inexperience. Later Glacken quotes Count Volney's views on forest clearance, which are close to those cited in chapter 4 for Upper Canada: "Forest clearance was required for the extension of civilization, for public health, and for the promotion of agriculture necessary for this extension, but it threatened also to defeat these purposes by diminishing the water supply in springs and books and thus perhaps even bringing about permanent aridity" (Glacken 1973, 691).

There is abundant evidence from the early American naturalists, whom Glacken cites, that "what they feared (most) was that European man in the New World was failing to understand the organic cycle in nature, from life to death and from decay to life, and its importance to human welfare". (Glacken 1973, 698, see note 122 for references).

4. The expansion of the United States at the expense of Mexico had historical consequences, especially starting from the midnineteenth century. As Elliot Young puts it: "The US–Mexico border established in 1848 cut straight through preexisting political, economic and cultural communities. The nation-state project of severing these communities, however, remains even today only partially completed" (Young 2004, 6). He argues, in his 2004 study of *Catarino Garza's Revolution on the Texas-Mexico Border* that: "The ongoing and increasingly tight economic, political and cultural connections between the United States and Mexico (and the rest of the Americas as well) shows us that rather than borderlanders becoming ethnics and ceasing to be borderlanders, they maintain hybrid borderland identities even after national boundaries have been established" (Young 2004, 15). Part of the interest of Garza's revolt, as Young makes clear, is the fact that although it took place on behalf of Mexicans inside Texas, their struggle was to remain independent of both Mexico and the United States, rather than choose an adherence to one of these countries. Such a position, of course, found favor with neither country.

Chapter 3

1. Robin Fedden in his classic study, based on his experiences as a mountaineer in the 1950s wrote:

The vegetation on the two sides of the Pyrenees was as different as their formation. The beechwoods through which we climbed were characteristic of the northern slopes, where close forests mantle the mountainsides. . . . From our small peak we could appreciate the differing nature of the two faces of the Pyrenees. (Fedden 1962, 31)

2. "The curious position of the Val d'Aran, like a geographical fault, no doubt accounts for the fact that it is Spanish territory though lying to the north of the main watershed. Elsewhere the latter, with one or two exceptions, firmly divides Frenchmen and Spaniards" (Fedden 1962, 119).

3. Writing of his travels in the mid-1950s Fedden was still able to recall very large flocks of sheep in the high pastures:

As we sat there . . . another flock of sheep appeared from the dead ground below our vision. They were the first of the summer migrations from sere valleys to the richer pastures of the Val d'Aran and the north. They lapped, perhaps 2,000 of them, in a wave up the slope, hesitating yet pressing forward like foam up a beach. The consignment probably of several valleys, they bore the brands of many owners. It was an immemorial movement and the crooks that the hired shepherds held must have been among the oldest implements in the world. (Fedden 1962, 98)

4. These transformations have been observed in most of the various parts of the Spanish Pyrenees. In her study of a Basque shepherding community Sandra Ott examines the cooperation and reciprocity that formed the basis of communal institutions, like those of the Val d'Aran. However in a new foreword, Ott discusses developments that have changed this pastoral community since her book was first printed. She comments: "In the summer of 1992, Sainte-Engrace staged its first *pastorale* (folk opera) since July 1976. It served an intriguing function by providing all age groups with a common sense of identity as 'people of Sainte-Engrace.' For some of the younger people, it also heightened awareness of a shared identity with Basques from other provinces, both in France and in Spain" (Ott 1981).

5. The limitations of Fedden's rather romantic approach are obvious when he is describing the impact of the enormous hydroelectric installations in the Spanish Pyrenees. He writes:

Since 1953 certain valleys have felt the maleficent touch of progress. Hydroelectric works have come to San Mauricio, the lower Rio Malo, the upper Aiguamoch and the Rio Fougeras. Fortunately it seems that dams can be maintained without the presence of human beings. When the landscape has been scarred the surgeons leave. . . . A development more prejudicial to the area was the breaching of the Viella tunnel which in 1955 took a road across the seventy-five roadless miles that previously separated the passes of the Portalet and the Bonaigue. It opened up the heart of the range. But the damage is less than might be supposed. There are no hotels and the motor-cars hurry though. (Fedden 1962, 119–120)

His confidence would have been undermined had he visited the valley a decade later in the late 1960s. There were two ski-stations and the beginnings of a very vibrant tourist industry, culminating today in every conceivable facility: restaurants, hotels by the score, shopping malls, and even a heritage museum depicting the world Fedden had described forty years earlier. Among the objects of material culture for sale are vernacular Aranes houses, in the form of dolls houses, for children (or adults). History and livelihood have been translated into tradition, and tradition into heritage. Interestingly much of the Val d'Aran has been subjected to Catalanization, in the form of street names for example. Catalan, although always spoken by the Aranes, was never their principal language but a second or third language.

Chapter 4

1. Francis Codd, the young British doctor whose experiences were explored in chapter 1, also provides evidence, through his letters home, of a growing sense of responsibility for the institutions of his adopted country. Soon after arriving, on June 19, 1847, he declaims against the absence of the rule of law. The Ottawa valley is peopled by "such a set of savages" and "[there is] no law or civil power within 100 miles to control them," he writes. In the same letter he mentions the ugly brawls between rafts men in which he, as the local doctor, inevitably becomes involved. The people cannot be trusted because "for the most part they are an infernal set of rogues, and there is no court of law nearer than Perth" (Redclift 2004, 46).

Chapter 7

1. Mexico's presentation of self to the outside world was particularly evident in the World Fairs at which it participated from 1880 until the 1930s. The Mexican participation in the Paris Exhibition of 1889 exemplified the Porfirio project of modernization, and was designed to show how much Mexico had advanced. Subsequent exhibitions, like those of Rio de Janeiro in 1922 and Seville in 1929, were designed to show how much the country had benefited from a revolution (Trillo 1996).

2. The Cruzob sent a message to an academic conference, held in Merida in 1997, on the history of the Caste War. The message ended: "The Maya are a living people, and our traditional authorities are a present institution, not of the past as some would wish to see them. . . . As you know we have ideas and a voice that must be heard, and if this does not happen we are always ready for more centuries of resistance, educating our sons in our traditions, preparing always for a rebirth of our ancient grandeur. They still make war on us" (Reed 2001, 361).

3. The growth of mass tourism on the Mexican Caribbean has led to the "discovery" of activities with strong tourist appeal. Many of these are entirely genuine, but they have been enhanced by the press and media for their tourist value. A good example of the rediscovery of heritage on the Caribbean coast has been the preparation of anthologies of music from Quintana Roo, which it is claimed had been forgotten. A recent collection of recordings dates back to 1943. (See *Por Esto!* 2003.)

References

Aglietta, M. 1979. *A Theory of Capitalist Regulation*. London: New Left Books.

Alford, V. 1937. *Pyrenean Festivals*. London: Chatto.

Andrews, A., and G. Jones. 2001. Asentamientos colonials en la costa de Quintana Roo. *Temas Antropologicos* (January 23).

Arzapalo Marin, R., and R. Gubler. 1997. *Persistencia Cultural entre los Mayas Frente Al cambio y la Modernidad*. Mérida: Ediciones Universidad de Yucatán.

Baraona, R., and O. Delgado. 1972. El sistema de tenencia precaria y la explotacion del trabajo de los aparceros. In *El Proyecto de Reforma Agraria en la Region Arrocera del Ecuador*. Santiago: FAO.

Barcena, I. 2000. Hacia un desarrollo sostenible? In I. Barcena, P. Ibarra, and M. Zubiaga, eds., *Desarrollo Sostenible: Un Concepto Polemico*. Bilbao: Universidad del Pais Basco.

Barke, M., J. Towner, and M. T. Newton, eds. 1996. *Tourism in Spain*. Wallingford: CAB International.

Bebbington, A. J., S. Guggenheim, E. Olson, and M. Woolcock. 2004. Exploring social capital debates at the World Bank. *Journal of Development Studies* 40 (5): 33–64.

Bebbington, A. J. 2002. Sharp knives and blunt instruments: Social Capital in development studies. *Antipode* 34 (4): 800–3.

Beinart, W., and P. Coates. 1995. *Environment and History: The Taming of Nature in the United States and South Africa*. London: Routledge.

Bennett, J. W., and S. B. Kohl. 1995. *Settling the Canadian-American West 1890–1915*. Lincoln: University of Nebraska.

Berthold-Bond, D. 1993. *Hegel's Grand Synthesis: A Study of Being, Thought and History*. New York: Harper.

Berthoud, G. 1972. Introduction: Dynamics of Ownership in the Circum-Alpine Area. *Anthropological Quarterly* 45 (3): 423–55.

Bessiere, J. 1998. Local development and heritage: Traditional food and cuisine as tourist attractions in rural areas. *Sociologia Ruralis* 38: 21–34.

Beteta, R. 1999. *Tierra del Chicle*. Chetumal, Mexico: Govierno del Estado de Quintana Roo.

Bhaskar, R. 1989. *The Possibility of Naturalism*, 2nd Ed. Brighton: Harvester.

Bigsby, H. 1955. The shoe and the canoe, or pictures of travel in the Canadas. In G. Craig ed., *Early Travellers in the Canadas*. Toronto: Macmillan.

Blankstein, C., and C. Zuvekas. 1973. Agrarian reform in Ecuador: An evaluation of past efforts and the development of a new approach. *Economic Development and Cultural Change* 22 (1): 328–51.

Blomley, N. 2003. Law, property and the geography of violence: The frontier, the survey and the grid. *Annals of the Association of American Geographers* 93: 121–41.

Botero, M. F. J. 1988. La historia oral de los Mayas de Quintana Roo. Lic. Dissertation. Escuela Nacional de Antropologis y Historia, Mexico City.

Broek, J. O. M. 1941. *Frontiers of the Future*. Berkeley: University of California Press.

Bromley, D. W., and M. M. Cernea. 1989. The management of common property resources: some conceptual and operational fallacies. *World Bank Discussion Papers*, no. 57. Washington, DC: World Bank.

Bromley, D. W., D. Feeny, M. A. McKean, P. Peters, J. Gilles, R. Oakerson, C. Ford Runge, and J. Thomson, eds. 1992. *Making the Commons Work: Theory, Practice and Policy*, San Francisco: ICS Press.

Buckner, P. A. 1993. *English Canada: The Founding Generations*. London: Canadian High Commission.

Bunker, S. G. 1985. *Underdeveloping the Amazon*. Chicago: University of Chicago Press.

Burns, R. K. 1961. The Ecological Basis of French Alpine Peasant Communities in the Dauphine. *Anthropological Quarterly* 36 (3): 130–55.

Burns, R. K. 1963. The Circum-Alpine culture area: A preliminary view. *Anthropological Quarterly* 36 (3): 1–43.

Buttel, F. 2000. Response to Frank, Hironaka and Schofer. *American Sociological Review* 65: 117–20.

Calder, J. 2003. *Scots in Canada*. Edinburgh: Luath Press.

Campistol, J. R. 1951. *Francia, La Corona de Aragon y la Frontera Pirenaica: la lucha por el Valle de Aran*. Madrid: Consejo Superior de Investigaciones Cientificos.

Carballo Sandoval, A. 1999. Community involvement in sustainable ecotourism: The case of the Mexican Caribbean area. Geographical Paper 140. University of Reading.

Careless, J. M. S. 1967. *The Union of the Canadas: 1841–1857.* Toronto: Mckellard and Stewart.

CEDEGE (Comision de Estudios para el Desarrollo de la Cuenca del Rio Guayas). 1970. *Tenencia de la Tierra y Reforma Agraria—Un estudio socio-economico y legal.* Guayaquil: T. Ingledow.

CEDEGE. 1975. *Proyecto de Proposito Multiple Guayas.* Guayaquil: T. Ingledow.

Cesar Dachary, A., and S. M. Arnaiz Burne. 1998. *El Caribe Mexicano: Una frontera olvidada.* Chetumal: University of Quintana Roo.

Chan Colli, M. 2001. XXXII Aniversario luctuoso del General Francisco May. *Nicte T'an* (April): 4–6.

CIDA (Comite Interamericano de Desarrollo Agricola). 1965. *Ecuador: Tenencia de la Tierra y Desarrollo Socioi-Economico del Sector Agricola.* Washington, DC: InterAmerican Committee for Agricultural Development.

Coke, E. T. 1955. A journey from Quebec to the Maritimes in 1832. In G. Craig, ed., *Early Travellers in the Canadas.* Toronto: Macmillan.

Cole, J. W., and E. R. Wolf. 1974. *The Hidden Frontier: Ecology and Ethnicity in an Alpine Valley.* New York: Academic Press.

Cole Harris, R., and J. Warkentin. 1991. *Canada before Confederation.* Ottawa: Carlton University Press.

Collantes, F., and V. Pinilla. 2004. Extreme depopulation in the Spanish rural mountain areas. *Rural History* 15 (2): 149–66.

Collier, A. 1994. *Critical Realism, an Introduction to Roy Bhaskar's Philosophy.* London: Verso.

Connolly, P. 1994. Urban planning and segmented land markets in Cancun. In G. Jones and P. M. Ward, eds., *Methodology for Land and Housing Market Analysis.* London: UCL Press.

Cooper, F. 2004. Empire multiplied: A review essay. *Comparative Studies in Society and History* 46 (2): 247–72.

Cowan, H. I. 1961. *British Emigration to British North America.* Toronto: University of Toronto Press.

Craig, G., ed. 1955. *Early Travellers in the Canadas.* Toronto: Macmillan.

Croall, J. 1995. *Preserve or Destroy: Tourism and the Environment.* London: Gulbenkian Foundation.

Cronon, W., ed. 1996. *Uncommon Ground: Rethinking the Human Place in Nature.* New York: Norton.

Crosby, A. 1986. *The Colombian Exchange.* Wesport, CT: Greenwood Press.

Crow, B., and A. Thomas. 1982. *Third World Atlas.* Milton Keynes: Open University Press.

Cueva, A., ed. 1975. La crisis de los anos 60. In *Ecuador: Pasado y Presente.* Quito: Universidad Central.

Curtis, W. 1969. *The Capitals of Spanish America*. New York: Praeger.

Dachary, A. C., and S. M. Arnaiz Burne. 1998. *Cozumel: Los Anos de Espera*. Mérida: Fundacion de Parques y Museos de Cozumel.

Dasgupta, P., and I. Serageldin, eds. 2000. *Social Capital—A Multifaceted Perspective*. Washington, DC: World Bank.

Dauberry, C. 1955. Bytown and the Rideau anal in the 1830s. In G. Craig, ed., *Early Traveller in the Canadas*. Toronto: Macmillan.

De la Cuadra, J. 1958. El montuvio Ecuatoriano. In J. De la Cuadra, ed., *Obras Completas de Jose de la Cuadra*. Quito: Ediciones Casa de la Cultura.

De Vries, T. A. 2002. *Chicle Commercialization: Institution, Sustainability and Green Markets*. MA dissertation. Miami: Florida International University.

Dickens, P. 1997. Beyond sociology: Marxism and the environment. In M. Redclift and G. Woodgate, eds., *The International Handbook of Environmental Sociology*. Cheltenham: Edward Elgar.

Duchrow, U., and F. Hinkelammert, eds. 2004. *Property for People, Not for Profit: Alternatives to the Global Tyranny of Capital*. New York: Zed Books.

Eckersley, R. 2004. *The Green State: Rethinking Democracy and Sovereignty*. Cambridge: MIT Press.

Ehrentraut, A. 1996. Globalization and the representation of rurality: Alpine open-air museums in advanced industrial societies. *Sociologia Ruralis* 36: 4–26.

Ekman, A. K. 1999. The revival of cultural celebrating in rural Sweden: Aspects of tradition and transfer. *Sociologia Ruralis* 39: 280–93.

Ellen, R., S. Parkes, and A. Bicker, eds. 1997. Introduction. In *Indigenous Environmental Knowledge and Its Transformations*. Amsterdam: Harwood.

Ellen, R. 2000. Local knowledge and sustainable development in developing countries. In K. Lee, A. Holland, and D. McNeill, eds., *Global Sustainable Development in the 21st Century*. Edinburgh: Edinburgh University Press.

El Universo, Guayaquil, January 20, 1969.

Encyclopedia de Quintana Roo. 1998. Vol. 3. Cancun: Mensa.

European Union Regional Policy Unit. 2000. *Structural Policies and European Territory: The Mountains*. Luxemburg: Office of Official Publications.

Evans, N. J., and R. Yarwood. 2000. The politicization of livestock: Rare breeds and countryside conservation. *Sociologia Ruralis* 39: 280–93.

Everest Tourist Guide to Cancun and the Riviera Maya. 2002. Cancun.

Febvre, L. 1973. Frontier: The Word and the Concept. In P. Burke, ed., *A New Kind of History: From the Writings of Febvre*. London: Hutchinson.

Fedden, R. [1962] 2002. *The Enchanted Mountains: A Quest in the Pyrenees*. London: John Murray.

Fidler, I. 1955. The advantages of Upper Canada over the American states. In G. Craig, ed., *Early Travellers in the Canadas*. Toronto: Macmillan.

Fine, B. 1999. The developmental state is dead. Long live social capital. *Development and Change* 30 (1): 1–19.

Fine, B. 2001. *Social Capital versus Social Theory: Politics, Economics and Social Science at the Turn of the Millennium*. London: Routledge.

Forero, O., and M. Redclift. 2004. Chicle, the Mayan frontier and the persistence of coyotaje. Paper delivered at the Institute for the Americas. University of London. November.

Foster, R. 1960. *The Nobility of Toulouse in the Eighteenth Century*. Oxford: Oxford University Press.

Fowler, T. 1955. The journal of a tour through British America. In G. Craig, ed., *Early Travellers in the Canadas*. Toronto: Macmillan.

Fox, J. 1996. How does civil society thicken? The political construction of social capital in rural Mexico. *World Development* 24 (6): 1089–103.

Frank, D. J., A. Hironaka, and E. Schofer. 2000. The nation-state and the natural environment over the twentieth century. *American Sociological Review* 65: 96–116.

Friedmann, H., and P. McMichael. 1989. Agriculture and the state system: Rise and decline of national agricultures, 1870 to the present. *Sociologia Ruralis* xxix (2): 253–75.

Glacken, C. 1973. *Traces on the Rhodian Shore*. Oxford: Oxford University Press.

Glusker, S. 1998. *Anita Brenner: A Mind of Her Own*. Austin: University of Texas Press.

Goldmann, M., ed. 1998. *Privatizing Nature: Political Struggles for the Global Commons*. London: Pluto Press.

Gomez Ibanez, D. A. 1975. *The Western Pyrenees: Differential Evolution of the French and Spanish Borderland*. Oxford: Clarendon.

Gonzalez Durán, J. 1974. *La Rebelión de los Mayas y el Quintana Roo chiclero*. Mérida: Editorial Doris.

Goodman, D., and M. Redclift. 1991. *From Peasant to Proletarian: Capitalist Development and Agrarian Transitions*. Oxford: Basil Blackwell.

Goodman, D. E., and M. R. Redclift. 1991. *Refashioning Nature: Food, Ecology and Culture*. London: Routledge.

Goodman, D., B. Sorj, and J. Wilkinson. 1987. *From Farming to Biotechnology: A Theory of Agro-industrial Development*. Oxford: Basil Blackwell.

Gray, J. 2000. The common agricultural policy and the re-invention of the rural in the European community. *Sociologia Ruralis* 40: 30–52.

Greenwood, D. 1978. The demise of agriculture in Fuenterrabia. In J. B. Aceves and W. A. Douglass, eds. *The Changing Face of Rural Spain*. Cambridge, MA: Schenkman.

Hamerly, M. 1970. A social and economic history of the city and district of Guayaquil during the late colonial and independence periods. Unpublished PhD. thesis. University of Florida, Gainsville.

Hannigan, J. 1995. *Environmental Sociology: A Social Constructionist Approach*. London: Routledge.

Hannigan, J. 2000. Response to Frank, Hironaka and Schofer. *American Sociological Review* 65: 120–2.

Hardt, M., and A. Negri. 2001. *Empire*. Cambridge: Harvard University Press.

Harriss, J. 2002. *De-Politicized Development: The World Bank and Social Capital*. London, Anthem Press.

Hayter, R., T. Barnes, and M. Bradshaw. 2003. Relocating resource peripheries to the core of economic geography's theorizing: Rationales and agenda. *Area* 35: 15–23.

Hermans, D. 1981. The encounter of agriculture and tourism: a Catalan case. *Annals of Tourism Research* 8: 463–79.

Hirsh, F. 1976. *The Social Limits to Growth*. London: Routledge and Kegan Paul.

Hobsbawm, E. 1979. *The Age of Capital: 1848–1875*. London: Penguin.

Horta Duarte, R. 2004. Facing the forest: European travellers crossing the Mucuri River Valley, Brazil in the nineteenth century. *Environment and History* 10 (1): 31–58.

Howison, J. 1955. The pioneer society of Upper Canada after the War of 1812. In G. Craig, ed., *Early Travellers in the Canadas*. Toronto: Macmillan.

Humphreys, R. A., ed. 1940. *British Consular Reports on the Trade and Politics of Latin America, 1824–1826*. London: Athlone Press.

Ilberry, B. W., and M. Kneafsey. 1998. Product and place: Promoting quality products and services in lagging rural regions of the European Union. *European Urban and Regional Studies* 5: 329–41.

Jaramillo Botero, M. F. 1988. *La Historia Oral de los Mayas de Quintana Roo*. BA dissertation in ethnology. Escuela Nacional de Antropología e Historia, Mexico City.

Jenkins, V. S. 2000. *Bananas: The American History*. Washington, DC: Smithsonian Institution Press.

Jones, G. 2003. Imaginative geographies of Latin America. In P. Swanson, ed., *The Companion to Latin American Studies*. London: Edward Arnold.

Kallen, C. 1990. Eco-tourism: The light at the end of the tunnel. *E-Magazine* (July–August): 32–47.

Kautsky, K. 1927. *The Materialist Conception of History.* Reprinted Yale University Press, 1988, J. Kautsky, ed.

Kenny, M. 1966. *A Spanish Tapestry: Town and Country in Castile.* New York: Harper Row.

Koch-Kraft, A. 1995. Freedom in the North: Canada. In D. Hoerder and D. Knauf, eds., *Fame, Fortune and Sweet Liberty: The Great European Emigration.* Bremen: Temmen.

Konrad, H. W. 1991. Capitalism on the Tropical-Forest Frontier. In J. T. Brannon and G. M. Joseph, eds., *Land, Labor and Capital in Modern Yucatán.* Tuscaloosa: University of Alabama Press.

Knowles, V. 1992. *Strangers at Our Gates: Canadian Immigration and Immigration Policy 1540–1990.* Toronto: Dundurn Press.

Lang, T., and M. Heasman. 2004. *Food Wars.* London: Earthscan.

Lapointe, M. 1997. *Los Mayas Rebeldes de Yucatán.* Mérida: Maldonado Editores.

Latour, B. 1987. *Science in Action: How to Follow Scientists and Engineers through Society.* Milton Keynes: Open University Press.

Law, J. 1992. Notes on the theory of the actor-network: Ordering, strategy and heterogeneity. *Systems Practice* 5: 377–93.

Lebergott, S. 1993. *Pursuing Happiness: American Consumers in the Twentieth Century.* Princeton: Princeton University Press.

Lefebvre, H. 1991. *The Production of Space,* tr. D. Nicholson-Smith. Oxford: Basil Blackwell.

Leff, E. 2000. Sustainable development in developing countries: Cultural diversity and environmental rationality. In K. Lee, A. Holland, and D. McNeill, eds., *Global Sustainable Development in the 21st Century.* Edinburgh: Edinburgh University Press.

Lowenthal, D. 1997. In T. Griffiths and A. Robin, eds., *Empires and Ecologies: Reflections on Environmental History.* Edinburgh: Kiele University Press.

Macdonald, N. 1966. *Canada, Immigration 1841–1903.* Aberdeen: Aberdeen University Press.

MacPherson, C. B. 1962. *The political theory of possessive individualism: Hobbes to Locke.* Oxford: Oxford University Press.

MacPherson, C. B., ed. 1978. *Property: Mainstream and Critical Positions.* Toronto: University of Toronto Press.

McKean, M. A. 2000. Common property: What is it, what is it good for, and what makes it work? In C. C. Gibson, M. A. McKean, and E. Ostrom, eds., *People and Forests: Communities, Institutions, and Governance.* Cambridge: MIT Press.

Malloy, R. P. 1995. Adam Smith and the modern discourse of law and economy. In R. P. Malloy and J. Evensky, eds., *Adam Smith and the Philosophy of Law and Economics*. Dordrecht: Kluwer Academic.

Marin, R. A., and R. Gubler. 1997. *Persistencia cultural entre los Mayas frente al cambio y la modernidad*. Mérida: Ediciones Universidad de Yucatán.

Martins, L. 2000. A naturalist's vision of the tropics: Charles Darwin and the Brazilian landscape. *Singapore Journal of Tropical Geography* 21 (1): 19–33.

Mintz, S. 1986. *Sweetness and Power: The Place of Sugar in Modern History*. New York: Penguin Books.

Mol, A., and F. H. Buttel, eds. 2002. *The Environmental State under Pressure*. London: Elsevier.

Moreno, A. 1973. *Ecuador: Capitalismo y dependencia*, 2 vols. Quito: Ediciones Amenecer.

Murdoch, J., and M. Miele. 1999. Back to nature: Changing worlds of production in the food sector. *Sociologia Ruralis* 39: 465–81.

Neale, W. C. 1998. Property: Law, cotton-pickin' hands and implicit cultural imperialism. In R. C. H. Gilman, ed., *Property in Economic Context*. Philadelphia: University of America Press.

Norgaard, R. 1984. Co-evolutionary agricultural potential. *Economic Development and Cultural Change* 32 (3): 74–96.

Norgaard, R. 1984. *Development Betrayed*. London: Routledge.

Nye, D. 2003. *America as Second Creation: Technology and Narratives of New Beginnings*. Cambridge: MIT Press.

Ojeda, L., et al. 1971. Dominacion politica en la Cuenca del Guayas. unpublished manuscript. Quito.

Ott, S. 1981. *The Circle of Mountains: A Basque Shepherding Community*. Reno: University of Nevada Press.

Paz, O. 1985. *The Labyrinth of Solitude*. New York: Avalon Press.

Pigram, J. J. 1997. *Tourism, Development and Growth: The Challenge of Sustainability*. London: Routledge.

Plant, G. F. 1951. *Overseas Settlement*. Oxford: Oxford University Press.

Playa Magazine. August 1999. Playa Del Carmen.

Popper, F. J. 1995. Progress of the Nation: The Settlement History of the Enduring American Frontier. *Western Historical Quarterly* (Autumn): 623–49.

Popper, F. J. 1997. Is there still a frontier? The 1890 census and the modern American west. *Journal of Rural Studies* (October): 75–89.

Popper, F. J., and D. Popper. 1999. The Buffalo commons: Metaphor as method. *Geographical Review* (October): 63–87.

Popper, F. J., D. Popper, and R. Lang. 2002. From maps to myth: The census, Turner and the idea of the frontier. *Journal of American and Comparative Culture* 13 (Spring): 67–95.

Por Esto! 2003. Preparan antologia de la Musica Quinanarroense. April 9. Cancun.

Prescott, J. R. V. 1965. *The Geography of Frontiers and Boundaries,* London: Hutchinson.

Putnam, R. 1993. *Making Democracy Work: Civil Traditions in Modern Italy.* Princeton: Princeton University Press.

Quintana, M. E., and L. A. Palacios. 1937. *Monografia y Album de Los Rios,* Quito.

Ramos Díaz, M. 1999. La bonanza del chicle en la frontera caribe de México. *Revista Mexicana del Caribe* 7: 172–93.

Redclift, M. R. 1971. *Community and Social Transactions in a Spanish Pyrenean valley.* D.Phil. thesis. University of Sussex, Falmer, Sussex.

Redclift, M. R. 1973. The future of agriculture in a Spanish Pyrenean village and the decline of communal institutions. *Ethnology* 12 (2): 16–31.

Redclift, M. R. 1975. Agrarian reform and peasant organization in the Guayas basin, Ecuador. Paper before the Peasants Seminar, Centre for International and Area Studies, University of London, January.

Redclift, M. R. 1976. Agrarian reform and peasant organisation in the Guayas basin, Ecuador. *Inter-American Economic Affairs* 30 (1): 623–47.

Redclift, M. R. 1983. *Development and the Environmental Crisis: Green or Red Alternatives?* London: Methuen.

Redclift, M. R. 1987. *Sustainable Development: Exploring the Contradictions.* London: Methuen.

Redclift, M. R. 1996. *Wasted: Counting the Costs of Global Consumption.* London: Earthscan.

Redclift, M. R. 2000. *The Frontier Environment and Social Order.* Chichester: Edward Elgar.

Redclift, M. 2001. Changing nature: The consumption of space and the construction of nature on the "Mayan Riviera." In M. Cohen and J. Murphy, eds., *Sustainable Consumption.* New York: Elsevier.

Redclift, M. R. 2004. *Chewing Gum: The Fortunes of Taste.* New York: Taylor and Francis.

Redclift, M. R., and C. L. Sage, eds. 1994. *Strategies for Sustainable Development.* Chichester: Wiley.

Redclift, N. 1978. *The Transformation of the Peasantry in the Spanish Pyrenees.* D.Phil. thesis. University of Sussex, Falmer, Sussex.

Reed, N. 2001. *The Caste War of Yucatan*. Stanford: Stanford University Press.

Remmers, G. 1994. Ecological wine-making in a depressed mountainous region of southern Spain. In J. van der Ploeg and A. Long, eds., *Born from Within*. Assen, Netherlands: Van Gorcum.

Reyes, O. 1960. *Breve Historia General del Ecuador*: 1809–1940, vol. 2. Quito: Ediciones Gales.

Rider, N. 2002. *Yucatan and Mayan Mexico*. London: Cadogan Guides.

Roige, X., F. Estrada, and O. Beltran. 1997. *La Casa Aranesa: antropologia de l'arquitectura a la Val d'Aran*. Tremp: Colleccion Polaris, Generalitat de Catalunya.

Rosado Vega, L. 1998. *Un Pueblo y Un Hombre*. Chetumal: Editorial Norte Sur.

Sahlins, P. 1989. *Boundaries: The Making of France and Spain in the Pyrenees*. Berkeley: University of California Press.

Salvatore, R. D. 1996. North American travel narratives and the ordering/othering of South America (c. 1810–1860). *Journal of Historical Sociology* 9 (1): 85–110.

Sayer, A. 1992. *Method in Social Science: A Realist Approach*, 2nd ed. London: Routledge.

Schmidt, A. 1998. *Von Raum zu Raum. Versuch uber das Reisen*. Berlin, Merve Verlag. Quoted in Maerk, J., and E. Muller. 2000. Running still: Reflexiones epistemologicas acerca de espacio, viaje y turismo. In J. Maerk and I. Boxhill, eds., *Tourism in the Caribbean*. Chetumal: Universidad de Quintana Roo.

Schwartz, W. 1999. Afterword: Postcolonial times, the visible and invisible. In F. Driver and D. Gilbert, eds., *Imperial Cities: Landscape, Display and Identity*. Manchester: Manchester University Press.

Schweizer, P. 1988. Shepherds, workers intellectuals: culture and centre-periphery relationships in a Sardinian village. *Stockholm Studies in Social Anthropology* 18: 1–24.

Serageldin, I., and A. Steer, eds. 1994. Making development sustainable: From concepts to environmentally sustainable development. Occasional Paper Series, no. 2. Washington DC: World Bank.

Simonian, L. 1995. *Defending the Land of the Jaguar: A History of Conservation in Mexico*. Austin: University of Texas Press.

Small, S. 1998. *An Irish Century, 1845–1945*. Dublin: B. Roberts.

Smith, S. S., and J. Kulynych. 2002. It may be social, but is it capital? The social construction of social capital and the politics of language. *Politics and Society* 30 (1): 149–86.

Soler I Santalo, J. 1906. *La Val D'Aran*. Tremp: Garsinen Ediciones.

Sosa Ferreyro, R. A. 1969. *El Crimen Del Miedo, Costa Amic*. Mexico City: Ediciones Forma.

Spaargaren, G., A. Mol, and F. Buttel, eds. 2006. *Governing Environmental Flows: Global Challenges to Social Theory*. Cambridge: MIT Press.

Stanfield, M. E. 1998. *Red Rubber, Bleeding Trees: Violence, Slavery and Empire in Northwest Amazonia, 1850–1933*. Albuquerque: University of New Mexico Press.

The State of Quintana Roo. 2001. Mexico City: Ediciones Nueva Guia.

Stephens, J. L. 1988. *Incidents of Travel in Yucatan*, vol. 2. Mexico City: Panorama Editorial.

Taylor, G. R. 1972. *The Turner Thesis*. Lexington, D.C. Heath.

Tenorio Trillo, M. 1996. *Mexico at the World Fairs: Crafting a Modern Nation*. San Francisco: University of California Press.

Thompson, E. H. 1932. *People of the Serpent: Life and Adventure among the Mayas*. Boston: Houghton Mifflin.

Thompson, M., and S. Rayner. 1998. Cultural discourses. In S. Rayner and E. Malone, eds., *Human Choice and Climate Change*, vol. 1. Columbus, OH: Battelle Press.

Thoreau, H. D. [1854] 2004. *Walden*. Princeton: Princeton University Press.

Trillo, M. T. 1996. *Mexico at the World Fairs: Crafting a Modern Nation*. Berkeley: University of California Press.

Tucker, R. P. 2000. *Insatiable Appetite: The United States and the Ecological Degradation of the Tropical World*. Berkeley: University of California Press.

Turner, F. J. 1920. *The Frontier in American History*. New York: Holt.

Turner, J. K. 1965. *México Bárbaro*. México City: Cordemex.

Updike, J. 2004. Introduction. In H. D. Thoreau, *Walden*. Princeton: Princeton University Press.

Villa Rojas, A. 1978. *Los Elejidos de Dios. Etnografia de los Mayas de Quintana Roo*. Mexico City: Instituto Nacional Indigenista.

Villavicencio, X. 1860. *Geografia del Ecuador*. Quito: Ediciones Forma.

Violant, I. S. 1949. *El Pireneo Espanol*. Madrid: Editorial Plus Ultra.

Wahab, S., and J. J. Pigram. 1997. *Tourism, Development and Growth: The Challenge of Sustainability*. London: Routledge.

Wallman, S. 1977. The shifting sense of "us": Boundaries against development in the western Alps. In S. Wallman, ed., *Perceptions of Development*. Cambridge: MIT Press, pp. 23–47.

Weinberg, D. 1975. *Peasant Wisdom: Cultural Adaptation in a Swiss Village*, Berkeley: University of California Press.

Weld, C. R. 1955. Lumbering and Farming near Peterborough in the 1850s. In G. Craig, ed., *Early Travellers in the Canadas*. Toronto: Macmillan, pp. 13–41.

Whymper, E. 1972. *Travels amongst the Great Andes of the Equator* [E. Shipton, ed.]. London: Charles Knight.

Wolf, T. 1892. *Geografia y Geologia del Ecuador*. Leipzig: Tanzieg.

Woolcock, M. 1998. Social capital and economic development—Towards a theoretical synthesis and policy framework. *Theory and Society* 27 (2): 151–208.

Wynne, G. 1999. Remaking the land god gave to Cain: A brief environmental history of Canada. *Canada House Lecture Series 62*. London: Canadian High Commission.

Young, E. 2004. *Catarino Garza's Revolution on the Texas–Mexico Border*. Durham: Duke University Press.

Zuvekas, C. 1976. Agrarian reform in Ecuador's Guayas River basin. *Land Economics* 52 (3): 73–94.

Index